the series on school reform

Patricia A. Wasley
Coalition of
Essential Schools

Ann Lieberman
NCREST

SERIES EDITORS

Joseph P. McDonald
Annenberg Institute
for School Reform

Incorporating the following books from the
PROFESSIONAL DEVELOPMENT AND PRACTICE SERIES

Restructuring
Urban
Schools

A Chicago Perspective

G. Alfred Hess, Jr.

Foreword by Michelle Fine

Teachers College, Columbia University
New York and London

Published by Teachers College Press, 1234 Amsterdam Avenue, New York, NY 10027

Library of Congress Cataloging-in-Publication Data

Hess, G. Alfred, 1938–
    Restructuring urban schools : a Chicago perspective / G. Alfred Hess, Jr. ; foreword by Michelle Fine.
      p.   cm. — (The series on school reform)
    Includes bibliographical references (p.   ) and index.
    ISBN 0-8077-3476-4 (alk. paper). — ISBN 0-8077-3475-6 (pbk.)
     1. School management and organization—Illinois—Chicago.
    2. School improvement programs—Illinois—Chicago. 3. Educational change—Illinois—Chicago.   I. Title. II. Series.
    LB2802.C5H47   1995
    371.2′009773′11—dc20   95-24148

ISBN 0-8077-3475-6 (paper)
ISBN 0-8077-3476-4 (cloth)

Printed on acid-free paper
Manufactured in the United States of America

02 01 00 99 98 97 96 95   8 7 6 5 4 3 2 1

DEDICATION

This book is dedicated to the staff of the Chicago Panel on School Policy, whose work with schools and school system data in Chicago underlie most of the findings presented here. I have been enlightened by their insights, corrected by their arguments, and enriched by their colleagueship.

This book is also dedicated to the memory of John Kotsakis, Assistant to the President for Education Reform in the Chicago Teachers Union. John was one of the earliest advocates of reforming the Chicago Public Schools and played major roles in the Mayor's Education Summit, the Corsortium for Chicago School Research, and the CTU Quest Center for School Restructuring. He was a valued friend and colleague whom I deeply miss.

Contents

Foreword

Fred Hess is always, and at once, an educator, activist, researcher, preacher, worrier, and idealist. No different from his past pursuits, this book, too, carries his signature with brilliance, honesty, and clarity. Moving between voices of hope and despair, Fred invites readers into Chicago to reveal from the inside how profoundly the most remarkable school reform movement of the 20th century has shaken the foundations of public education.

In this foreword I offer three kinds of thoughts: thoughts on Fred as he has trespassed marvelously across the worlds of educational researchers and activists for 20 years; thoughts on Chicago school reform, to credit what it has accomplished and how it has enabled so many other cities to imagine "what could be"; and finally thoughts on this book, *Restructuring Urban Schools: A Chicago Perspective*, which marks a classic, reflective, fleshy study of school reform in vivo.

As to *Fred*: Those of us who know Fred ponder (and gossip) often—how can he wear all those hats neatly upon what seems like such a cool head? How can he manage to have his heart deep in the reform law, his mind buried in its evaluation, and his anxieties percolating into its future? Working across the hyphens of activist-researcher, qualitative-quantitative, passion-distance, and even, at times, wandering across the dreamer-cynic divide (Fine, 1994), Fred is an exemplary "border crosser" (Giroux, 1991). He seeks to unravel and advance theory and practice; he wants to know and compel through stories and numbers; he yearns to clarify signs of social possibility and evidence of educational apocalypse. Speaking through a discourse of "controlled passion"—undoubtedly refined through his years of importing research into the world of community organizing, and activism into the hovels of educational anthropology—he not only crosses borders, he smuggles jewels of passion, insight, control, and compassion into every corner he occupies/invents.

On *Chicago*: I admit I am one of those unabashedly, unreconstructed, unashamed fans of Chicago school reform. I never "grew up" as so many of the conservative critics of Chicago school reform have implored us all to do . . . to make room for the voucher legislation that breathes down reform's throat. In the early 1900s, just post reform law, with Michael Katz and Elaine Simon of the University of Pennsylvania, and the generosity of the Spencer Foundation, I had the marvelous opportunity to "hang out" in Chicago, to float as an academic voyeur in a social movement the depth of which I had never seen in public schools and local communities. Since the passage of the law, the city has been abuzz with the delights and dilemmas of public education. There are wrinkles, even disasters, but the evidence of "success" continues to be compelling on two counts.

First, Chicago school reform has unleashed a sense of *public energy around public schools* unprecedented in this century, unknown in this country, feared in many jurisdictions. While other cities struggle with questions of "parental involvement," usually cast in the most degenerated and cynical forms of bake-sales or tutors, Chicago models broad-based adult activism in governing schools, selecting principals, making critical budgetary decisions. This is an image that other cities across the country are either running in fear from or grappling to create anew in our own communities. A true measure of success.

On a second front, Tony Bryk and colleagues of the Consortium on Chicago School Research, have been particularly compelling in demonstrating a *strong empirical relation between democratically run schools and classroom-based improvements in teaching and learning* (1994). Dewey would be proud. The rest of us, who have long been advocating for dual strategies of reform in which parents/communities are engaged, and teachers are primary decision makers around school-based practice, finally have the data to confirm. Chicago school reform has been able to create many school contexts, across the city, marked by a powerful braiding of democratic governance and electric teaching and learning.

With an eye on *Restructuring Urban Schools: A Chicago Perspective*: This book, as you will see, reads like a novel, with lots of rich scenes, clever turns of language, textured character development. Readers wander into the halls of the State legislature, peek into classrooms in individual schools, catch glimpses of community-based coalition meetings, and, at moments, sink into Fred's internal "angst" about reform. Most fundamentally, this text self-consciously journeys across levels of analysis.

Traveling between state policy, district organization, school-based practices, and community-based politics, *Restructuring Urban Schools: A Chicago Perspective* models a most important corrective on case studies which typically focus on state policy *or* district organization *or* classrooms *or* student outcomes. To tell the story of school reform, researchers must be able to "code switch," that is, journey between levels. While the typical text on school reform glances a bit romantically at a teacher and her or his children, we all know that 90% of the headaches that teachers must endure happen "north" of the classroom. Teachers work in severely constrained and constraining "limit situations" (Martin-Baro, 1994) of inequitable financing, administrative policies that undermine classroom practice, administrators who don't respect teacher work, inadequate materials, tracking, colleagues who are "bumped" out of their schools routinely and who can't, therefore, be relied upon to build communities, the absence or inanity of centralized professional development opportunities. The bureaucratic lives endured by educators are wearing, corrosive, damaging. Knowing all that we know, researchers fetishistically focus our urban gaze on these teachers' classrooms. We draw the teacher, her children . . . and sometimes the shadows of parents present or absent. We present the "field" as if only three groups exist to admire/lay blame upon. Whited out are conditions of inadequate financing, overcentralized bureaucracy, and racism that strangle all three. In refreshing contrast *Restructuring Urban Schools: A Chicago Perspective* self-consciously "outs," applauds, and holds accountable all levels of Chicago's public school system. In its sweet way, as only Fred could do, this text demands an end to analyses that hold teachers and students monogamously hostage to our scholarly portraits.

The Fred Hess who wrote *Restructuring Urban Schools* is honest, provocative, and reflective. He will warm your hearts with hopes for radical change. He will worry you with evidence of the now familiar "one step forward, two steps back" chronology of urban school reform. Throughout his text he bleeds a passion and reveals a belief in the possibilities of all children and all schools.

Fred has sent us this book as an archive of reform, an analysis of Chicago's history, a call for action. Read it, get outraged and mobilize, for the winds of privatization and fiscal abandonment are sending shivers down all of our local spines. As we speak, the future of democratic public education hangs precariously from an underfunded cliff.

Michelle Fine

REFERENCES

Bryk, A. S., Deabster, P. E., Easton, J. Q., Lupescu, S., & Thum, Y. M. (1994, May). Measuring achievement gains in the Chicago Public Schools. *Education and Urban Society*, pp. 306–319.

Fine, M. (1994). Working the hyphens: Reinventing self and other in qualitative
    research. In N. Denzin & Y. Lincoln (Eds.), *Handbook of qualitative re-
    search* (pp. 70–82). Thousand Oaks, CA: Sage.
Giroux, H. (1991). Postmodernism as border pedagogy. In H. Giroux (Ed.),
    Postmodernism, feminism and cultural politics. Albany: State University
    of New York Press.
Martin-Baro, I. (1994). *Writing for a liberation psychology*. Cambridge, MA:
    Harvard University Press.

Acknowledgments

I want to thank John Q. Easton, for five years the Chicago Panel's director of monitoring and research, who took an idea, fleshed it out, helped secure funding to implement it, and recruited, trained, and supervised the staff who have made our monitoring and research project possible. Specific recognition is due to John for his joint authorship of earlier versions of Chapter 4 and Appendix A. In 1994, John left the Chicago Panel to become Director of the Chicago Public Schools Department of Research, Evaluation, and Planning.

Particular recognition is due to Susan Leigh Flinspach and Susan P. Ryan, who have provided the long-range continuity to our qualitative research in 14 Chicago schools, and who contributed to the original version of Chapter 6. Sandra L. Storey, Tony Monfiletto, and Todd Rosenkranz have contributed greatly to the statistical and financial databases that have made possible the quantitative analyses included in this study. I am also indebted to the other members of the Chicago Panel's research and monitoring staff, program staff, and support staff, without whose assistance and forbearance this book could not have been completed.

I want to acknowledge my debt to the scores of colleagues in the movement to reform the Chicago schools. Many of the ideas in this book were formed in the crucible of debate and action among and by these members of the reform community. In particular, I would single out Donald Moore, Gwen Laroche, Anne and Stan Hallett, Bill McKersie, and Sylvia Puente. I am grateful to the officers, Board of Directors, and member organizations of the Chicago Panel who provide direction and encouragement for the work of the staff. The support of the Chicago Panel by the city's foundations and corporate community made all our work possible. The specific foundations providing funding for the monitoring project have included the Chicago Community Trust, the Field Foundation of Illinois, the Lloyd A. Fry Foundation, the John D. and Catherine T. MacArthur Foundation, the Lyle A. Spencer Foundation, and the Woods Charitable Fund. The Joyce Foundation has provided major support to the Chicago Panel for its school finance research and advocacy efforts.

I want to express my gratitude to Ann Lieberman, Series Editor, and Susan Liddicoat at Teachers College Press, who encouraged me to see this project through to completion and whose suggestions have helped to reshape the manuscript. I am also grateful for the support and advice of Michelle Fine and Bill Ayers, whose comments on an earlier draft of the manuscript helped immeasurably to improve the final product.

Finally, I want to thank Chuck and Ann Felton, summer neighbors, whose friendship and support kept me going during the early days of this project. And special thanks and love are extended to my wife, Mary, and my children, Randy and Sarah, whose interests, projects, and desires were constantly being put off because I was "working on the book." Without the warm support of my family, I could not have completed this work.

CHAPTER 1

Developing a Uniquely
Chicago Perspective

I am a Chicagoan, unabashedly in love with my city. I was not born in the Windy City, but it has been my home for nearly 30 years. I came to Chicago as a young man to learn about life in the inner city and to try to find ways to help meet the needs of the city's inner-city residents. I joined a community of people living and working on the Westside, seeking to revive a neighborhood called Fifth City, and I owe much of my perspective to community leaders like Lela Mosley who taught me what life was like in the city.

One of my earliest memories of Chicago is a giant civil rights rally with Martin Luther King at Soldier Field in 1966, followed by a march to the doors of the Chicago Board of Education to protest the continuing segregation of Chicago schools. Later, my son attended those schools as one of the declining number of white students in the system. He went through Stewart Elementary and was in one of the first classes to enter Arai Middle School in the port-of-entry Uptown area, before graduating from Mather High School. One perplexing feature of his time at Mather I would not understand until years later. Randy would regularly arrive home shortly after 1:30 p.m. He explained that his last period was a study hall with 400 kids in the auditorium, and he could study better at home. Since he was back at school by 3 p.m. for soccer practice or to work as an aide in the driver's education program, I didn't worry about it. Only years later, when I studied eight Chicago high schools in a matched-pairs study to determine why some schools had higher dropout rates than others, did I discover that first- and last-period study halls were a systemwide way to reduce the school day of Chicago students, thereby saving money by reducing the number of needed teachers. Thus students were encouraged to come to school late or leave early.

In 1980, after earning a doctorate in educational anthropology as a vehicle for making a career shift from community organizing, I had the opportunity, through a post-doctoral fellowship in ethnography and public policy at Northwestern University, to begin studying schooling in Chicago. The focus of my "post-doc" was the development of a court-mandated desegregation plan, 14 years after King's march on the Chicago Board of Education. My perspective on Chicago was forged from my experiences of living and working in its inner-city communities and struggling with such perpetual delays in dealing fairly with its poor and minority citizens. In 1980, I did not realize I was embarking on a decades-long effort to reform and reshape the Chicago Public Schools.

What I did know was that I had made a choice. As I was completing my doctorate, I began looking for work outside the field of community organizing and adult education, which I had been doing since coming to Chicago in 1966. I received several invitations to apply for academic jobs in universities and colleges in other parts of the country. I realized then that I had to choose between seeking an academic position or seeking work in a particular place: Chicago. I decided to stay in the city. This choice of "place" over "position" has had a fundamental influence on my work, keeping me focused on relevant and practical solutions to real problems rather than designing elegant solutions to theoretical problems. In the process, with my colleagues, I have developed approaches to many fundamental questions that depart from the conventional academic wisdom about public education, approaches I would probably never have understood had I chosen to seek a "position" rather than committed myself to work in a "place."

The post-doc started my studies of the city's schools. It led to a part-time position at Northwestern, directing the placement of undergraduates in field study sites across the city. That part-time position both gave me the opportunity and created the economic necessity for me to find consulting projects studying education in Chicago.

One of those projects was with the Chicago Panel on Public School Finances (Hallett & Hess, 1982). I was hired by the Panel's first executive director, Anne Hallett, to study changes in the Chicago Public Schools budget as a result of its virtual bankruptcy in 1979–80 and to assess the effects of those changes on the educational program available to students in the city. This was an unusual assignment for an educational anthropologist to undertake, and it forced me to develop an expertise in school finance that eventually led to membership on the national board of directors of the American Education Finance Association. I am probably the only anthropologist ever to have served on the AEFA board, and undoubtedly the first school finance expert to serve as president of the Council on Anthropology and Education.

Anne's faith that I could master this new field had been nurtured by her husband, Stan Hallett, who had secured the fellowship at Northwestern that allowed me to pursue my graduate program and who had been my mentor at the university. The Halletts remain two of my most valued colleagues in the effort to improve Chicago and its schools. When Anne resigned as the Panel's director to leave the city for a brief period in 1983, I was fortunate enough to be asked to take her place.

For more than a decade, I have led the Chicago Panel in its efforts to understand the problems of the Chicago Public Schools, to help design efforts to overcome those problems, and to study the effectiveness of the solutions we helped devise. Along the way, I learned much about public education in large urban school systems, particularly in Chicago. I had to teach myself and my colleagues about the intricacies of urban school finance and about how budget decisions reveal the real priorities of leaders of the school system. I learned much about the hypocrisy of the state's political leaders, who proclaimed that education was their highest priority while state support for public schools fell from 48% of their costs to less than 33%. And I discovered the structural inequities that keep low-income and minority students from receiving adequate school funding to allow them the educational opportunity to overcome their disadvantaged condition. I came to see that for the children of the affluent, education was seen as the way into the future, while in low-income and minority communities, education was seen by politicians, unions, business leaders, and professional educators as a jobs-and-contracting program for adults that had little to do with the success or failure of students.

Along the way, I helped to expose the mismanagement of the school system's administration and the horrendous dropout rates, which exceeded 40% (Hess & Lauber, 1985). I traced the sending and receiving patterns of school enrollment that funneled the best students into the selective and majority-dominated high schools while consigning the rest to "holding pen" neighborhood schools that could only be described as a system of "educational triage" (Hess, 1986). I investigated why some high schools were more successful than others in graduating the same kinds of students, but in the process discovered how the school system systematically shortchanged all its high school students (Hess, Wells, Prindle, Kaplan, & Liffman, 1986). I helped my colleagues to realize that the system was failing its students from their earliest years, for we could successfully predict who would eventually graduate and who drop out on the basis of second-, third-, and fourth-grade data (Hess, Lyons, & Corsino, 1989).

Thus, for me and for my colleagues, in the effort to turn around the Chicago Public Schools, school reform was a necessity, not an optional research proposal. Articulating goals that affirmed that all Chicago students can learn at levels comparable to other students across the nation was an attack on uncaring administrators and burned-out principals and teachers. Reallocating the system's resources was an effort to trim the fat and to redress fundamental inequities that had existed for decades. Establishing a system of school-based management was an effort to give parents, community residents, and committed school staffs the opportunity to put students first, instead of last, when educational decisions were being made. These were the efforts of friends of the Chicago Public Schools who were trying to help that struggling system get back on the right track (Hess, 1991). But these were not the actions of unthinking supporters. These were the actions of what John Watkins (1992), out of the Coalition of Essential Schools context, calls "critical friends."

And therefore, once the Chicago School Reform Act of 1988 (P.A. 85-1418) was formulated and enacted into law, we continued our effort to be helpful by studying the implementation of the reform act. Once again, this was not simply an academic opportunity that we were fortunate enough to be given. This was a responsibility to try to see what things were working and what things were not, and to figure out what could be done about those things that were not working. We believe our studies of the Chicago school reform effort will be informative for researchers, practitioners, and interested observers across the United States and perhaps beyond. We have tried to be rigorous in our research methodology in order to be able to present the best possible data. But we do not pretend to be detached and disinterested observers. We are passionately committed to the effort to improve the educational opportunities of Chicago's students. The Chicago School Reform Act was an effort to turn that commitment into possibilities for the city's children. We are intensely interested to see whether that legislation and the efforts to improve Chicago schools that it has spurred will result in those improved educational opportunities. Thus it is not the reform act itself that commands our attention, but the educational opportunities for young Chicagoans that it either detracts from or enhances.

In this book, I report on our studies of the implementation of the reform effort and try to share with the reader the successes and failures, the possibilities and the problems encountered in trying to reshape an ineffective urban school system. I discuss our efforts to try to make the playing field more level for low-income and minority young people. And I try to expose some of the assumptions that are taken for granted about public education in the United States that may need to be changed if low-income, minority students in the inner city are to receive an adequate educational opportunity.

I do not claim to provide, in this book, a reasoned and comprehensive view of all potential educational improvement strategies, although I do try to position the Chicago reforms in the larger national reform context. I am trying to reflect on the attempt to improve urban schools from a uniquely Chicago perspective and a thoroughly engaged perspective.

I should be quick to point out, however, that I do not pretend that this book represents *the* Chicago perspective. One of the real strengths of the Chicago reform effort is that it represents a broad movement by thousands of people to improve our city's schools. Each of them could provide their own perspective on the Chicago reforms, and each would be valuable and important. In this book, I try to present the views of many participants in this reform effort. Their views vary widely, as the reader will see. Each of their voices is important. The unique compilation of those voices and perspectives brought together in this book is *my* Chicago-based perspective on restructuring urban schools.

ESTABLISHING A RESEARCH PERSPECTIVE: TO CATALOGUE OR CRITIQUE?

When you are an anthropologist doing policy-relevant work in education and something like the Chicago School Reform Act "happens" to you, it is hard to ignore it.* It presents a major opportunity and a major responsibility. How should anthropologists or other social scientists respond to major social changes happening in their own culture, right in front of their eyes? Unfortunately, many have simply ignored it. Despite living in the metropolitan area, they seem to have said, "It's not the people I study" or "It's not my specialty." Others have taken one school and focused all their energy on seeing how this systemwide policy change impacts one situation, probably involving a marginalized population. Still others, already engaged in ongoing efforts, have adapted their work to include this intrusion from the larger social context.

But for those interested in doing policy-relevant research, an effort needed to be made to assess the effect of this policy initiative on the whole city, or at least on the whole school system. At the Chicago Panel,

---

*The following portion of this chapter was originally prepared as an address to the Council on Anthropology and Education during its 1991 meetings in Chicago. A revised version appeared under the title "School Reform and Anthropology: To Catalogue or Critique" in the *Anthropology and Education Quarterly, 23*(3), 175–184, September 1992. Reprinted by permission of the American Anthropological Association.

we designed a large-scale, multisite monitoring and research project that uses both quantitative and qualitative approaches. The quantitative studies combine budget data, student test scores and dropout rates, large-scale surveys, and staffing characteristics. These data are being analyzed using the most sophisticated statistical techniques, such as hierarchical linear modeling (Raudenbush & Bryk, 1986), to see which changes at which of the city's 540 schools are most associated with improved student achievement. At the same time, we are studying much more intensively the happenings at 14 representative schools to understand the dynamics and workings of the implementation of the school restructuring policy initiative. We have provided periodic reports of these studies throughout the 5-year primary implementation period. (See Appendix A for a discussion of our research methodology.)

But such an opportunity is not an unmixed blessing. Aside from the tremendous escalation of effort that it requires, assessing a public policy initiative of this scale presents some daunting challenges to a qualitative researcher. Ethnographic studies are typically small in scale, involve a single site, often are restricted to a small number of informants, and frequently involve a culture that is exotic to the researcher. Anthropologists tend to be happier studying simpler societies in their own context or marginalized groups on the edges of our own mainstream culture. This propensity frequently leads us into studying the dissonance experienced by minority subgroups, whether they be based on race, gender, or ethnicity. And this propensity has produced some of our very best work, such as John Ogbu's study of *Minority Education and Caste* (1978).

But assessing the effects of the school reform movement in Chicago is very complex, is huge in scope, and requires a focus on the mainstream cultural core within which our cities now operate. In the last decade, there appears to have been a growing concern in anthropology to examine the American mainstream, from Marvin Harris's *America Now* (1981) to Holland and Eisenhart's *Educated in Romance* (1990). Interestingly, it seems that most anthropologists studying the American mainstream do so from a post-positivist orientation, perhaps to achieve the same distance and otherness that anthropologists bring to their studies of the exotic and the marginalized. For an anthropologist who has been deeply involved in policy-relevant research on the Chicago Public Schools for a decade, assessing the effects of the Chicago reform effort also requires some critical reflection on one's own role.

One day, several years into the reform effort, some members of the research team working on the Chicago Panel's 5-year monitoring and research project were going over a draft report we were preparing. That report was intended to describe the then-current status of school improvement planning in the 14 representative schools we had been studying. The task had been to analyze these 14 documents to see what patterns might be emerging and to assess them for their likely effect on the 14 schools. On the one hand, we were struggling to objectively report what was in the documents we were analyzing. On the other, we were imposing an evaluative screen which contended that "add-on" programs were less likely to produce significant changes in student achievement levels than were efforts to dramatically alter the normal instructional practices in regular classrooms of the schools. Some team members were reluctant to go beyond the bounds of the documents themselves. But, at the same time, others were being excessively negative about the add-ons in order to sharpen the contrast with those fewer schools that were making serious efforts to change their current instructional practices in regular classrooms.

I found myself asking the team not to limit themselves to the documents alone, but to discuss them with our informants in the various schools to get a greater understanding of *why* some things were included in some improvement plans and excluded from others. Then we started discussing why we were preparing this report at this point, just 2 years into a 5-year study of reform implementation. We discussed the fact that we hoped these 14 schools, and others across the city to which we would distribute the study, would read the report, see what they had planned and what they had omitted that others had included, and then *change* their plans and their future behaviors. The report was not intended simply to catalogue what had been happening in the school improvement planning dimension of Chicago school reform. The report was intended to critique it and to lead to changes in the very process we were studying!

Now for those familiar with the works of Jurgen Habermas (1971, 1978) and anthropologists like George Marcus and Michael Fischer (1986), such a suggestion does not sound so terribly radical. But for positivistically trained researchers, such implications of policy-relevant studies can be shocking. This is the challenge facing most researchers working in the educational arena today. Are we there merely to catalogue what is going on, to sit back in our armchairs and postulate theories, or are we also there to seek to have a profound impact on how schooling is done in our societies? Do we simply catalogue? Or do we also critique? And if we critique, is that critique detached and dispassionate? Or is it engaged and active?

QUESTIONS RAISED BY CASE STUDIES
IN SCHOOL RESTRUCTURING

A few years ago, I edited a series of studies about efforts to restructure schooling across America (Hess, 1992b). In the process of examining these studies from different cities and reform movements, several questions were raised for me.

Is There a Role for Qualitative Researchers in Studying Educational Policy?

Anthropologists and other qualitative researchers have not been widely involved in the major educational policy debates in America during the last half century. The anthropologists who have been active have frequently been so through other guises: as sociologists of education, graduate school professors of education, state board of education researchers, or school reform activists.

To seize this opportunity for engaging in major educational policy debates, there must be a body of qualitative researchers whose primary focus is on the major issues being debated. Successful policy research is cumulative, not a side foray away from an otherwise unrelated academic career. It requires a body of policy-focused researchers who exchange information about the implementation of various policies over many years. But, in contrast with meetings of sociologists, political scientists, and educational researchers, a review of the schedule of a typical meeting of anthropologists reveals a dearth of such topics. When such topics do appear on the agenda, they frequently deal with the fringes of major policy debates, focusing on the impact of major policies on small, exotic subgroups, while ignoring the impact of the policy on the populations that form a major component of our society.

Apart from the outstanding work of Lois Weis (1991), Michelle Fine (1991b), Annette Lareau (1991), and Margaret LeCompte (LeCompte, Wiertelak, & Eilletto, 1991), there has been little debate among anthropologists about the major policies being propounded through America 2000 (the national education goal-setting process); about the reform efforts of the teachers unions; or about the education reforms undertaken by cities, states, or national governments. There has been little discussion about the effects of the school-based management movement on reinvigorating the relevant claims of diverse local communities against the legitimate interests of the state in imposing its will on children and parents through schools. These are the types of topics that must come to the fore if qualitative research is to have an impact on educational policy. These are some of the topics I propose to address in this book.

Can Policy Research Be Objective?

Policy-relevant research demands involvement. The related question is: Can we still be objective? Others, such as K. Howe and Eisenhart (1990) and Maxwell and Pitman (1992), have much more adequately reviewed the literature on research methodology, but it seems evident that significant participation in policy formation, assessment, and alteration requires more commitment and less detachment than traditional academic research focused on expanding basic knowledge. I leave to others the argument that basic knowledge development also requires a more critical methodology than that supported by positivistic assumptions. My own career has been substantially shaped by Sartre's (1970) observation that "one knows the world by seeking to change it." Such a sentiment is a hallmark of most policy-relevant research and has far-reaching implications for research methodologies, perspectives, and ethics (Deyhle, Hess, & LeCompte, 1992).

In my own experience in public-school-oriented research in Chicago, effective policy-relevant research requires a combination of the roles of advocate and reliable researcher/informant. Policy makers and those shaping their opinions and actions need reliable information that is accurate, timely, and appropriate to the decisions they are facing. But they also require advice about how that information should be used. They need recommendations as to what should be done about the policy problems that such research seeks to address.

Policy-relevant research is not policy-neutral. It leads toward the making of policy decisions that settle on one possible action or set of actions while eliminating others. Frequently such decisions are not made on the basis of ultimately demonstrable truth, but in response to the best choice among feasible current alternatives, which may later be succeeded by other, (hopefully) better, alternatives. This means that policy-relevant research is regularly assessing the relative value of various policy alternatives or seeking to expand the available alternatives by proposing new ones; it is perpetually replacing its own earlier efforts.

In policy-relevant research, everyone has a position. Reliable policy research examines all the possibly relevant data and then assesses their impact on the policy decisions to be taken. Less reliable policy-relevant research allows the researcher's advocacy position to shape what information is included and what is omitted. Thus, for policy-relevant research, the question involves the reliability of the researcher in including all relevant materials and the integrity of the researcher in avoiding serious distortions of the interpretation of the data included. For policy-relevant research, the issue is not the complete disinterest of the researcher, but his or her reliability and integrity.

POLICY AND PLACE—THE STRENGTH
OF QUALITATIVE RESEARCH

Policies are sometimes designed in the rarified atmospheres of political think tanks; or they may be fashioned in the hard give-and-take of political skirmishing. They may be created by the programmatic decisions of bureaucratic administrators, or they may emerge from negotiations between employees and management. In most cases, policies are created at some distance from the locations where they must be implemented. Rarely can any policy or set of policies take into account all the possible elements that may affect their implementation. But policies, ultimately, must be implemented in particular places, in particular circumstances, and by specific persons. And that plays to the strength of qualitative research.

The strength of qualitative research is in describing what happens in local situations and in explaining how a policy is implemented. In addition, qualitative research, combining observation of events and interviewing of the major actors in the process of implementation, has an advantage in explaining why things happen the way they do. Studying the implementation of policy at first hand, qualitative researchers are able to give policy makers a better understanding of the problems local actors are having as they struggle with putting a policy into practice and the progress they are making. They help policy makers to see needed correctives and to have patience when the public and the media demand unreasonably quick judgments about the effectiveness of recently adopted policies. But to provide such assistance, qualitative researchers have to participate in the policy debates, be aware of the critical issues being discussed and decided, and find appropriate venues to examine the policies being implemented. Then they must be willing to make interim reports long before they are ready to produce a final product—reports that, by their appearance, may alter the implementation they are studying. As one of the authors in the set of studies that prompted these questions notes, such involved research is messy indeed (Watkins, 1992). But it is the kind of messy research that policy makers need in order to make, or to refrain from making, important policy decisions.

Tom Carroll (1992) has pointed out that qualitative researchers bring important values and skills to the process of policy formation. Policy debates tend to be heavily dominated by rhetoric about what a projected policy promises to accomplish and by studies of the outcomes that have resulted. Frequently omitted from this debate is much evidence about how these policies actually were being implemented, what the problems were, and what, if any, midcourse corrections might have been appropriate to help particular policies be more successfully implemented. Such implementation studies provide a special opportunity for qualitative researchers. I hope the reader will find that this book stands in that tradition.

One of the strengths of qualitative research is its ability to describe *what* is actually happening as policies are implemented, *how* these actors are doing what they are doing, and *why* various actors in the implementation process are acting as they are, either to make the implementation successful or to frustrate it. Without such implementation studies, politicians and the general public are quick to jump to premature conclusions about the viability of particular reforms.

As one of the people deeply engaged in the Chicago school reform movement, I am asked 10 or 15 times a week, "Well, how's reform going? Is it successful?" The question of success cannot yet be answered adequately in Chicago or in most other cities studied in our 1992 volume (Hess, 1992b). Answers will not emerge for another 3 or 4 years, in all likelihood. But policy makers, the media, and the public want more immediate assessments.

While it is still too early to measure success, qualitative researchers *can* discuss whether the policy is being implemented in the fashion that was envisioned or whether it is already off-track and encountering unforeseen impediments. They can also provide a context for the problems encountered in implementing any change in policy: Are these the problems envisioned in the policy design or are they unanticipated obstacles? And, as the final results begin to become available, these implementation studies can help to answer the *why* question: Why was the policy successful or why was it unsuccessful? Was the policy the wrong policy? Was it undermined by unanticipated opposition? Was the policy appropriate but the implementation design faulty? Did other, unrelated, events intrude to create an impossible situation or to guarantee success for a policy that otherwise might have failed miserably? Is the policy replicable in other settings, or was it successful because of a unique and idiosyncratic set of circumstances that are unlikely to be duplicated elsewhere? These are important questions, that are frequently overlooked in the political judgments about adopted policies; these questions are best answered by qualitative research.

I have tried to suggest that qualitative researchers bring peculiarly valuable skills to the process of policy formation and implementation. But if we are interested in taking on such a more engaged role, we must focus our discussions on the major policies being debated. While not abandoning our concerns for those who are different, we must come in from the margins and focus on the mainstream. To do so will stretch our minds, our methods, our ethics, and our common tribal culture. The opportunities are great, and we are peculiarly suited to meet a pressing need in our society.

COMBINING QUALITATIVE AND QUANTITATIVE TECHNIQUES

In this book, I use qualitative approaches, along with quantitative data, to describe what the Chicago school reform effort has been and to analyze its strengths and weaknesses. Qualitative approaches help to explain what is occurring in particular situations and help us to understand the dynamics at work in this reform effort. But knowing the dynamics alone is not enough. We also want to know how extensively things are changing. We want to know how widely beliefs are shared. We want to know how many schools are making significant changes. We want to know how many more resources are available in schools, both in dollars and in staff. We need to know how unevenly the resources for public schools are distributed, both across the state and within the Chicago school district. And we want to know how much student achievement and behavior have changed. These are the hard evidence that change is or is not occurring. These are the basis for generalizations that can only be hinted at from qualitative data alone. But without the qualitative data, the numbers are sterile and easily lead to questionable interpretations.

In this book, I extract from the Chicago experience some policy-relevant lessons that challenge basic assumptions about public education in the United States. I look at those assumptions, describe their shortcomings, and put forward the alternative assumptions that I believe underlie much of the reform effort in our nation. For better or worse, the effort to transform the Chicago Public Schools is based on these alternative assumptions.

CHAPTER 2

Chicago: A School System—
Not Students—"At Risk"

All too frequently, the discussions of "at-risk" students proceed from the assumption that these students exist at the margins of the regular student enrollment.* This is particularly the case, I have noticed, with scholars working from national data sets such as the High School and Beyond survey (HS&B). So Hammond and Howard (1986) suggest that black and Hispanic students (whose dropout rates are reported at an unbelievably low 17% and 19%, respectively, by the HS&B survey) "display some rather interesting anomalies in their statistical behavior." They suggest that dropping out can best be understood as behavior at one end of the performance spectrum:

> At the other extreme are students whose performance suggests that they have essentially dropped out (or have been dropped out) of the academic process though they have remained in the school building. Still further to this side are students for whom school attendance is not only minimally productive, but even painful. For them dropping out is a rational response to an intolerable situation. (Hammond & Howard, 1986, p. 55)

Such an analysis leads the authors into an individualized and psychologized definition of the problems of "at-risk" students and to the proposal of remedies that call for all teachers to have high expectations for black students.

Similarly, Wehlege and Rutter (1986) describe dropouts as marginalized students who "do not expect to get as much schooling as their peers" and who experience "conflict with and estrangement from institutional norms and rules (p. 381)." The authors propose a solution that is based on this presupposition that "at-risk" students are primarily

*This chapter first appeared in Robert Rossi (Ed.), *Schools and Students at Risk: Context and Framework for Positive Change*, New York, Teachers College Press, 1994.

marginal students on the edges of normal student bodies. They propose alternative schools within regular schools that could be more attentive to the special needs of "at-risk" students. These alternative schools would have a few teachers who work intensively with those who are "at-risk" in groupings of students that are small and mutually support-ive. But how applicable are such approaches to the urban schools that many "at-risk" students attend?

At Chicago's Austin High School, where the longitudinal dropout rate for the class of 1982 was 62.1%, only 18.4% of the entering ninth-graders could read within a range that might be considered "normal" (above the 27th percentile nationally, or no more than 2 years below grade level; Hess & Lauber, 1985). For the class of 1985, the dropout rate increased to over 80%. In segregated urban schools like Austin, where 54.2% of the students are from low-income families, or nearby Crane, where 73.2% are low-income students, "at-risk" students are not on the margins of the student body. They *are* the student body. And, it may be argued, these students are rejecting, in massive numbers, the structures and performance of contemporary urban schools as being inadequate to meet their needs.

It is for this reason that reform activists in Chicago abandoned the effort to add specialized programs in individual schools to meet the needs of individual "at-risk" students and began to focus on the prob-lem of changing "at-risk" schools. The Chicago reform activists were convinced that it was inappropriate to "blame the victims" and there-fore sought to provide opportunities for schools to change to become more effective with low-income students. Instead of trying to change the young people, the Chicago reform effort sought to change their schools.

Other scholars have expressed similar concerns about the way we talk about students with whom our schools have not been very success-ful. Michelle Fine (1990) has suggested that the debate over "at-risk" students has been designed to distinguish such students from the rest of "us." She accuses conservative scholars of bartering over the bodies of such students as if they were "public property, while the minds, collec-tive educations, and critiques of those most likely to drop out are ren-dered simply irrelevant to the arguments postured" (p. 56). She suggests that some scholars consider these students to be "the worrisome 25%," while others, such as Chester Finn (1989), see them as a "manifestation of linked social pathologies and inherited characteristics" (p. 15). Fine continues: "Either way, they are not 'us.' And they are not even very closely related to us" (1990, p. 56). Fine goes on to document the way in which the current discussions emphasize this distinction while diverting attention from other, more productive debates about how to change schools so that these students might be successful.

Similarly, Swadener and Niles (1991), based on their ethnographic work with parents of families frequently characterized as "at-risk," suggest that "the deficit model of 'at risk,' with its pervasive implications that there is 'something wrong' with the child and the family, does little to enhance parent communication and often undermines the potential for partnerships with parents" (p. 13). They continue:

> By suggesting an alternative "at promise" view, it is our intent to convey the importance of considering the possibilities in all children and the promise of partnerships with parents. This view locates many of the problems faced by children and families outside the family so that attention can be focused on the larger contexts within which families struggle today. (p. 13)

Both Fine and Swadener and Niles develop more fully than can be done here the social-reproduction argument that American schools are not equally accessible to children of all social classes. They suggest that the current structure of our public schooling efforts contributes to the lack of success of "at-risk" students. The Chicago School Reform Act was drafted out of a similar concern. While I will not adopt Swadener and Niles's "at-promise" connotation, I share their concern about changing the structures and expectations that now dominate thinking about schools in the United States.

Linda Darling-Hammond (1994) has also commented on the systemic nature of inequity in public education in the United States.

> The fact that U.S. schools are structured so that students routinely receive dramatically unequal learning opportunities based on their race and social status is simply not widely recognized. If the academic outcomes for minority and low-income children are to change, however, aggressive action must be taken to change the caliber and quantity of their learning opportunities. (p. 1)

Years before Darling-Hammond wrote these words, school activists were detailing how unequal the learning opportunities were for low-income and minority students in Chicago.

PREVALENCE AND NONSUCCESS OF "AT-RISK"
STUDENTS IN THE CHICAGO PUBLIC SCHOOLS

As Chicago reformers were mounting a legislative effort to foster extensive change, the data they were presenting showed a school system that was made up predominantly of students who were not being successfully educated. During the 1987–88 school year, 80.2% of all elementary school students qualified for a free or reduced-price lunch. There were 96 elementary schools in which every student qualified and another 112 in which more than 90% did. Two-thirds of the system's primary and intermediate students attended schools in which at least 80% of the students were from low-income homes. Only 32 of Chicago's 440 regular elementary schools had fewer than 30% of their students from low-income backgrounds, and these schools were attended by fewer than 5% of the city's public elementary school students (see Appendix B).

During the 1989–90 school year, the first under the reform act, using the much more restrictive census definition of poverty, there were 165,842 elementary students (42% of the elementary-aged children) who qualified for federal Chapter I support for disadvantaged students, but the funds were so limited that resources were concentrated into only 288 of the city's 491 public elementary schools and served only 50,733 students, almost exclusively in pull-out programs. Despite the relaxation of federal regulations, only 5 Chicago elementary schools were permitted by the system's bureaucrats to use the funds for school-wide programs. Thus most low-income students in Chicago schools were not served by these federal funds at all, and most of those who were served had to experience the labeling effect of participating in a pull-out program, which probably negated whatever benefit the program itself provided.

For years, special education programs in the Chicago Public Schools had been in chaos. This catastrophically mismanaged program was highlighted in the 1982 report of Designs for Change, entitled *Caught in the Web* (Moore & Radford-Hill, 1982). The authors charged that Chicago steered black students into educationally mentally handicapped (EMH) classes at rates triple those of other major cities. They claimed that as many as 7,000 of the 12,000 EMH students were misclassified. More recent data indicate that as many as 4,000 Chicago students (1% of the total enrollment) have been tuitioned out to privately run specialized schools or residential placement centers at a cost of more than $50 million a year.

Desegregation as a School Improvement Strategy

As reform was beginning in Chicago, the system was a predominantly minority school system. Only 12.3% of the students were white;
59.6% were black; 25% were Hispanic, and 3.1% were Asian or Native
American (Chicago Panel, 1990). Just over 9% were limited in their
English proficiency. The Chicago Public Schools had had a long history
of *de facto* segregation. Though the system had been legally desegregated in 1874, residential segregation, reinforced by Chicago Real Estate
Board policy and restrictive covenants incorporated into property titles
until as late as 1969, combined with the system's emphasis on neighborhood schools, led activists in the 1950s to claim that 91% of Chicago
schools were attended by 90% or more of one race (for a brief history
of desegregation efforts in Chicago, see Hess, 1984). However, it was
not until 1980, when white enrollment had dropped to 18%, that the
system entered into a consent decree with the U.S. Department of Justice to desegregate. At that time, 9 of the city's high schools had more
than 70% white students, enrolling 45% of all white high school students in the city. Only a quarter of white high school students attended
schools where more than half of the enrollment was minority. By contrast, 85% of black high school students attended schools with fewer
than 15% white students. At the elementary school level, there were 74
schools with more than 70% white enrollments, and 347 schools with
fewer than 15% white students; these segregated elementary schools
enrolled 93.1% of all black students and 58.2% of all Hispanic students
(Hess & Warden, 1987).

Thus, students who might be considered "at-risk" because they
belonged to a racial or ethnic minority were generally isolated in schools
primarily attended by similar students. At the elementary school level,
students in these racially isolated schools achieved at lower levels than
did students attending schools with more white students. On the eighth-
grade Iowa Test of Basic Skills in 1985–86, the median grade-equivalent
score for students in schools with at least 30% white students was 8.5,
3 months below the national norm; the median for students in schools
with less than 15% white students was 6.8, 2 full years below the normal grade level.

The implementation of the 1980 desegregation agreement eliminated the few remaining predominantly white schools in the system, but
left the vast majority of minority students attending the more than 300
schools that were 100% minority in enrollment. Our assessment of the
effect of the desegregation program was that only 4% more minority

students were attending schools in desegregated settings at the end of
the decade than had been doing so before the desegregation agreement
was signed (Hess & Warden, 1988). One of the primary mechanisms
used in the desegregation plan was a doubling of the number of magnet
schools. The study showed that these schools were disproportionately
funded and provided disproportionate benefits to white, middle-class
students. Thus, despite increasing desegregation funding from $9.8 mil-
lion in 1980–81 to $77.3 million in 1985–86, for the most part minority
students continued to attend schools in which low-income students
were aggregated and were performing less successfully than were students attending the system's relatively few integrated schools. But due
to the small number of remaining white students, desegregation, as a
school improvement strategy, had done about as much as it could do
(Easton & Hess, 1990).

A System of Educational Triage

Economically disadvantaged and minority students in Chicago were
not being successfully educated. In addition to the intolerably high
dropout rates already mentioned, Chicago students were scoring badly
on every form of standardized measure being reported. But, as noted in
the Panel's initial dropout study, the most disadvantaged students were
shunted into one set of schools, while the most successful were
"drawn" into another set of schools in a system of "educational triage"
(Hess, 1986). Students with the best elementary school preparation were
enrolled in one set of high schools, while those with the worst scores
were shunted to neighborhood schools, predominantly in low-income
inner-city neighborhoods. Overage students were funneled into the
worst schools and prevented from attending the more selective high
schools. The best schools were more than a third white in enrollment,
while the worst enrolled only 6% white students—and most of those
students were in only 4 of the 21 schools. The percentage of low-
income pupils was twice as high in the worst schools as in the best (see
Table 2.1).

This means that half of all low-income high school students, half of
all students entering high school overage (which usually means they
were retained in grade at least once in elementary school), 45% of all
black, and 49% of all Hispanic students were shunted into neglected
schools that then lost more than half of their students before graduation.
The aggregate dropout rate for these schools was 55.8%, and none of
them graduated as many students as dropped out. On the other hand,
half of all white students were enrolled in selective high schools or those

TABLE 2.1. **High School Characteristics and Dropout Rates by Percentage**

Dropout Rates	White	Low Income	Reading Below Normal	Overage	Dropouts
Low Rates	33.5%	28.3%	27.8%	13.3%	25.2%
Mid Rates	27.7%	34.4%	58.2%	26.7%	45.2%
High Rates	5.9%	51.9%	69.9%	34.5%	55.8%

which enrolled few minority or low-income students. These selective or exclusive schools, in aggregate, had dropout rates below the national average and less than half the rates of the neighborhood "dumping ground" schools. The triage assignment of students created great disparities in school success at the high school level.

While the median score of 1 Chicago high school was at the 78th percentile on the ACT (American College Test) in 1988–89, 31 schools were in the 1st (lowest) percentile. Only 6 of 58 Chicago high schools ranked at the 10th percentile or higher (Chicago Panel, 1990). The story was similar on other measures and nearly as dismal in the elementary schools as in the high schools.

When we studied elementary schools (Hess & Greer, 1987), we discovered that 20% of these schools enrolled nearly two-thirds (63.1%) of all white eighth-graders; in these schools, only 11.4% of the students were from low-income families. In aggregate, only 18% of graduates of these elementary schools started high school reading at below-normal rates and only 19% eventually dropped out. These schools tended to be smaller than most schools in the system, and they had more experienced faculties. By and large, they sent their students to the system's selective and exclusive high schools. Students in the other 80% of Chicago elementary schools included few (13.5%) white students and generally one-third to one-half of their students were from low-income backgrounds. When we tracked the sending patterns from elementary schools to high schools, we found these schools dividing their graduates, sending the more successful to the selective and exclusive high schools and the less successful to high schools in their own neighborhoods. Needless to say, dropout rates for students sent to the selective and exclusive schools were generally 20 percentage points lower than for students sent to inner-city neighborhood high schools.

The school system was failing its students, most of whom were "at-risk" when they entered the system. It tended to aggregate the students least likely to be successful in "at-risk" elementary schools. It sorted out the most successful elementary students and enrolled them in more selective or exclusive high schools. It left the rest to attend more neglected inner-city neighborhood high schools. To compound this problem, it focused its resources on schools with fewer "at-risk" students in attendance.

Federal compensatory funds were concentrated in schools that overwhelmingly enrolled low-income students, but the effects of these funds were undercut by lower levels of basic resources provided to those schools. State compensatory funds were blatantly diverted to provide bureaucratic overhead (see Appendix B). The lower spending at the schools with more low-income students in part reflected the fact that these schools also were staffed with the most inexperienced teachers (Hess & Greer, 1987).

If one begins to define "at-risk" as referring to students who come from economically disadvantaged families, and adds to that being from minority families that are racially isolated, and then includes lack of academic preparation, it is clear that such students are disproportionately enrolled in inner-city and rural school systems. In urban systems, such students frequently are further isolated in inner-city neighborhood elementary schools; they are less prevalent or underrepresented in selective schools and in schools in more exclusive neighborhoods. Such is the case in Chicago.

What Chicago activists saw was *a school system* that was "at-risk," not a system of schoolchildren who were "at-risk." It was a school system in which most of its students started school at a disadvantage and remained in that condition throughout their school years. The system's resources, however, were husbanded for those students who showed the most promise. These students were steered into a few well-performing schools that were provided with the most experienced teachers and frequently were provided extra resources. Those individual students who had overcome the risks, who had battled *Against the Odds* (Hess et al., 1989) to maintain good attendance and achieve good grades from their teachers, were steered into the system's better high schools. Meanwhile, most "at-risk" kids were concentrated in "holding pens" until they reached an age when they could officially drop out. Many had unofficially dropped out years before. If the facts were equally available, I suspect many other large urban systems could be similarly assessed.

Responses to the Problems

Following the Chicago Panel's publication of several of its dropout studies, we convened a symposium of university scholars and leaders from the city's nonprofit school-support agencies to examine solutions to the dropout problem. This symposium quickly dismissed the ad hoc proposals that treated potential dropouts as marginalized students. It adopted a sociological, rather than psychological, perspective to address student failure. The members built a matrix of student needs and potential solutions that covered all years from infancy to age 18 and included both hours spent in school and those spent out of school. It was agreed that a comprehensive approach would be needed. Otherwise, students could be expected to continue making what were apparently "rational" decisions to drop out of school: If a student was unprepared for high-school-level work when he or she graduated from eighth grade, and had been unable to accumulate any course credits during the first two years in high school, dropping out would seem more rational than investing another 4 years in the current school system. However, under the psychological scenarios advocated by academics, these dropouts could now be blamed for future life failures because they did not make it through a system that was stacked against them.

Chicago reformers decided it was the system that had neglected and stacked the odds against low-income and minority kids. Primarily, it was the system that was failing the kids, rather than the kids who were failing in the system. Such a conclusion was incomprehensible to Chicago school system administrators, who were more comfortable with psychological explanations of the failures of individual students. It is equally incomprehensible to many academics, social workers, and policy makers, whose actions serve to maintain these poorly performing urban school systems and whose jobs depend on the existence of a pool of "at-risk" students as clients.

When we described the ways in which Chicago high schools regularly shortchanged their students through 20% shorter subject periods, chaotic classrooms, and phantom study halls (Hess et al., 1986), the school superintendent's only response was that we were trying to "trash" the school system. When asked by the news media why the system could not do better by its students, Dr. Byrd could only respond by blaming the number of low-income students in the system ("Byrd Defends School Anti-Dropout Role," 1987). Refusing to only blame the victims, Chicagoans set out to reform the school system.

Thus the Chicago School Reform Act empowered the parents of

"at-risk" students by giving them the opportunity to win democratic control of local school councils governing their schools and by providing extra resources to the schools enrolling the most low-income students. This was a revolutionary move that one educational traditionalist, the dean of a local school of education, characterized as "giving the keys of the asylum to the inmates."

CHICAGO: A SYSTEMIC ATTEMPT TO ADDRESS THE NEEDS OF "AT-RISK" STUDENTS

In far too many settings across the United States, low-income minority students attend schools that are themselves at risk of failing their enrolled students. While these "at-risk" students may not come to school with all of the advantages of their more affluent agemates, at least in terms of the behavior characteristics that schools currently value and reward, they bring other strengths and maturities that are frequently ignored or devalued by school staffs trying to emulate their more "successful" neighbors located in more affluent communities. Instead of emphasizing the strengths their students bring to school and adapting their programs to successfully guide these students in the learning enterprise, these "at-risk" schools too frequently try to force their students to abandon the characteristics that make them successful on the streets of their own inner-city communities and replace them with the behaviors middle-class schools have traditionally rewarded. Without examining their own assumptions about what will make young people successful, these schools continue to emphasize the behaviors appropriate in bucolic small towns and suburbs and use learning patterns characteristic of a manufacturing century in an economy increasingly focused on information and service (see introduction to Part I and Chapter 8).

In this context, it is at least reasonable to raise the question as to whether it is the students or the schools that are most "at-risk" of failure. The assumption, at least among reformers in Chicago, is that *it is our schools that are more seriously failing our city's students*. Rather than blaming the students who are failing in our schools, we suggest it is the schools that are failing our young people. If our schools are unwilling to build on the strengths our students bring with them or are unable to restructure themselves to better meet our students' needs, then it is the schools, even more than the kids, that must be changed.

The Chicago school reform movement is an effort to address more adequately the previously unmet needs of low-income minority young people by creating a systemic opportunity for schools to restructure.

The Chicago School Reform Act embodies a very different philosophy of meeting their needs. It is a grand experiment in attempting to force schools to change to meet the needs of their students rather than assuming it is the students who must change to conform to the expectations of schools, schools that were originally created to produce citizens for a manufacturing age.

PART I

Marking the Progress of School Reform in Chicago

The Chicago School Reform Act was signed into law on December 12, 1988, in a ceremony that also celebrated the move into a new facility for the Washington Irving Elementary School. Teachers and students marched a half-mile from the century-old facility behind their principal, Madelaine Miraldi, and Governor James R. Thompson; in the gymnasium in the new building they convened with other political leaders and members of the school reform movement. Following speeches and back-slapping, the governor signed the law that set the public schools in Chicago on a radically different path.

The Chicago school reform effort stands out as the chief example of one current reform strategy: the devolution of authority from a large, centralized school district and its bureaucracy to local, democratically elected governance units at the school level.

The image of "school-based management" (SBM) carries many different connotations. It may be used to describe participatory management that includes teachers in school decision making. It may mean greater flexibility for principals in organizing their still largely autocratically run schools. It may be used to suggest tactical flexibility at the school level to meet national, state, and locally imposed goals, objectives, and strategies. Or it may mean a radical devolution of authority under which local units set their own goals and objectives, which may be at variance with the president's or governor's or other policy maker's ideas of what the one best educational system ought to look like (cf. Tyack, 1974). The Chicago school reform effort is the largest and most radical SBM experiment in the United States in granting authority to local parents, community representatives, and school professionals as a strategy for improving student achievement. It is a strategy that is in competition with other, more centralized approaches that emphasize the importance of coherence in the whole national educational enterprise.*

A BRIEF HISTORY OF RECENT SCHOOL REFORM EFFORTS

A convenient marker of the beginning of the current U.S. school reform movement is the 1983 release of *A Nation at Risk: The Imperative for Educational Reform* (National Commission on Excellence in Education). In somewhat overblown rhetoric, the report announced that the nation's public schools were being inundated by a "rising tide of mediocrity" and that, had an outside power done to our educational system what we have allowed to happen, it would have been considered an act of war. More than a dozen other major reports criticizing America's public schools were issued during the early 1980s.

While several states, such as Arkansas and California, had already undertaken a number of school reform efforts, many others adopted legislation in the years immediately following the release of *A Nation at Risk*. The key word in these early school reform efforts was "accountability." The central theme was higher requirements to assure excellence: higher certification standards for teachers, higher graduation standards for students, and report cards that gave higher visibility to school performance levels. The legislation enacted in this "first wave of school reform" frequently did not include significant provisions to change the way schooling was conducted, though it sometimes included more funds to increase teacher salaries. A "sound bite" description of this phase of reform might be: "Work longer, harder, and smarter so that students might learn more."

Scholars and practitioners more intimately connected to public schools than the politicians and business and civic leaders who provided the major impetus for the accountability focus realized that more fundamental changes were necessary if student achievement was to be improved. The "second wave of school reform" focused on "restructuring" schools and school districts. Three different strategies emerged as vehicles to accomplish this restructuring.

Enhancing teacher professionalization is a concept that encompasses a wide variety of approaches, from reshaping the preparation of

*This paragraph and the next three sections first appeared as part of the introductory article to the special issue of *Education and Urban Society* (Hess, 1994b) entitled *Outcomes of Chicago School Reform*, for which I served as editor. © 1993 by Corwin Press, Inc. Reprinted by permission of Corwin Press, Inc.

teachers in schools of education, to retraining the entire teaching faculty of a city such as Pittsburgh, to giving teachers a share in the decision making at local schools (a worker-participation strategy touted by business gurus such as Deming [1982] under the image of "total quality management").

A second strategy, *using market pressures to improve schools via enrollment choice*, was given impetus by the publication of *Politics, Markets, and America's Schools* (Chubb & Moe, 1990). This strategy is most widely debated under the image of vouchers, government grants for a year's education that parents can redeem for their children at any school of their choice. This strategy is frequently referred to as the "voting with one's feet" approach. Opening up public school enrollment choices, such as those pioneered in Minnesota (Perpich, 1989), have been seen as a way to avoid diluting state support for public schools while preserving the market pressure on schools to improve.

The third strategy, *parent involvement through school-based management*, had its roots in parent advisory councils mandated for federal Chapter I programs prior to 1980 and in the decentralization and community control efforts of the late 1960s and 1970s. When the Chicago School Reform Act was adopted in 1988, it stood as the culmination of this strategy.

CURRENT TRENDS IN SCHOOL IMPROVEMENT EFFORTS

The interaction of these various strategies for improving schools has produced an interesting realignment of actors during the 1990s. One development of the focus on heightened accountability of schools for their students' achievement has been *outcomes-based education*. The essence of this approach is the notion that schools should be accountable for the success of their students (the outcomes), not for complying with a long list of state regulations and mandates (the inputs). The theory here is that if the state, or the federal government, wants to establish goals or standards that schools should meet, then schools should not have the means of meeting those goals dictated in such detail that they have none of the flexibility required to change what they currently are doing in falling short of the goals. The logical end result of this strategy would be to eliminate virtually all state and district regulations on schools, except those necessary to assure the civil rights of minorities or those with special needs. Some self-professed conservative groups, such as the Eagle Forum, have associated outcomes-based education with specifically liberal curricula and have mounted a concerted attack on districts adopting an outcomes-based approach. The illogic of associating the outcomes-based approach with any specific curriculum content is ignored by such groups, but it is also frequently ignored by its liberal defenders.

A second strategy that has emerged from the accountability movement emphasizes improving and enhancing the inputs and components of the current schooling system. Advocates of this strategy originally focused on answering the criticism that current outcome measures focus on the use of standardized tests, which frequently emphasize basic skills rather than critical thinking or performance. They sought to develop more "authentic assessments" of what students should know and be able to do. Incorporated within this strategy was the effort to improve the capacity of the teaching force through restructuring the "preservice training" to be offered to potential teachers and by raising the expectation level for teacher capacity, both by shifting teacher training into a master's degree program of graduate education similar to professional training in other fields and by initiating a national certification board that would grant a higher level of certification for a limited number of teachers, similar to the board certification won by physicians with specialized skills. The ultimate manifestation of these efforts has been the call for *coherence in the nation's educational system*, most clearly articulated by Marshall Smith and Jennifer O'Day (1991), which argues that if we are to reach a set of national goals, then our assessments must measure achievement in terms of those goals, our curriculum should include the content and skills covered by the assessments, and our teachers should be trained in implementing that curriculum. Since Smith left the deanship of the Stanford School of Education in 1993 to become the Under Secretary in the U.S. Department of Education, that philosophy has underlain much of the Clinton administration's educational agenda.

A third strategy has emerged that is a more direct descendant of the movement toward school-based management. The effort to devolve authority from the district and state levels to the school level draws from both teacher professionalization and parent empowerment antecedents. From advisory councils and shared decision making, the movement for school-based management has emphasized giving school actors more power to determine the program of their local school. The Chicago school reform effort emphasized freeing schools from local school district regulation. In some states, such as Washington, carefully chosen schools were given waivers from state regulations to enhance this local control. In Minnesota in 1990, and in a number of states since, charter schools have been authorized by state legislatures. Charter schools are public schools that are supported with public funds and provide a free education for their students; frequently they are freed of the many restrictions and regulations of state school codes as long as they meet the goals included in their charters. To some extent, there is a similarity between charter schools in the United States and "grant-maintained" schools in England. If the goals of such charter schools focus on student achievement levels, there is also a compatibility with the outcomes-based education strategy. In some instances, charters are granted to groups of teachers seeking to organize teacher-run schools; in other cases, nonprofit boards are created to run the schools; for-profit companies also could be allowed to run publicly chartered and supported schools, as has actually been authorized in Massachusetts.

HOW RADICALLY SHOULD SCHOOLS CHANGE?

One cross-cutting issue among advocates of these various reform strategies involves the extent of the changes envisioned for public schools in the United States. Much of the impetus for reforming schools came out of the search for schools that made a difference for their students. As an antidote to the early work of James Coleman (1966) and Christopher Jencks and his colleagues (1972) that implied that schools do not make any difference in student achievement, that the socioeconomic status (SES) of students was all that mattered in predicting achievement levels, a series of researchers, including Ron Edmonds (1979) and Wilbur Brookover and Lawrence Lezotte (1979), identified inner-city schools that were effective in educating low-SES students. These researchers then identified the characteristics associated with these *effective schools* (see Purkey & Smith, 1983). The most well-known of these characteristics were strong instructional leadership from the principal, clear goals and high expectations for students, order and discipline, maximized learning time, and assessment and curriculum alignment to keep track of student progress. Other less frequently mentioned characteristics included school-site management, parental involvement, and collaborative planning and collegial relationships.

Implicit in a reform movement focused on creating schools that foster these characteristics, and that presumably will be effective in ensuring high student achievement, is the vision that effective schools will look a lot like the best of our current schools (most of which are located in the suburbs of our metropolitan areas) except that the student body may be composed of economically disadvantaged, and frequently mostly minority, students.

Similarly, a strategy focused on creating a *coherent national sys tem of public education* that integrates a common vision from goals through assessment, teacher instruction, and curriculum assumes that we already know what schools should look like: very much like the best of current schools. In short, both of these approaches are at best incremental in their vision of required change. The advocates of these strategies can safely argue that most change in public education has been incremental. That certainly has been the case for most of the twentieth century.

However, a growing number of scholars and practitioners are arguing that we are at a more radical turning point in the history of public education in the United States. They claim the current factory-model image of public schooling is no longer adequate. Bernard Avishai (1994) suggests that the batch processing of homogeneously grouped (at least by age) young people is designed to produce disciplined graduates who would be obedient workers used to taking directions. Tom Carroll (1992) argues that this design of schools does not fit the new shape of our national economy as we move out of the manufacturing age and into an information age. Avishai agrees that the information age, with its technological interconnectivity and its disparate, collaborative efforts of work teams separated geographically, demands a new structure for public schools. Such a vision demands more radical changes than those envisioned by incrementalists such as the champions of effective schools or the advocates of a coherent national policy.

The Chicago School Reform Act was designed to foster the development of effective schools across the city. It was framed out of the conviction that schools could make a difference for low-income and minority students, that social class was not destiny in terms of educational outcomes. It was crafted with the conviction that school actors had to be free to design programs that would meet the needs of their own students, programs that school staffs could "buy into" rather than programs imposed on them. But it was shaped out of the conviction that local school actors would not be likely to defy central office administrators to meet their students' needs unless they were primarily accountable to the parents of students and residents of the local community. Thus school-based management that involved a devolution of real power and of accountability was the most attractive vehicle available. This vehicle leaves open the possibility of radical departures from the current images and practices of public schooling, but it must be recognized that the Chicago School Reform Act, with its roots in the images of effective schools, is more likely to lead to incremental change than to radical restructuring.

A PLAN TO MONITOR REFORM IMPLEMENTATION

Even before the new reform-launching interim board of education was appointed, the Chicago Panel had outlined a comprehensive 5-year research design for monitoring the implementation of the school reform effort and had begun to secure funding for the project. John Q. Easton was attracted away from the public schools to direct the monitoring and research effort. As noted in Chapter 1, part of the project involves staff observing in 14 Chicago schools that are representative of the students enrolled in the Chicago Public Schools. Virtually every meeting of the local school council (LSC) in these schools was attended and recorded. Principals were interviewed each year. Teacher leaders from the Professional Personnel Advisory Committee (PPAC) and from the LSCs were also interviewed, as were the chairs of each LSC. Quantifiable data from all Chicago schools were compiled into annually produced databooks and analyzed for special reports. A 7-year longitudinal study of student achievement was launched. These efforts produced more than a dozen reports during the first 5 years of reform implementation. (See Appendix A for the methodology of the study.)

In addition, the Chicago Panel was one of the initial cooperating agencies that founded the Consortium on Chicago School Research. Headquartered at the University of Chicago and led by Anthony Bryk, the Consortium also developed a wide-ranging research agenda, which included surveys of 13,000 elementary school teachers and of every principal in the school system. Easton headed the work group that designed, conducted, analyzed, and reported on the 1991 teacher survey (Easton et al., 1991a). He served on the work group for the survey of principals (Bennett et al., 1992), which was staffed by another Panel employee, Darryl Ford. The Consortium's work also benefited from an ongoing study of the dynamics of reform in 12 purposively selected schools, conducted by the Center for School Improvement at the University of Chicago. Finally, in 1993, the Consortium conducted shorter investigations of six successfully restructuring schools. During the summer of 1993, these various approaches were drawn together in an integrative report entitled *A View from the Elementary Schools: The State of Reform in Chicago* (Bryk, Easton, Kerbow, Rollow, & Sebring, 1993). By participating with other skilled researchers through the Consortium, the Panel was able to assure that some of its research goals were achieved that otherwise would have been neglected due to a shortage of resources. The diversity of perspectives brought together under the aegis of the Consortium enriched the study of reform in Chicago in a way that no single agency could have done.

The chapters that follow are based on the research conducted by the Chicago Panel and the Consortium on Chicago School Research. In this part of the book, I provide a summary of the process of reform and its implementation and some insights into the reform effort. The chapters reflect assessments of the process as it was underway. It will be many years before the full impact of the Chicago reform effort can be adequately assessed.

CHAPTER 3

Restructuring the Chicago Public Schools: The Plan of Action

On December 2, 1988, the Illinois State Legislature voted to adopt the Chicago School Reform Act (P.A. 85-1418).* The act fundamentally changed the structure of public education in the city by creating local school councils consisting of teachers, parents, community representatives, and principals. Based, in part, on the business theory of participatory decision making, the councils are the vehicle through which the goals of Chicago school reform are to be achieved.

Chicago school reform has been called the most radical experiment in the history of public education. Its success or failure will have a major impact on how American children are educated. This chapter depicts the evolution of Chicago's particular type of school reform, from the actual restructuring of the Chicago Public School system to mobilizing support for school reform from citizen activists, parents, business executives, state and national efforts, and the media.

This chapter describes the restructuring reforms enacted by the state legislature and examines the reasons that led the General Assembly to act in this way. It suggests the ways in which the Chicago experiment are and are not applicable to school reform efforts in other venues.

THE CHICAGO PUBLIC SCHOOLS: IN NEED OF REFORM

The Chicago School Reform Act builds on the unique history of the Chicago Public School system. In 1985, the Chicago schools enrolled some 435,000 students, down from a high of 585,000 in 1968 (Chicago

*This is a revised version of my article, "Restructuring the Chicago Public Schools." Used by permission of Simon & Schuster Macmillan from *Education Reform in the '90s*, edited by Chester F. Finn and Theodore Rebarber. Copyright © 1992 by Vanderbilt University, Educational Excellence Network.

Board of Education, 1985). The school system was recovering from a fiscal crisis in 1979–80, when it had failed to meet its payroll and required a state financial bailout. This bailout included subjecting many of its financial decisions to the review and approval of an oversight board, the Chicago School Finance Authority (CSFA). Under the terms of the bailout, the system was forced to cut more than 8,000 positions from its budget (Hallett & Hess, 1982).

The school system was also operating under a desegregation consent decree and, as noted in Chapter 2, had virtually eliminated all predominantly white schools. However, in a school system that had only about 15% white enrollment, that left the vast majority of minority students continuing to attend completely segregated schools and not benefiting significantly from desegregation (Hess & Warden, 1987).

The system had involved parents in advisory roles since 1970 (Cibulka, 1975). Local advisory councils had been established at virtually all schools. Chapter I parent advisory councils were maintained at Chicago schools after the federal government allowed their discontinuance in 1982. Bilingual advisory councils were functioning in most schools serving large numbers of students with limited English proficiency (Chicago provided special instruction to students who collectively spoke more than 80 different languages). Further, the local school advisory councils or PTAs had been involved in the selection of school principals for nearly 15 years, interviewing candidates and recommending their three preferences, which were almost always followed in the general superintendent's recommended appointments.

However, the system was not being very successful in educating the children enrolled in its schools. In January 1985, Designs for Change, a Chicago-based educational research and advocacy group, released a study showing that only one out of three graduating seniors was capable of reading at the national norm and that at inner-city schools, the proportion was much lower than that (Designs for Change, 1985b). Two months later, the Chicago Panel on Public School Policy and Finance released a complementary study showing that 43% of entering freshmen dropped out before graduation, with dropout rates in inner-city schools reaching 67% (Hess & Lauber, 1985). When combined with the Panel's earlier study showing that the 8,000 positions cut during the 1980 financial crisis were disproportionately teachers and other student-contact staff (Hallett & Hess, 1982), a picture was created of a school system failing its students and more interested in protecting bureaucratic jobs than improving its schools. It was from this base that the school reform movement was launched.

THE INEFFECTIVENESS OF PREVIOUS STATE REFORM EFFORTS

In 1985 Illinois, like other states before it, enacted statewide school reform legislation in response to the report *A Nation at Risk* (National Commission, 1983). The 1985 reform act (P.A. 84-126) was long on accountability and short on serious efforts to improve the state's schools (Nelson et al., 1985). It did not seriously address the shortcomings of the Chicago schools, though the reports of high dropout rates and low graduate reading scores appeared as the bill was being debated. In a special section devoted to Chicago, the act did create local school improvement councils (LSICs) at every school, which were encouraged to engage in school improvement planning and given the right to review discretionary spending by the principal.

However, the accountability provisions may have been more important in the long run, because they helped highlight how poorly Chicago schools were performing. In 1987, the state report card showed that 33 of 64 Chicago high schools scored in the 1st (lowest) percentile of all high schools in the country on the American College Test (ACT). In fact, Chicago schools dominated that lowest percentile, which only included 54 schools nationwide. Only 7 Chicago high schools scored higher than the 10th percentile. At the elementary grades, 60% to 70% of all students were reading below the national norms on the Iowa Test of Basic Skills.

It is not surprising that state school reform had little effect on Chicago. Chicago is not very different from other large urban school systems. Dropout rates in Boston, for instance, when calculated the same way we did in Chicago, were 53% (Camayd-Freixas, 1986), and that did not include the 35% the Massachusetts Advocacy Center (1988) reported never made it to high school. Using similar statistics, the Dade County Public Schools, which include both the city of Miami and its suburbs, reported a 28% dropout rate (Stephenson, 1985). New York reported a 33% rate, though knowledgeable critics pointed out that that figure would be much higher if New York counted the kids transferred into the night school and then allowed to drop out ("Dropout Program Is Sought," 1988).

Meanwhile, suburban schools graduated upwards of 95% of their students. In fact, in Illinois, according to the state report card, some suburban districts graduated up to 105% of their students! Because the state report card was initially based on a comparison of the size of the graduating class with the ninth-grade class four years previously, schools with large numbers of transfers in, primarily those in the fast-growing suburbs, graduated more students than they had earlier had in the ninth grade. The urban dropout rates reported previously were based on longitudinal tracking of individuals, called cohort analysis studies, in contrast to the comparisons of aggregate enrollment, called attrition studies.

In short, urban schools are not like suburban schools, a fact recognized by most people. Rural schools are often different from either urban or suburban ones. But state policy makers too frequently ignore these differences, except to complain about their costs to the state. Urban districts are frequently described as "black holes," and the color reference is usually intentional. Rural districts are thought to be too small and inefficient. Both cost the state too much and perform too poorly. Suburban districts cost the state little and perform well. Even without much state aid, they spend much more on each pupil than the rest of the state.

If we all know these differences exist, why do state and federal officials continue to search for the "one best solution" (cf. Tyack, 1974)? Why do we try to enact the one set of policies that will fix all these schools? In fact, the problems faced by urban schools are quite different from those faced by suburban schools and by rural schools, and the solutions for each must be different as well.

The Council of Great City Schools (1987) reports that, in the United States, a quarter of all youth live in central cities. Students who attend urban schools are predominantly from disadvantaged homes, and these students dominate inner-city schools. In Chicago, more than half of the entering freshmen at Austin High School come from low-income homes, and 82% of those freshmen are reading at least two grades below normal. These disadvantaged students dominate the school enrollment. Yet from a policy perspective, we treat Austin like any other high school in the state!

In addition, in most states urban school districts are organized differently than other school districts in the state. Outside of Chicago, the average school district in Illinois has 1,385 students in about four schools of 300 to 350 students each. In 1991, Chicago enrolled 410,000 students in 542 regular attendance centers and 55 other specialty sites. There were 36 high schools and 10 elementary schools each with more students enrolled than in the average Illinois district! In the suburbs, most districts had 10 or fewer administrators. In Chicago, in 1988, there were 4,380 persons who worked in one of the administrative units in the central or subdistrict offices. There were another 38,000 employees working in the system's schools. Unlike most other districts in the state, urban school systems are administered by large, rigid bureaucracies, far removed from their large schools, which are neither successfully educating inner-city young people nor saving money.

The Chicago School Reform Act restructuring of an urban school system is an attempt to create a solution geared to the urban school problem. It would not necessarily be appropriate for problems in suburban or rural schools, except in those states using large county districts with their own bureaucracies. There may be aspects of the Chicago restructuring effort that would be appropriate in other settings, but the effort as a whole is aimed at the urban problem. States with large urban centers may find elements of the Chicago experiment that would address their own urban problems.

THE CHICAGO RESTRUCTURING PLAN

The restructuring of the Chicago Public Schools was mandated by P.A. 85-1418, the Chicago School Reform Act. There are three major components to the act: a set of goals, a requirement to reallocate the resources of the system toward the school level, and a system of school-based management that is centered on the establishment of local school councils at every school.

School Reform Goals

The 123-page Chicago School Reform Act contains 10 goals to serve as the measures of school improvement over a 5-year period. In essence, these goals require that students perform at national levels in achievement, attendance, and graduation rates and that the school system provide an adequate and rounded education for each enrolled student.

The specific goals are as follows:

1. assuring that students achieve proficiency in reading, writing, mathematics, and higher order thinking that equals or surpasses national norms;
2. assuring that students attend school regularly and graduate from high school at rates that equal or surpass national norms;
3. assuring that students are adequately prepared for further education and aiding students in making a successful transition to further education;
4. assuring that students are adequately prepared for successful entry into employment and aiding students in making a successful transition to employment;

5. assuring that students are, to the maximum extent possible, provided with a common learning experience that is of high academic quality and that reflects high expectations for all students' capacities to learn;
6. assuring that students are better prepared to compete in the international market place by having foreign language proficiency and stronger international studies;
7. assuring that students are encouraged in exploring potential interests in fields such as journalism, drama, art and music;
8. assuring that individual teachers are granted the professional authority to make decisions about instruction and the method of teaching;
9. assuring that students are provided the means to express themselves creatively and to respond to the artistic expression of others through the visual arts, music, drama and dance; and
10. assuring that students are provided adequate athletic programs that encourage pride and positive identification with the attendance center and that reduce the number of dropouts and teenage delinquents (P.A. 85-1418, Sec. 34-1.01.A).

While these goals are quite wide-ranging, it was generally agreed among the reform advocates and the monitoring agencies that the primary goals were the first two: raising student achievement to the national norms and raising attendance and graduation rates to the national norms. To achieve these goals systemwide would be a tremendous challenge, and at least in terms of graduation rates, probably unreasonable, given what is known about the elementary school effects on student graduation rates (cf. Hess et al., 1989). However, the act asks that these goals be met *at each school in the district!*

The Reallocation of Resources

One of the primary criticisms of the Chicago Public Schools during the 1980s was the continual growth of the central bureaucracy while local schools were starved for adequate numbers of teachers, texts, supplies, and other resources. These criticisms were based on budget analyses presented by the Chicago Panel during the board's annual budget hearings. These analyses were built on the Panel's initial research into the budget cuts surrounding the fiscal crisis of 1979–80 (Hallett & Hess, 1982). The determinative analysis came in 1987, in testimony on the general superintendent's proposed budget following a 19-day school strike (Chicago Panel, 1987). That testimony showed the growth of the administrative bureaucracy in each year since 1981, while total student enrollment was dropping. In 1981, there were 6.3 administrative staff for every 1,000 students; by 1986, the ratio had grown to 8.6 per 1,000 students. This growth in the bureaucracy was built from the low point in total staffing reached through personnel cuts following the fiscal crisis, cuts that were proportionately lighter for administrators than for teachers: 18% of classroom teachers were cut during the crisis, while only 13% of administrative staff were cut (Hallett & Hess, 1982). (See Appendix B for a fuller picture of the financial condition of the Chicago Public Schools.)

In addition, the Panel had identified an illegal diversion of state compensatory aid from serving disadvantaged students into supporting the central bureaucracy (Chicago Panel, 1988). Illinois, unlike most other states, has a poverty-impaction aspect in its school aid formula that is based on the proportion of economically disadvantaged students in enrollment. Districts with a proportion higher than the state level (about 18% in 1987–88) received additional weighting for those students in the school aid formula. In 1987–88, the Chicago Public Schools received $238 million in compensatory aid as part of total state aid of $832 million. Under 1978 legislation, Chicago was to distribute 60% of this state compensatory aid (called State Chapter I aid) to attendance centers on the basis of free-lunch counts, while 40% was to be distributed to attendance centers on the basis of total enrollment. In fact, the Chicago Board of Education diverted nearly a third ($42 million) of the funds targeted for disadvantaged students to support central administrative costs under the pseudonym of "Program Support." In addition, contrary to the intent of the law, but unfortunately not directly proscribed in this state law as it is in federal law, the board used these state compensatory funds to provide basic services, such as kindergarten, guidance counseling, and librarians, in schools with heavy concentrations of disadvantaged students while providing the exact same levels of these services at other schools with regular Education Fund resources.

The Chicago School Reform Act was drafted to include two provisions to alter the disproportionate allocation of resources within the school system. The first requirement was to place a cap on administrative costs. The intent of the reformers was to limit the proportion of the school system's budget that could be spent in the administrative units (the central office and the then 23 administrative subdistrict offices). However, difficulty was encountered in finding a nonarbitrary criterion for assessing what was "disproportionate." The initial legislation required not exceeding the proportion of expenditures in the fiscal year 1985 budget (FY 1985 was the year during which the then general superintendent had assumed office). One legislator wanted to use the FY 1981 year as the base. The associate superintendent for finance of the Illinois State Board of Education proposed an alternative that seemed less capricious. His suggestion, which was adopted, was to limit the proportion of noninstructional costs in the system to the average proportion of all other school districts in the state for the preceding year. The advantage of this recommendation was the obvious fairness of the criterion. The disadvantage, in practice, is that the state's codes of noninstructional expenditures include a number of items at the school level, such as teacher retraining, that the reformers explicitly intended to be supported by additional resources. However, the state associate superintendent predicted that his recommendation would free up about $40 million through downsizing the central administration; these funds would be available for redistribution to local schools. That figure was the key target figure for the second half of the reallocation design.

The Chicago Panel, along with two of its member organizations, the Chicago Urban League and the United Neighborhood Organization (a coalition of four constituent groups in primarily Hispanic communities), had been pressing the board of education to change the basis for its allocation of State Chapter I funds for several years (Hess & Warden, 1987). Although the general superintendent of the Chicago Public Schools acknowledged the propriety of the Panel's recommendation, he claimed such a shift in resources would be too disruptive of the school system. His response came at the same time that he was increasing central office staff while proposing to cut the number of teachers at the school level.

These reform groups were able to incorporate into the Chicago School Reform Act a provision to change the allocation procedures for State Chapter I aid. The first change was to prohibit the use of State Chapter I funds for any purposes outside local schools, except for 5% of the funds that had been used for desegregation purposes during the 1980s (the reform act, in numerous places, ensures that provisions of the act are not to be used to infringe on the system's desegregation efforts). This reallocation provision required that about $40 million of previously deducted "Program Support" funds be distributed directly to the schools, starting in the fall of 1989. In addition, another newly incorporated provision shifted the proportion of targeted funding from 60% to 100%, over 4 years (70% in the fall of 1989, 80% in 1990, etc.). Finally, one Chapter I reallocation provision, phased in over 5 years, required that none of the Chapter I funds would be used to support basic programs present in all schools. The resulting freed funds would be available for discretionary use at the school level. The act also required that any newly targeted aid (i.e., the difference between the 60% level in 1988–89 and the 70% level for 1989–90) be considered discretionary. This "supplemental/discretionary" provision of the act required that an additional $10 million be shifted to the school level in 1989–90. As a result of these various provisions, the average elementary school received about $90,000 in new discretionary resources for the first year of implementation of school reform in Chicago. That figure would increase to about $491,000 in the fifth year.

School-Based Management Provisions

The primary vehicle for achieving the goals of the act and for utilizing the reallocated resources was the establishment of local school councils (LSCs) at each school site. These councils were to be the cornerstone of school-based management and decision making. The LSCs were given three major responsibilities: to adopt a school improvement plan (SIP), to adopt a budget to implement that plan based on a lump sum allocation, and to decide whether to terminate the incumbent principal and select a new one or to retain the incumbent—in either case to sign the selected principal to a 4-year performance-based contract.

Complementary to the establishment of the LSCs, a number of other provisions in the reform act altered the responsibilities and authority of other actors in the school system: teachers, principals, district superintendents, the general superintendent, administrative units, and the board of education itself. These changes are enumerated below.

Local School Councils. Local school councils were mandated for each school site. These councils are composed of six parents, two community representatives, two teachers, and the principal. In high schools, they include one student. These student members were nonvoting members until 1991, when they gained a vote on most matters. Under the original legislation, the parent representatives were elected by a vote of the parents with children attending the school; parents who are also employees of the system are not eligible to vote for parent representatives or serve on LSCs as parent reps. The community representatives were elected by residents living within the geographic boundaries of the school enrollment area who were neither parents of enrolled students nor employees of the school system; employees may not serve as community reps. Two teachers were elected by all employees assigned to each school, exclusive of the principal. The principal is considered elected by his or her assignment to the school (P.A. 85-1418, Sec. 34-2.1).

This particular configuration of membership was designed to give parents a major voice in the educational decisions affecting their children. It was also designed to avoid the problems encountered in New York City, where employees, for several decades, were able to dominate elections to the 32 community boards of education that govern elementary schools in that city. Employees were given representation on each LSC, but only through the teacher and principal positions.

On November 30, 1990, this segmented voting pattern was declared by the Illinois Supreme Court to be in violation of the one-person/one-vote mandate of the federal and state constitutions. In June 1991, a new selection process was enacted under which parents and community residents select both parent and community representatives. Teachers are nominated by a vote of the faculty, but appointed to LSCs by the Chicago Board of Education.

District Councils. District councils were established for each administrative subdistrict in the city (P.A. 85-1418, Sec. 34-2.5). Each council is composed of one parent or community representative from each school in the district. These councils were given powers similar to those of LSCs to retain, terminate, or select a district superintendent (DS). The district superintendent was changed from being a line officer with authority over principals and school employees and answerable to the general superintendent into being a monitor and facilitator of school improvement responsible to the district council. The DS is charged to facilitate the provision of training to the LSCs, to mediate disputes at the local school, to settle election disputes, and to monitor both the establishment of a school improvement plan at each school and its implementation. If the DS judges that a school is not progressing adequately in adopting or implementing its improvement plan, he or she can recommend to the district council that the school be put on a remediation plan, which he or she develops for the school. If the school does not begin to improve under the remediation plan, the district council can place it on probation, under which a board of education improvement plan will be established to correct identified deficiencies at the school. If no improvement in correcting the deficiencies is noted after 1 year, the board may: (1) order new LSC elections, (2) remove and replace the principal, (3) replace the faculty, or (4) close the school.

The district council is to play a coordinating function for schools in geographic proximity to one another. Each subdistrict council elects a representative to a systemwide board nominating commission.

The Board Nominating Commission. The board nominating commission was charged to propose three nominations to the mayor for each appointment to the new board of education. An interim board of education was to be appointed by the mayor to serve 1 year. The new permanent board would contain 15 members on staggered 4-year terms. The initial nominating commission was charged to propose 45 candidates to the mayor by mid-April 1990. From the 15 slates of three nominees, the mayor was to select one appointee for each slot. If he found a slate did not contain any satisfactory candidates, he could reject the entire slate and request that a new one be recommended to him (P.A. 85-1418, Sec. 34-3.1). In fact, Mayor Richard M. Daley did reject about half the initial slates presented to him, and the first permanent board was not fully selected and seated until 17 months after the interim board had been selected.

The Interim Board of Education. As a result of a spring 1989 amendment to the Chicago School Reform Act, an interim board of education composed of seven members was appointed during May 1989, two months earlier than originally planned. Following the election of Richard M. Daley as mayor in April, the legislature advanced the implementation date of the reform act to give him a freer hand to get reform underway. The interim board of education, in addition to providing governance to the district between the initiation of the implementation of reform and the installation of the new permanent board of education, was charged with five major responsibilities: to institute a nationwide search for a general superintendent, to adopt a systemwide set of reform goals and objectives, to reduce administrative expenditures to meet the cap on noninstructional costs, to adopt a budget reallocating resources in line with provisions of the reform act, and to negotiate a contract with the system's employee groups (P.A. 85-1418, Sec. 34-3).

The Permanent Board of Education. The new permanent board of education was given most of the powers of the prereform board, with the exception of the powers granted to local school councils and district councils. To recognize the existence of the new, semi-autonomous LSCs, the basic descriptive term for the responsibility of the board was changed from "*management of*" to "*jurisdiction over* the public education and the public school system of the city" (P.A. 85-1418, Sec. 34-18). Specific new responsibilities included assuring the following:

- Proper reallocation of State Chapter I funds
- Establishment of an open enrollment plan by school year 1991–92 (later postponed to 1994–95)[1]
- Establishment and approval of "systemwide curriculum objectives and standards which reflect the multi-cultural diversity in the city" (P.A. 85-1418, Sec. 34-18)
- Protection of the civil rights of special education and bilingual pupils
- Reduction of overcrowding
- Opportunity for students to meet new state university entrance requirements
- Encouragement of new teacher-recruitment efforts
- Provision of training for personnel for their new responsibilities
- Establishment of a fund to meet special priorities the board might determine while distributing funds to attendance centers in an equitable manner

The powers and duties section concludes with the notation, "Nothing in this paragraph shall be construed to require any additional appropriations of State funds for this purpose" (P.A. 85-1418, Sec. 34-18.1-28).

Teacher Empowerment. While other school-based management efforts across the country have focused on giving teachers new participation in decision making at the local school level, the Chicago plan gives more council seats to parents and community representatives than to the professional staff. In most other school districts experimenting with school-based decision making, there are few new powers given to the school-improvement-planning teams, which mostly gain a voice in decisions previously made by principals by themselves. Frequently, the new school-level powers are restricted to waivers granted on a case-by-case basis by the board of education or the relevant employee union. In the Chicago plan, however, extensive programmatic, budgetary, and personnel control are granted to the LSCs. Since the intent of the Chicago reform act was to establish a new level of staff accountability for student achievement to parents and the community through the LSCs, it was deemed critical to assure that the councils were dominated by parents and community representatives.

At the same time, the importance of involving teachers in decision

---

1. It should be noted that an examination of the 1990–91 enrollment pattern of the Chicago Public Schools revealed that 28% of elementary students and 54% of high school students attended different schools than those in their neighborhoods to which they would have been geographically assigned; that is, they were already exercising enrollment choice.

making was recognized in the relationship mandated at the school level between the LSCs and the professional staff. Primary responsibility for school improvement planning was vested in the principal, who is advised by the Professional Personnel Advisory Committee (PPAC). The PPAC is to be composed of "certified classroom teachers and other certificated personnel who are employed at the attendance center" (P.A. 85-1418, Sec. 34-2.4a). The size and operation of the PPAC is to be determined by the certificated personnel at each school. The PPAC is established "for the purpose of advising the principal and the local school council on matters of educational program, including but not limited to curriculum and school improvement plan development and implementation" (P.A. 85-1418, Sec. 34-2.4a).

The Principal. Although never stated explicitly in the description of the principal's powers and duties, the Chicago School Reform Act is built on the assumption that the principal is the chief instructional leader in each school. The principal is given new powers and duties to enable his or her performance of that role. But principals are made directly accountable to local school councils for the effectiveness of their performance. At the point of contract renewal, principals who are judged ineffective may be terminated, with no tenure rights other than those they hold as teachers.

Principals are given the right to select teachers, aides, counselors, clerks, hall guards, or any other instructional program staff for vacant or newly created positions "based on merit and ability to perform in that position without regard to seniority or length of service" (P.A. 85-1418, Sec. 34-8.1). For the first time, the engineer in charge and lunchroom manager are also made accountable to the principal, though still not completely under his or her control.

Principals are also given the responsibility for initiating, in consultation with the LSC and the PPAC, a needs assessment for the school, for designing and recommending a school improvement plan for consideration by the LSC, and for drafting a budget for amendment and/or adoption by the LSC. Thus the principal is placed in the role of being the instructional leader of the school, charged to propose ways to improve the school that will win the approval of the parents, community, and teachers who make up the school community. The principal is given additional powers in staff selection, planning, and budget flexibility, and given additional resources with which to work. In exchange, the principal's continued employment is dependent on his or her ability to convince the LSC that he or she is being effective in exercising that leadership.

The Chicago School Finance Authority. Primary responsibility for monitoring the proper implementation of the Chicago School Reform Act was vested in an already existing oversight body: the Chicago School Finance Authority. The CSFA was established in 1980 to oversee the finances of the Chicago Public Schools, but with the return to fiscal stability of the system, its powers had been reduced to annual reviews of the board's budgets to assure that they were balanced (the CSFA could prevent the opening of schools if the budget were not balanced) and to paying off the large bonded indebtedness incurred to bail out the system from 1980 through 1982. The Chicago School Reform Act requires the board of education to submit to the CSFA and gain approval of an annual plan for reforming the school system. The CSFA is charged to assure that the major elements of the reform act are then appropriately implemented by the board of education (P.A. 85-1418, Sec. 34A). However, since the sanctions available to the CSFA are largely limited to reporting inappropriate actions to the General Assembly and other public officials, its oversight function for reform is significantly less empowered than its ongoing charge to assure the financial stability of the system.

Thus the relationships between the various primary actors in the public school system were fundamentally changed by the Chicago School Reform Act. By changing these relationships, the reform activists who wrote the law intended to give new opportunities to local school actors to shift the relationships between themselves and their students so that their students would have improved opportunities to learn. While recognizing that the shifting of these reporting, accountability, and decision-making relationships would not automatically result in different teacher–student relationships, the framers of the law were convinced that the learning nexus could not be changed under the existing set of bureaucratic relationships. Their vision of changed schools was based in the literature about effective inner-city schools that was being widely discussed during the 1980s.

THE THEORETICAL BASIS FOR CHICAGO SCHOOL REFORM

The major components of the Chicago School Reform Act were not selected randomly or as the haphazard result of political compromises, though compromises were required on several lower-level issues. The primary theoretical bases for the reform act are found in the research results associated with the effective schools literature and in the participatory management theories that find their educational manifestation in school-based management practices. Educational bankruptcy safeguards had been adopted in states like New Jersey to provide a way for state educational leaders to assure the effectiveness of local school districts.

Effective Schools

The effective schools literature gained visibility through the efforts of Ronald Edmonds (1979), a professor and researcher first at Michigan State University and then at Harvard University; later he became a high-level administrator in the New York City public schools, where he tried to implement the findings of his research. Edmonds sought out successful inner-city schools in which disadvantaged students were learning at or above national norms. He then contrasted these schools with comparable schools that were less successful. He and his Michigan State collaborators (e.g., Brookover & Lezotte, 1979) were able to identify a series of characteristics of what he called "effective schools." Chief among these characteristics was the conviction among the faculty that all students can learn successfully.

While such an assertion seems self-evident, inner-city educators had been making excuses for the poor performance of students in their systems based on the 1966 Coleman Report. James S. Coleman, principal investigator for a major study of urban schools for the federal Office of Equal Educational Opportunity, had found that the only variable that consistently correlated with low student achievement was the social and economic status of the student's family. The federal government used that research to initiate federal aid to disadvantaged students, now popularly known as federal Chapter I programs. However, in schools of education across the land, future school administrators were brainwashed through use of the Coleman findings into having lower expectations for students from poor neighborhoods. Edmonds set out to show that these lower expectations became self-fulfilling prophecies. He was able to demonstrate that when faculties held high expectations for the abilities of their students, those students were more likely to achieve at the national norms.

Edmonds also showed that the leadership of the principal is a key characteristic of an effective school. While no particular style of leadership was associated with this effectiveness in Edmonds' studies, the effectiveness of that leadership was related to the ability of the principal to establish a philosophical consensus about the educational program in his or her school. In addition, effective schools used frequent student assessments (testing) for diagnostic purposes, designing educational programs that were specifically geared to meet the changing educational needs of the enrolled students. These schools were also seen to be schools with clearly defined and maintained discipline and an orderly educational climate.

The Chicago School Reform Act was designed as an effort to foster the development of these characteristics in every city school. The leadership of the city's school system had used the poverty level of its students as an excuse for low performance for years. In an interview in a major city newspaper, General Superintendent Manford Byrd cited the poverty level of the city's students as the reason dropout rates were so high and test scores so low ("Byrd Defends School Anti-Dropout Role," 1987). As noted in Chapter 2, he explicitly rejected the findings of a Chicago Panel research report (Hess et al., 1986) that suggested the system was shortchanging the city's high school students by scheduling students into nonexistent study halls and using other scheduling mechanisms that reduced daily instruction to less than 4 hours (despite state law requiring 5 hours of instruction and a pattern of even higher average minutes of daily instruction across the suburbs). He denied that this lack of comparable instruction time was contributing to lower achievement and called the report a "trashing" of the public schools.

It was obvious to the activists in the Chicago school reform movement that few school faculties would operate out of the conviction that all students could be successful learners as long as they, and their principals, were responsible to administrative leadership that was more concerned to eliminate threats to bureaucratic stasis than to assure the high achievement of the system's students. This conviction was supported by research conducted by several local university professors a few years earlier.

Van Cleve Morris, Robert Crowson, Cynthia Porter-Gehrie, and Emmanuel Hurwitz (1984), at the University of Illinois: Chicago, had studied a number of principals in the Chicago school system. They coined the term "creative insubordinates" to describe those principals whom they found to be peculiarly successful. These were the principals who were willing to break the rules "creatively" to see to it that their schools performed effectively for their students. To the reformers, it was evident that the multitude of sanctions, both explicit and potential, which were part of the Chicago Public Schools bureaucratic chain of command, produced a repressive effect on principal creativity and leadership at the school level. While the "creative insubordinates" ignored the potential for sanction by their superiors, most principals lacked the intestinal fortitude to ignore the threats of their immediate superiors (the district superintendents, as formerly constituted) and other central administration bureaucrats.

The Chicago School Reform Act broke the repressive control of principals under the bureaucratic chain of command and shifted the locus of their accountability from their administrative superiors to LSCs dominated by parents. It was assumed that the primary concern of parents and community representatives would be the achievement levels of the students enrolled in the school. The reformers believed that principals would be empowered to exercise the instructional leadership necessary for effective schooling only when the potential for bureaucratic sanctions was removed and when they were given the capacity to shape the composition of the faculty of the school over time and provided new flexibility and resources for school improvement planning.

Participatory Decision Making

A second basis for the design of the reform act is the theory of participatory management, which was sweeping across the American business community during the 1980s. The movement in business toward decentralization and site-based management was rooted in the conviction that employees will be more productive when they participate in the decisions that affect their efforts. In public education, that theory was embedded in the notion of school-based management or shared decision making. Activists in the Chicago school reform effort had examined several particular manifestations of school-based management.

Karl Marburger (1985), of the National Committee for Citizens in Education, was consulted several times on his experiences with school-based management in school systems across the country, including St. Louis, Salt Lake City, and New York. In Marburger's experimental sites, school improvement councils were half parents, half staff. They enjoyed no additional powers at the school level beyond those previously experienced by the school staff. Their power at the school site was dependent on the extent to which principals wished to share the power they exercised. Marburger emphasized that, as he conceptualized it, school-based decision making was a voluntary sharing of power by the general superintendent and by principals at local schools. Given the intransigence of the Chicago general superintendent and the perceived number of ineffective principals, the Marburger approach was rejected.

More promising was the approach taken by several local affiliates of the American Federation of Teachers (AFT), to which the Chicago Teachers Union belonged. Under experimental implementation in Hammond (Indiana) and Dade County (Miami), school improvement councils were formed at participating local schools (O'Rourke, 1987; Hanson,

Morris, & Collins, 1992, respectively). They were given the permission to develop school improvement plans that might violate individual restrictions of either board of education regulations or provisions of the union contract. By agreement between the board of education and the union, waivers could be granted for potential violations of those regulations or provisions.

Elements of the AFT approach were incorporated in the Chicago School Reform Act. Although LSCs would not be dominated by teachers and professional staff members, as the councils were in Hammond and Dade County, teachers were given a role on the LSCs. However, the major parallel with the AFT approach is vested in the Professional Personnel Advisory Committee, which is designed to work collaboratively with the school principal on designing a school improvement plan, on matters of curriculum, and on other instructional matters. The reform act explicitly calls for the provision of waivers from both board of education policies and employee collective bargaining agreements (P.A. 85-1418, Sec. 34-2.3). Since the Chicago Teachers Union had initiated the discussion of contract waivers, it is not surprising that waiver language was added to the contract negotiated during the summer of 1989 to reflect that provision of the reform act.

Educational Bankruptcy

One other important provision was included in the reform act on the basis of experiments in school reform elsewhere in the nation. In New Jersey and several other states, so-called school bankruptcy laws had been enacted under which the state board of education could declare a school district educationally bankrupt and move to take over control of the district from local officials. In response to concerns that LSCs would become unaccountable for improvement at their schools, a similar provision was incorporated in the school reform act, as described above. However, reformers placed their primary reliance on the accountability of biannual elections for members of the local school councils. As in most other jurisdictions in this country, the primary responsibility for the effectiveness of LSCs lies with the electorate.

THE NECESSITY OF A LEGISLATIVE APPROACH

Even with this description of the major components of the Chicago School Reform Act and the theoretical bases on which the reform effort rests, the question still remains: Why was a legislative approach necessary? The answer to this question lies in the particular history and context of school reform in Chicago. Some dimensions of the answer have already been described above.

As just recounted, less radical school-based management approaches have been undertaken voluntarily in other locales. In St. Louis and in several community elementary districts in New York City, school-based plans were being implemented with the consultation and assistance of Marburger and his associates. In Salt Lake City, under Superintendent Donald Thomas, school councils had been in operation for a dozen years, though their effectiveness was questioned by outside researchers (Malen & Ogawa, 1988). In Hammond, Dade County, and several other cities with AFT locals, school-based management was incorporated in the union contract.

In each of these situations, the key ingredient was the willingness of the superintendent of schools to engage in some dimension of power sharing. Similarly, at the local school level, a required element was the willingness of the principal to enter into a power-sharing arrangement. Only in Hammond, after years of implementation, was there any requirement that principals be willing to engage in power sharing or face removal.

In Chicago, these conditions simply did not exist. As has already been demonstrated, the general superintendent seemed to be focused on power accumulation rather than power sharing. His budget proposals progressively drained resources from the schools while expanding the bureaucratic empire. He accused those who questioned his priorities of "trashing" the public schools and at a public meeting referred to their support by foundations as "pimping off the miseries of low-income students." In sharp contrast to the approach of his counterparts in such school districts as Dade County, Hammond, Rochester (New York), or Cincinnati,[2] his relationships with the teachers union and other employee groups were confrontational rather than collaborative. The confrontation between the administration and the unions culminated in a 19-day school strike in the fall of 1987. The school reform effort gained significant momentum as a result of that strike.

In the obvious absence of any inclination for voluntary agreements

---

2. The general superintendents and AFT local presidents from these four cities were guests at a conference in Chicago on June 30, 1987, just 2 months prior to the longest teachers strike in the city's history. The conference was jointly sponsored by the Chicago Teachers Union and Chicago United, a coalition of major business and civil rights groups in the city. Superintendent Byrd refused the invitation to attend or even to bring greetings to his colleagues from these other major urban school systems.

that might lead toward improvement of the Chicago Public Schools, an effort was mounted through the Mayor's Office to coerce the school system and its employees into a set of agreements patterned after the Boston Compact (Cippolone, 1986; Schwartz & Hargroves, 1986). In October 1986, Mayor Harold Washington convened an educational summit focused on what he called "the learn–earn connection." Washington, facing a reelection campaign the following spring, perceived potential vulnerability in two related areas: high minority youth unemployment and high dropout rates/low qualifications of graduates of the public schools. He called together some 40 representatives of the business community, the school system, the teachers union, area universities, and civic groups to address these issues. Politically inspired, the original intent was that the summit would last about 6 months, but the mayor reconvened the summit for a second year following the 1987 school strike.

The first year of the education summit was built on the false premise that the school system would be willing to take steps to reform itself if it were offered jobs for its qualified graduates. The assumption was that promises of expanded job opportunities for qualified graduates would induce the school administration to take steps to increase the number of its students who both graduated and had higher achievement levels. The fallacy was in the assumption that central office administrators cared what happened to students after they left high school. School systems receive no inducements for the success of their students after they leave the system. As long as pupils are enrolled, the system receives state aid tied to some student-based formula. But even this aid is no inducement to retain students, for the aid formula in Illinois provides less than half of the per-pupil costs of education in most school districts, while property tax support is not affected by enrollment declines (e.g., declines resulting from high dropout rates; cf. Hess & Lauber, 1985). The fallacy was in assuming that school administrators would be willing to undergo the pain of restructuring and resource reallocation (e.g., firing or reassigning their friends and colleagues) in order to secure a benefit for graduating students. Needless to say, summit-sponsored negotiations between the business community and the school system failed during the summer of 1987. They foundered on the general superintendent's demand for $83 million in additional support before the system would agree to any significant effort to improve its schools.

During the second year of the mayor's education summit, reconvened after the disastrous 19-day school strike, the fears and desires of system administrators and union representatives were largely ignored. Under immense political pressure following the strike, neither administrators nor union leaders were willing to refuse to participate in school reform agreements that were dominated by the desires of parent and business representatives. However, it was also obvious to most participants that administrators and board members had little intent to implement any significant aspects of the summit agreements. Mayor Washington had died during the second year of the summit and had been replaced by a weak acting mayor, Eugene Sawyer, who showed little inclination to pressure the school administration to adopt significant reform.

In addition to the contextual issues that made legislation appropriate, there were certain legal requirements that had to be changed if school reform was to be effective. The compromise enacted in 1978 about the use of State Chapter I funds had been abused by the board of education. It was necessary to require the board to distribute the money entirely to schools on the basis of enrollments of low-income children, to equalize basic programs, and to make these compensatory funds discretionary. These elements required amendment of the 1978 statute. Similarly, the creation of LSCs with real power required replacement of the local school improvement council provisions of the 1985 reform act. In a similar vein, the effort to change the relationships of some employees, so that engineers and lunchroom managers would be responsive to principals, required changing existing school code provisions. The new governance and certification provisions also had to be inserted in place of existing provisions of the school code. Thus legislation was needed to correct previous statute mandates.

New legislation was also required to constrain certain behavior. The Chicago Panel had demonstrated the insatiable growth of the central bureaucracy, eating up the newly acquired resources of the school system. If school reform was to work and new discretionary funds were to be available at the school level, this propensity for top-heavy growth had to be constrained. Thus a cap on the size of the administration was written into the statutes, along with monitoring authority for the state board of education.

For all these reasons, mandating legislation would be needed if school restructuring and reform were to be implemented in Chicago. The Chicago School Reform Act, P.A. 85-1418, was the vehicle enacted to require reform in the city's schools.

INITIAL REFORM IMPLEMENTATION

With the state legislature's enactment of the Chicago School Reform Act (P.A. 85-1418), attention shifted from the state capitol back to Chicago. To examine the legislatively required changes in various dimensions of the school system, the general superintendent created a reform task force, with 18 individual task forces. However, resistance to the mandates of the act was high, by both administrators and members of the board who were originally scheduled to be replaced by an interim board on July 1, 1989.

The primary election for a permanent mayor to serve out the balance of Mayor Washington's term was scheduled for March 1989, with the general election in the following month. Richard M. Daley, son of Chicago's former mayor, became the leading candidate. He made education reform the centerpiece of his electoral campaign. Several Northside school reform activists took visible roles in his campaign and in shaping his school reform platform. Once again, school reform was caught up in mayoral, and thereby racial, politics.

Daley, the white son of a former four-term mayor, was running against Sawyer, a black. Sawyer had been selected by the city council as acting mayor to succeed Harold Washington, the city's first black mayor. He was chosen over Tim Evans, another black who had been Washington's council floor leader, primarily on the votes of white aldermen and a few black aldermen who had been Democratic machine loyalists. Thus, Washington's black–Hispanic–progressive coalition split apart following his death. While some black political leaders backed Sawyer, emphasizing the need to "keep the seat," others saw him as a dupe for the old-line, white machine leaders. Anti-machine blacks backed Evans, who established the Harold Washington Party to oppose Daley in the general election. With the black community divided and Hispanics wooed by Daley, the former mayor's son easily defeated Sawyer in the primary and Evans in the general election. With Daley's electoral victories, school reform had an active booster in City Hall. But the cost to reform was high. School reform, already viewed suspiciously by some in the black community as threatening local black leadership of the school system, was now seen as a program of this "new Daley" who had wrested the mayor's office back out of black hands.

The new mayor was able to forge an alliance with the Speaker of the House to achieve two significant victories in the spring 1989 legislative session: The date of implementation of school reform was pushed forward to May 1, 1989, and an increase in the income tax was passed to provide new revenues to both the city and the board of education. On May 26, Daley appointed a new interim board of education, dominated by persons with direct contacts to the school reform movement.

During the late spring, summer, and early fall of 1989, the interim board accomplished four of the five major tasks assigned to it under the reform act ("Interim board accomplishes," 1989). It cut 544 jobs out of the central administration and reallocated the resulting resources (nearly $40 million) to local school budgets as discretionary funds for the forthcoming LSCs. It negotiated a contract extension with its employee groups to assure a smooth opening of schools in the fall. It negotiated the dismissal of the general superintendent and hired his replacement. And the interim board successfully conducted elections for the local school councils. On October 12 and 13 some 313,000 persons chose, from among more than 17,000 candidates, the 5,400 parents, community representatives, and teachers who were to sit on the new LSCs. The interim board failed in its mandate to submit a systemwide reform plan to the overseeing Chicago School Finance Authority before the opening of the school year (a draft plan outline was submitted to satisfy the legal filing requirement; it was then returned to the board to be amended and resubmitted at a later date).

With the election of the 540 local school councils, the major effort at reform moved to the local school level. In the first school year (1989–90), LSCs were to design and adopt a school improvement plan; they were to adopt a school budget for the ensuing school year; and in half the system's schools, the councils were to determine whether to terminate the incumbent principal and select a new one or to offer the incumbent a new 4-year, performance-based contract (the remaining schools would make a determination about their principals during 1990–91). With few exceptions, LSCs carried out all of these responsibilities.

Citywide training and organizing efforts were extensive during the first year of implementation, with reform groups offering extensive training to LSC candidates in the months prior to the October elections. These groups also mobilized to get out the vote for the elections. Following the elections, they provided up to 30 hours of training for individual school councils that requested this outside assistance. The reform groups also mobilized widespread support for school reform by involving more than 100 organizations in a Citywide Reform Coalition to address continuing problems in improving the quality of education in Chicago schools. Finally, the reform groups, through their own more focused coalition, the Alliance for Better Chicago Schools (ABCs), continued to put pressure on the interim board and the new general superintendent to force timely and appropriate support from the central administration for school-based decision making.

The following chapters describe more fully the successes and shortcomings of LSCs in carrying out the responsibilities given to them under the Chicago School Reform Act.

CHAPTER 4

Year One: Contested Authority

The effort to reform the Chicago Public Schools formally was initiated with the appointment of the Interim Board of Education in May 1989.* Local school councils were elected in October of that year. A new general superintendent had been selected in September but did not start full-time employment in Chicago until January 1990. During the spring and summer of 1989, more than 80 principals had decided to retire and 50 branches of existing schools were made into independent schools, with interim principals appointed by the superintendent to launch reform in both of these situations. During the spring of 1990, local school councils (LSCs) selected permanent principals for these schools and for about 140 other schools. Through these diverse paths, the actors were assembled who would implement the Chicago School Reform Act. Their first year (1989–90) would be spent exploring the newly determined limits of their authority. Some would be gaining new opportunities and seeking every possible opening that could be developed. Others would be adjusting to reduced responsibilities. Some were confused. The first year of "school reform" would be a year of "sorting it all out."

To foster the intent to make "the individual local school the essential unit for educational governance and improvement" under the Chicago School Reform Act (P.A. 85-1418), the General Assembly devolved to the school level a number of powers previously exercised solely at the central administration or board level. However, a number of powers were explicitly reserved for centralized decision making, decisions that in other school-based management systems, such as in Great Britain (see Hess, 1992a), were also delegated to the school level. Many of these reserved decisions had direct impact on decisions that might be made at

---

*This chapter draws heavily on G. A. Hess & J. Q. Easton (1992), "Who's Making What Decisions: Monitoring Authority Shifts in Chicago School Reform." In G. A. Hess (Ed.), *Empowering Teachers and Parents: School Restructuring Through the Eyes of Anthropologists*. Reprinted by permission of Bergin & Garvey, an imprint of Greenwood Publishing Group, Inc., Westport, CT.

the school level. As noted in Chapter 3, among the reserved decisions are the responsibility to negotiate and sign contracts with employee unions, to adopt a systemwide budget, to adopt a systemwide school reform plan, to determine school enrollment patterns across the system, and to assure the continued implementation of desegregation programs operating under a consent decree with the federal government. In addition to all applicable local, state, and federal laws and regulations, LSCs are required to act within the constraints of employee contracts signed by the central board and within the policies established on the basis of these various reserved powers. Thus local schools are not entirely free to do as they please in deciding how to manage their educational programs and facilities.

During the second year of reform implementation, some issues arose that demonstrated that the locus of authority between schools and the central administration was still in dispute. In addition, there were some decisions for which authority was not contested but the impacts of which were seen by LSC members to be unfair and inappropriate.

AUTHORITY SHIFTS UNDER CHICAGO SCHOOL REFORM

Under the Chicago School Reform Act, LSCs were to become the primary site of school governance in Chicago. During the first year of implementation, there was considerable disagreement in the city, however, about what that shift entailed. In addition, there were some, both within the school system and outside it, who believed this central aspect of the Chicago School Reform Act was a fundamental error that should be undermined, if not reversed. Thus the first year of school reform could be described as a set of informal negotiations about how much authority LSCs now had and how much authority the central board and administration retained. These negotiations were not conducted in comfortable conference rooms with representatives of the contestants gathered around tables. They took place in decisions of the board of education, in memos from the superintendent, in defiant responses by school councils, and in court decisions. Several of these major decisions need to be examined before proceeding to an analysis of how authority came to be exercised at the local school level.

One central element of the reform act required the board of education to reallocate its resources in two ways. First, a cap was placed on administrative spending. The interim board's first act was to rewrite the superintendent's proposed budget to eliminate 544 central office staff positions and shift nearly $40 million to local school budgets. This shift funded the first-year effort in the other reallocation requirement, that funding to schools with high numbers of low-income students be progressively increased and that the use of those compensatory funds become, over 5 years, completely discretionary at the local school level (for a fuller description of this funding shift, see Appendix B). As a result of these requirements, the average elementary school received $90,000 in new discretionary resources in the first year of school reform, and that figure would increase to $491,000 in the fifth year. However, the interim board also entered into contracts with its employee unions during the summer of 1989 and again during the summer of 1990 that included raises totaling 26% over 4 years, for which new resources were not available (see Chapter 5 for further details). This forced the board to cut progressively the base level of funding for all schools during these years, undermining much of the new discretionary budget power of the LSCs.

Two other sets of related decisions impinged on LSCs as they were first getting started. The very first decision LSCs faced, before they even elected officers, was where to meet. While this decision seems to have an obvious answer, in fact, this was not the case. The law required LSCs to meet in a public place where their meetings could be observed by the public. However, custodians refused to open school buildings at night without overtime pay, and the board, having used up its available resources in giving pay raises, refused to fund that cost. Thus LSCs were required to scramble just to find places to meet. After several months, a compromise between the board and the engineers' union allowed LSCs to use schools two nights per month, at no extra cost to each school.

Similarly, within weeks of their election, LSCs were informed that they had to adopt spending plans for the current year's compensatory (State Chapter I) funds by December 1. This meant that, just as they were getting organized and before the members had had a chance to get to know one another, LSCs had to devote several meetings to deciding on the best use of fairly sizable amounts of money. This was a considerable disruption in the intended pattern of reform in the first year—that LSCs would spend their initial months getting trained and then doing an assessment of the needs of their school prior to exercising their three major responsibilities: adopting an improvement plan, adopting a budget, and selecting a principal. Instead, they were forced to make important budget decisions prior to receiving training and prior to conducting a needs assessment.

LSC OPERATIONS DURING THE FIRST YEAR OF SCHOOL REFORM

Local school councils were to be the essential unit of school governance and improvement under the Chicago School Reform Act. As noted in Chapter 3, they were given broad powers to adopt a school improvement plan, to adopt a budget, and to select the school's principal. They were also charged to advise the principal and staff on curriculum, textbook selection, discipline, and attendance. Chicago Panel staff found that these powers were exercised in different ways at different schools. In some schools, LSCs formally acted to make decisions that were not strictly within their purview under the law. In other schools, LSC decisions were hard to discern and frequently were little more than agreements with reports from the principal.

Across the system, all but 81 schools had adopted school improvement plans by the end of June 1990 and all but 40 had submitted budgets for 1990–91, according to the superintendent of schools ("'Fuzzy' School Plan Rejected," 1990). By mid-February 1991, 324 principals who were serving schools when the reform act was signed into law had been selected by their LSCs to continue in that role. That means some 203 schools (38.5%) were being served by principals who had come to their schools since reform was enacted. Five of the 14 schools in a sample of schools studied by the Chicago Panel selected a new principal. Systemwide, this was an unprecedented change in the persons exercising newly expanded authority at the local school level.

Staff from the Chicago Panel observed council meetings for the second half of the school year in 14 schools—10 elementary and 4 high schools. Two of these schools did not formally agree to participate in the observational study until the second year, and they are not included in much of the ensuing analysis. These 14 schools are representative of the school system as a whole in terms of racial characteristics, size, and geographic location, but, because of the small sample size, we do not claim that our observations can be automatically generalized to the system as a whole. However, these data do illustrate the distinctive ways that different local school councils operated. A report (Easton & Storey, 1990c) containing the data included in this chapter was sent to each LSC in the hope that it would help LSC members evaluate the effectiveness of their own councils through a stimulated process of self-analysis.

We examined *who* attended LSC meetings and who participated in the discussions of issues. We examined *what* issues were discussed and with what frequency. We looked at the school improvement plans that were adopted to examine the extent of authority LSCs were exercising.

And we examined *how* participants in this process, particularly principals, saw their roles changing under school reform. The details of meeting attendance and participation are presented more fully in Chapter 5, where the experiences of LSCs during the first two years of reform are compared. The first year's experience can be summarized as follows.

Attendance, Participation, and Topics of Discussion

LSC meetings during the first year of reform implementation averaged about 2 hours (127 minutes), with some councils averaging only about an hour-and-a-half and others meeting for nearly 3 hours. Usually 8 of 11 members were in attendance in elementary schools and 9 of 12 in high schools (high schools had a nonvoting student member on their LSCs). About 6 other adults would attend elementary LSC meetings and 18 others at high school meetings. Principals attended virtually every meeting; LSC chairs (always a parent) attended 88% of all meetings, the same attendance pattern as that of the 2 teacher members. Thus a core of the principal, chair, and 2 teachers were present at almost all LSC meetings. Parent members other than the chair attended three of every five meetings (62%), while community representatives attended two of every three meetings (67%). While most LSC members were quite constant in their attendance, 31% of nonchair parent members, 25% of community representatives, and half of the student members missed more than half the first-year LSC meetings. Thus LSCs in our sample of schools generally had a reliable core of members at each meeting, but a few of the councils struggled with some nonperforming members, and several requested individual members to resign due to poor attendance. The July 1991 amendments to the school reform act that met the requirements of the Supreme Court's decision created procedures for removing nonperforming LSC members.

Different members had different degrees of influence on decisions made by the LSCs. And different members participated more frequently on some topics than on others. As might be expected, principals participated more frequently than any other LSC members. Together, they addressed nearly two-thirds (66%) of all items discussed at LSC meetings during their first year. The chairpersons participated next most frequently (43%). Teachers participated 32% of the time, community members at 28%, and other parents spoke least frequently, to only 17% of discussed topics.

Not only did different members participate in discussions at different rates, they participated on some topics more than on others, as might be expected. Principals spoke more frequently about the school program, building and safety matters, and issues of finance and budgeting (speaking to more than 74% of these items when they were discussed). They rarely spoke on parent and community involvement items and participated less frequently on the range of other topics that we did not classify. Participating at a generally lower level, LSC chairs spoke to about half the discussions of LSC organization and procedures, building and safety matters, and personnel issues. Other parents rarely spoke to any of the issues, though, on average, at least one other parent spoke each time school programs, building and safety, and personnel were discussed. Teachers and community members spread their participation fairly evenly across all subjects.

During the first year of LSC meetings, the most frequently discussed topics concerned the programs of the individual schools (29%), with LSC organizational topics next most frequently on the agenda (28%). Most of the rest of the agenda involved issues of the building, security, or safety (13%); finance (11%); or personnel (11%). Surprisingly, parent and community involvement was rarely discussed at LSC meetings (4% of agenda items). Among the school program items, the curriculum and the nature of instruction were given the most attention. Each school was required to develop a school improvement plan (SIP). Some schools gave the improvement planning process much more attention, while in others SIP adoption was almost a routine decision. Similarly, in one school, overcrowding dominated the meetings of the LSC for months, while in most schools in our sample, it was not an issue.

Our analysis of LSC participation rates, when combined with our firsthand observation, led us to the conclusion that principals frequently played the role of *information provider* to the LSC. Frequently the items principals participated in started as items in the regular principal's report, an agenda item for virtually all regular LSC meetings. The chairpersons, who participated more evenly on the range of topics discussed, more frequently played the role of *facilitator*, helping the LSC to understand an issue or come to a decision. It is worth noting that the chairperson participated least frequently in school program issues, the arena in which the principal participated most frequently. Other parents and teachers participated most often on personnel and building and safety issues. Interestingly, teachers made fewer comments on school program items than did these parents. Community members were most likely to be heard on building and safety issues and on LSC organizational matters, and less frequently on school programs.

How Principals Initially Viewed Their Roles

Let us now examine the experiences of principals as the reform effort was being launched. As pointed out in Chapter 3, the Chicago School Reform Act was built on the conviction that an effective school would be led by an effective principal (Brookover & Lezotte, 1979; Edmonds, 1979; Purkey & Smith, 1983). Not all principals approached school reform enthusiastically. Members of the Chicago Principals Association filed suit to try to overturn the reform act, but there was no decision on this litigation during the first year of reform implementation. During interviews in the spring of 1990, only six principals in our original school sample identified changes in their role that they characterized as positive (Ford, 1991).

Two principals cited the increased discretion/flexibility that they now had as a result of school reform. One principal noted that she could get things done more quickly because she did not need approval from various layers of the bureaucracy. She also noted that she could acquire better teachers for the school by conducting her own interviews and making her own selection based on merit, not seniority. She also liked the discretionary funds that became available at her school. She put it this way:

> We were able to take State Chapter I money and allocate more money for books and supplies. We were able to allocate where we felt our needs were. And I've also written in four positions for summer school. We always have far more kids wanting to go to summer school than the board ever let us have. (Ford, 1991, p. 9)

Several principals commented on the additional assistance they received under school reform. One commended the additional wisdom brought by LSC members and the advantage of making decisions collaboratively. He commented, "It's inconceivable to me that a lot of people are going to come together and agree on something that isn't for the benefit of the children" (p. 9). Another principal commented that reform had given him 10 potential allies, but noted that the potential "ain't happened yet" (p. 9). Other principals commented on the new assistance they were receiving from professionals and universities. Yet another principal commented on the higher level of communications required by working with her LSC. She noted that she had always been a planner, but realized now that she had not always let others know what those plans were. She saw the new need to communicate as increasing the involvement of others.

Principals also appreciated the power they had to select staff. One commented:

> You might say that students have been better served because for the first time this year, when I had a vacancy, I didn't have to take the teacher [that] the Personnel Department sent me. I had a choice. I know of one case, . . . who I would have gotten, and I know that I made a better choice because this [other] teacher, the last seven schools he was in, every principal closed the whole . . . program just to get rid of him. That's how bad he was, and nobody wanted to go through due process [to terminate him] because it was easier to close the program for a year and later reopen it. (p. 5)

Interestingly, there was no evidence in our sample schools of principals seeking to use the relaxed procedures for remediation and dismissal of unsatisfactory teachers. This is a new power principals had not begun to use.

Some principals felt school reform had brought an increase in total power at the local school level. While others saw the power equation more as a zero-sum game, one saw it somewhat differently:

> One of the things about the school reform act is that it stresses a sharing of power and hopefully we will be able to illustrate that through sharing, we all have more power. Rather than diminishing power that we all have, we increase it. We increase our ability to accomplish by sharing power. That's the great hope of reform. (p. 5)

However, overall, principals were more prone to make negative comments about changes in their roles under reform. The most common complaint was about time. One principal said:

> The only thing I worry about is time: time, time, time. It's amazing, these people get on one small topic and you can spend an hour on it. Then, when you think about the many things that we have to cover, it adds up. But the one thing I am fully committed to is spending all the time that I am asked to spend. (p. 11)

Another principal echoed that complaint and reinforced the image of the principal as the information provider:

> The downside of school reform is that I just don't have enough time in my day. It's taken far more time. First of all, I'm spending a lot of time explaining to people who have no background knowledge. It's

just time consuming. I'm not decrying it; it's just time consuming.
(p. 11)

Other principals noted that the time demanded by the LSC elections and new activities related to council operations have entailed certain opportunity costs, particularly related to supervision and contact with other members of the faculty.

Another principal noted that she had taken on three new roles that she did not think appropriate. The first was that of being a public relations figure. She complained about the time she had to spend with parents on PR instead of doing her job. She suggested that if she did not spend a lot of time smiling at parents, her contract would not be renewed. Her concern was echoed by several colleagues who mentioned their fears about LSCs misusing the power to fire principals without good reason. This principal also noted that she had to spend time being a referee, trying to bring together two different factions in her school community. Finally, she complained that her post-reform role was primarily clerical:

> But you know, this is becoming very frustrating because it seems like everything is falling on my shoulders—dealing with the parents, dealing with the local school council, dealing with the teachers, getting all of the reports done—and it's very frustrating. . . . You know, I feel like a glorified clerk. You see what I'm saying, why I'm so frustrated—because that's all that I am, a glorified clerk. (pp. 11f)

Another principal, in commenting negatively about the way his council was operating, unknowingly revealed how some councils infringed on the powers legally mandated to the principal. He complained,

> Here we are, we're interviewing four persons for the position of Child Welfare Attendant. *We are interviewing.* Now, I have to adjust to that. That is my problem with it. I just honestly feel that I'm in the better position to know which of those four should be in that position. (p. 12)

Interestingly, this principal was uncomfortable with the LSC's being involved in personnel selection, but he was apparently unaware that this function was really his prerogative, not the LSC's. However, it may be that this principal had been intimidated by the other members of the LSC. Other principals were also worried about LSC members' exceeding their authority. One was particularly concerned that LSC members would not stick to policy issues, as board of education members are supposed to do, but would try to circumvent the principal to be directly involved in issues such as teacher evaluation, another responsibility clearly delegated to principals under the reform act.

Several principals commented on the new demands on them to work collaboratively with new groups of people, whether it be the LSC on budgeting or the Professional Personnel Advisory Committee on instructional matters. These cooperative efforts provided increased involvement but were not as efficient as when the principals did things by themselves.

But some principals saw this expansion of authority at the local level less charitably. One principal complained that she possessed more responsibility for education but had less help, the same salary, and her job on the line. She commented, "[We] have all this power, but on the other hand, we have a sword hanging over our heads" (p. 7). Another principal commented that she did not like the fact that two teachers would help to decide whether her contract would be renewed.

Nearly half of the principals echoed the concern about ultimate responsibility lying with the principal. Principals commented that "the final burden is on the principal" or "the ultimate responsibility is mine" or "let's face it, responsibility for this stuff really comes back basically to the principal" (p. 8). Still one principal expressed the relationship between the principal and the LSC a bit differently:

> The local school council is an oversight [authority] for the school—who operates through the principal. That's the kind of relationship we have—oversight committees or as liaisons, and they work through, not with. (p. 8)

For this principal, ultimate responsibility rested with the LSC, but that authority was delegated to the principal to implement LSC decisions.

What Improvements Were Planned?

Each of the 14 schools we were observing adopted an initial school improvement plan during the spring of 1990. Panel staff undertook an analysis of these plans to understand what schools intended to do to improve the quality of education they were offering their students.

The Chicago School Reform Act mandated that each LSC should create a 3-year school improvement plan that would lift student achievement, attendance, and graduation rates to the level of national norms, while providing "a common learning experience that is of high academic quality and that reflects high expectations for all students' capacities to learn'' (P.A. 85-1418, Sec. 34-2.4).

The legislation then provided a list of important components that should be included in school improvement plans, including a needs assessment; a list of objectives; the activities, staffing patterns, and training needed to reach the objectives; and a process for monitoring whether the objectives were being achieved.

Initial school improvement plans in the 14 studied schools varied widely. In three of the schools, the plans were rather cursory, with fewer than 10 objectives set forth. None of these three schools made any plans to address the curriculum or instructional program of the school. The only schoolwide programs they addressed were related to improving attendance and student discipline. Only one of these three sought to improve on the educational resource centers available to students (a high school seeking to open a math lab). About school organization, they made only minor suggestions that were essentially focused on adding time for students to learn rather than any form of reorganization of their current resources.

By contrast, three other schools addressed changes in virtually every aspect of their curriculum, intended to create new learning resource centers for students, and envisioned rather extensive reorganization in the ways teachers interact with students, including team teaching and regrouping to foster cooperative learning. It is apparent, from reading these plans, that these three school councils, from the very beginning, had much more expansive ideas about changes they wanted to see happen in their schools. It also seems obvious that, in these schools, teachers took a more active role in proposing changes that they thought would be beneficial to their students. Two of these schools had been involved in a year-long staff training and planning process under the system's desegregation programs. The third had employed professional, nonprofit planning facilitators to assist them in creating their plan. The remaining eight schools in our sample seem to fall somewhere in between the extremes represented by these two groups of schools.

When we looked at the relationship between the needs assessments conducted by schools and the school improvement plans LSCs adopted in this first year, we again discovered great variance. In a number of schools, the needs assessments were quite detailed and carefully pointed out specific problems that needed to be remedied. Frequently the school improvement plans then included quite specific approaches to attacking those problems. However, in other schools virtually no needs assessment was completed. In several, the needs statements seemed to be simply a restatement of the goal arenas incorporated in the school reform act (the central office had supplied all LSCs with a school improvement planning guide, which included planning pages for each arena included in the legislation). In these latter schools, the improvement steps were more cursory and seemed less likely to be realized.

As might be expected from Chicago-style restructuring, there were many different approaches to school improvement planning adopted in the 14 schools in our sample. One school decided to focus on boosting the self-esteem of its students as its major focus for improvement and therefore adopted an Afro-centric curriculum as the centerpiece of its reform. It intended to integrate that curriculum approach in all classrooms in the school. Other schools identified particular parts of their school program that were weak or in which students were not achieving as well as needed to meet national norms. They designed programs aimed at those specific problem areas. Still other schools saw their major problem as increasing attendance and focused on ways to get kids into school, while paying little attention to improving what these students would encounter when they did attend.

We were pleasantly surprised to discover that, with one exception, virtually all of the initiatives included within the 14 school improvement plans were well supported by current research on school improvement. There was some interest, in some schools, in moving toward cooperative learning and the general approaches included under the heading "student as learner." In many schools there was a focus on increasing time-on-task. There was an attention to moving beyond simply using basal readers to include literature, including the Junior Great Books approach, to move students toward an enjoyment of reading. It must be remembered that it had only been a few years since all Chicago classrooms were forced to use Chicago's peculiar form of mastery learning, which concentrated almost exclusively on subcomponents of reading and the use of worksheets, so that the movement back to basal readers in 1985 had been a major step forward. Many schools now seemed ready to take the next step. The major exception to this alignment with current theories in school improvement was one school that unapologetically decided to adopt homogeneous grouping of students to facilitate instruction. This unabashed tracking plan flew in the face of most recent research demonstrating the harmful effects it has on students labeled as the slow learners (Oakes, 1985; Rosenbaum, 1980; Slavin, 1988).

But across all the individual school plans, we were led to concur with staff from the school system's central office that most of these initial plans were not likely to create radical change in the schools we studied. They relied more on adding small increments than on making radical changes. Central office staff who analyzed plans from across the system put their assessment this way:

> Most school improvement plans stick to traditional methods of instruction, relying on a good basal reader or textbook supplemented by workbooks and seat work. More than one-fourth of the schools place major emphasis on remediation, extra study, or tutorial time for students below grade level or identified as at risk of failure.
>
> Evidence of innovation, in the sense of a sharp change of direction or the adoption of a wholly new approach, is rare in the plans. Far more of the schools, it seems, prefer to do more of what they are already doing or to do that better. Incremental change is what is seen, not uprooting and replanting.
>
> Nevertheless, the plans promise more change in the 1990–1991 school year than Chicago's public schools have seen in a long time. (Chicago Public Schools, 1990, p. 2)

On the basis of our examination of school improvement plans adopted at 14 schools, we had a similar concern. In three of the schools, fairly significant changes had been planned. In three others, the plans seemed to be pedestrian exercises. In the majority of schools, the plans called for more of the same in educational programming. That was not radical enough to create the kind of change many national critics of schools think is necessary.

SUMMING UP THE FIRST YEAR

The Chicago School Reform Act was a major effort to realign authority and decision making in a major urban school system. An explicit goal of the act was "to make the individual local school the essential unit for educational governance and improvement" (P.A. 85-1418, Sec. 34-1.01.B). The first year of implementation was the year in which most of the shifts in authority were to take place.

As a result of the legislation, there were undeniably new arenas for decision making being exercised at the local school level. Schools had chosen their educational leaders and signed them to 4-year performance contracts. In the process, they had chosen to dismiss some principals or to encourage others to retire. This ability to *change* principals was the new authority being exercised by LSCs. The fact that LSCs could make their own selection of a principal was an important element in the new process, but it represents a smaller increase in authority over the previous selection process than the addition of the ability to dismiss nonperforming or nonresponsive principals.

Similarly, the ability of principals to select teachers and other educational staff on the basis of merit rather than seniority was a welcome change for these school leaders. However, in some schools there were some differences over who exercised that authority at the local level. The legislation indicated that staff selection would be a responsibility of the principal. Whether through the principal's desire for broader participation, traditional practices already in place, or intimidation by the council, in some schools, LSC members were participating in the staff-hiring process.

It was also undeniable that there was a new outpouring of energy and enthusiasm directed toward planning for school improvement among the members of the local school communities. Whether exercised perfunctorily or engaged in with extensive training over a prolonged period of time, the process of creating a local school improvement plan mobilized more intense involvement in trying to change Chicago public schools than at any time in the system's postwar history. Sustaining that interest and involvement would be a major challenge for reform activists during the several succeeding years of implementing the legislation. Similarly, enabling local school improvement planners to envision scenarios for more radical educational change would become an important component of efforts to translate authority shifts into improved educational opportunities for the city's schoolchildren.

However, it must be noted that LSCs were experiencing frustrations in exercising their new authority because of decisions being made by the interim board of education and the school system's administration. Decisions about the system's budget and its contracts with its employee unions were properly the responsibility of the board of education under the reform act. But major changes in the terms of those contracts and in elements of the budget during the first year of implementation changed the conditions under which LSCs were planning. Dramatically increasing the compensation of teachers and other personnel forced the system to reduce the number of employees at local schools in order to be able to fund the raises. The decision to reduce the number of employees, rather than to redistribute them equitably as the legislation had anticipated, forced LSCs to divert the projected discretionary spending in the budgets adopted during reform's first year to maintain program efforts they had considered as part of their basic program.

Similarly, the central administration's refusal to reexamine the functions of central office personnel in any significant fashion left LSC members frustrated with the inadequate level of support they were receiving as they sought to deal with difficult problems such as overcrowding. A whole set of specific problems arose over which the central administration and individual LSCs disagreed as to who had the authority to determine a resolution. These tussles developed over regulations that were imposed by the central administration without prior notice, and the resulting disputes spawned calls for establishing a formal rule-making procedure similar to that used by the state board of education when it seeks to create rules and regulations that will have an impact on local school districts.

Still, with all the uncertainty and continuing "negotiation" on some issues, it was clear that major new decision-making authority had been devolved from the central office and board, authority that was being exercised at the local school level. Similarly, it was clear that many new actors were participating in exercising that local authority. In the schools we studied, the primary participants in most of the discussions leading up to local decisions were (in decreasing order) the principal, the LSC chair, the two teacher representatives, and the two community representatives. Other parents on the LSC participated less frequently during the first year of reform implementation, but because most votes were nearly unanimous, it does not seem that those parents were uninvolved or ignored. It is, perhaps, important to note that the near unanimity on most matters is an indication that the various constituencies on the local school councils were working collaboratively on behalf of their schools. Since the willingness of parents and teachers to work collaboratively was one of the major concerns expressed by some critics of the Chicago reform effort, that was a significant finding for the first year of implementation.

CHAPTER 5

A Midway Report:
Gathering Momentum

The initial implementation period of the Chicago School Reform Act was designed to be 5 years. Two and one-half years into that process, the Chicago Panel released a "Midway Report." The report (summarized in Hess, 1992c) indicated that school reform had been successfully launched; some schools were beginning to change in significant ways, but many more needed to act more radically than had been the case up to that point.

MAJOR EVENTS IN THE CHRONOLOGY OF REFORM

In the reports of the news media, reform in Chicago has been chronicled primarily through the events affecting the whole system. Thus what most Chicagoans and most national observers knew about school reform was shaped by the actions of the board of education, the general superintendent, the state legislature, the state supreme court, and the various reform groups and activists who had a major hand in designing the reform act. These events, elaborated next, have had a major impact on reform in Chicago, but they are only a part of the total story. The more important part of the story, told in the second part of this chapter, is what was happening at the local school level.

Actions of the Interim Board of Education

The school reform implementation process began with the mayoral appointment of the interim board of education in May, 1989. During the next 5 months, as noted in Chapter 3, the board accomplished four of its five "miracles," failing only to adopt an acceptable plan of reform until well into the second year of reform implementation ("'Fuzzy' School Plan Rejected," 1990; "Interim Board Accomplishes," 1989).

Prior to the effective date of the new reform act, the board of education that was scheduled to be replaced by the interim board had extended the contract of the then general superintendent, Manford Byrd, rather than complete the search they had begun prior to the final adoption of the reform act. The interim board reinstituted a national search for Byrd's replacement. The search focused on the superintendent in Memphis, and the board was about to extend him a offer to come to Chicago when a last-minute background check revealed that a public school employee had filed a complaint claiming she was the victim of sexual misbehavior by the Memphis superintendent. The Memphis superintendent was subsequently replaced, but then won election as mayor of that city.

Rather than reinstitute a completely new search, the board solicited suggestions from around the country. After a trip to California by several of its members, the board offered the superintendency to Ted D. Kimbrough, the superintendent of the 15,000-student Compton public schools. Kimbrough had been selected Black Superintendent of the Year in California. He had spent most of his career in the Los Angeles Public Schools, rising to assistant superintendent with responsibilities for legislative affairs. Thus he had had awards, big-city school system experience, and full responsibility for a small school district. Further, he had impressed interim board members by pulling up student test scores on his personal computer during a job interview in his own office. The interim board interview team flew back to Chicago singing Kimbrough's praises.

The litany of problems, however, began immediately after his election as general superintendent. He refused to leave California in time for the start of the new school year, deciding instead to complete his 30 years of California service to guarantee the best possible pension from that state. His Chicago contract included a huge annuity in addition to an annual salary of $175,000. Together with a housing allowance and other perks, his 3½-year contract would cost the interim board about $1 million. Soon after his arrival, it was discovered that he did not have the doctorate degree his resume had claimed and he did not possess the credits required for certification in Illinois. Special legislation was adopted to exempt him from that certification requirement.

The last 12 months of the interim board's 17-month tenure, extending into the second year of reform implementation, proved to be much less successful. Significant discord began to emerge during this period. Some of the discord derived from racial politics involving staff reductions and jockeying over the nominating process for appointments to the permanent board. Racial tension also escalated over the principal selection process under which half the city's schools selected an educational leader during the first year of reform. News accounts focused on a few schools where white principals were forced out by minority-dominated LSCs. However, when the staff of Designs for Change examined principal selection at all schools, they found no discernible pattern of racial or ethnic bias in principal dismissals (Andreoli, 1990), although there was a tendency for newly selected principals to more closely match the racial/ethnic enrollment in their schools.

Another arena of eventual discord involved employee contracts. Although the interim board had moved quickly to extend contracts with the school system's employee groups and to include in the extensions new provisions that matched new requirements under the reform act, it granted 5.4% raises to secure these agreements ("Teachers Union OKs Contract," 1989). With this contract settlement, the board began a process of fiscally irresponsible decision making that culminated, 2 years later, in a major fiscal debacle from which the permanent board was not able to extricate itself ("Board's Fiscal Mismanagement Undermines Long-Term Success," 1991).

The responsibility for fiscally undermining the school system must be borne by the interim board's vice-president, William Singer. Singer was Mayor Richard M. Daley's hand-picked finance leader on the newly installed "reform" board. Singer pushed through the cutting of 500 positions in the central and district administrative units, providing the resources to reallocate the initial discretionary funds to schools. But in negotiations with the employee unions in 1990, which he conducted virtually single-handedly, Singer let it be known early on that he was offering the employees raises of 21% over 3 years. The momentum generated by publicity about the supposed benefits from the proposed 3-year contract made it difficult for other members of the interim board to oppose the terms of the contract. Even the mayor was rumored to be privately angered by the precedent such a contract would set for police and firefighters as their contracts with the city expired. Little attention was paid to the lack of resources available to pay for the contracts.

Singer (1993) had criticized Mayor Daley's father for initiating the 1979–80 fiscal collapse of the Chicago Public Schools by forcing the members of the 1975 board of education to sign employee contracts that they could not afford. But when given the chance himself, and on behalf of the second Mayor Daley's political aspirations for reelection, Singer did exactly the same thing. (Daley would stand for reelection during the late winter of 1991.)

The interim board used a one-time, $40 million revenue bubble to fund the initial 5.4% raises in 1989. In the following year, 1990, it entered into the 3-year contract calling for annual 7% raises. To fund the first year (1990–91), the board had to replace the now-missing revenue bubble and find an additional $100 million in available funds. To help do so, it secured passage of legislation that allowed it to divert from $50 to $75 million each year from payments into its employee pension funds. It also had cut staff during the previous spring to create a surplus fund balance to carry into the first year of the contract ("Board's Budget Balanced by Smoke and Mirrors," 1990). Neither of these resources would be available to fund the increased costs of the second and third years of the contract. Questioned at a public hearing, Singer admitted the contract would create a budget deficit for the second year of $200–$400 million ("Board's Fiscal Mismanagement Undermines Long-Term Success," 1991).

The final arena of discord was the interim board's relationship to the administrative staff. The interim board established a pattern of micro-managing the system, providing little clear administrative direction and then second-guessing the actions of top administrators ("Needed: A New Spirit," 1990). The basic functions of the central administration were not redesigned, though staff had been severely reduced.

The Second Year

The new general superintendent, Ted Kimbrough, declared on his January 1990 arrival in Chicago that the second year of school reform (1990–91) would be focused on the local schools. Many reform groups warmly agreed that it was time to shift focus away from issues of governance and to concentrate on changes that would more directly impact student learning. Unfortunately, both the superintendent and the reform groups were to be disappointed.

On November 30, 1990, shortly after the new permanent board of education took office, the Illinois Supreme Court, ruling on a suit brought by the Chicago Principals Association (*Fumarolo et al.* vs. *Chicago Board of Education*), declared the Chicago School Reform Act to be unconstitutional. The suit had claimed that local school councils (LSCs) should not have the power to terminate principals because to do so would be to violate their rights of tenure, which, the plaintiffs claimed, had been extended under previous legislation and rules and regulations of the Chicago Board of Education. In addition, the suit charged, LSCs were not properly elected under the requirements of the federal constitution's "one person/one vote" requirements; therefore, LSCs could not constitutionally act to strip principals of their employment or take any other significant action.

The Supreme Court rejected the principals' claims about their tenure rights but agreed with them that LSCs were unconstitutionally elected because the constituency-based electoral process violated the principle of one person/one vote. Because parents could vote for six council members while community residents could only vote for two, the court ruled that the voting rights of community residents were diluted. Since the LSCs were the core of the reform legislation, the justices declared the whole act unconstitutional ("City School Reform Plan Is Ruled Illegal," 1990).

Thus the right of LSCs to terminate principals was upheld, if their own status could be corrected. Uncertainty reigned during December as various corrective legislative proposals were debated by members of the reform community. Most LSCs suspended operations, and few made significant decisions. On January 8, 1991, the Illinois General Assembly reenacted the Chicago School Reform Act (P.A. 86-1477), giving legislative authorization to all prior LSC acts and providing for the appointment of all sitting LSC members by the mayor; however, the legislators could not agree on an election procedure for the October 1991 elections ("Legislators Patch School Reform," 1991). The new election procedure, whereby parents and community residents would vote for five of the eight parent and community members while teachers would be appointed by the board of education following a staff advisory vote, was not adopted until July 1991 ("Edgar Signs 2 School Council Bills," 1991).

But before the electoral amendment could even be adopted by the General Assembly, a new discordant note was heard. On May 1, 1991, a month after the conclusion of the reelection campaign of Mayor Richard Daley, the general superintendent and the president of the board of education announced that the school system was facing a $315 million deficit for the next year, the second year of the employee contracts ("Kimbrough Reads the Riot Act, But Daley, Legislators Doubt Need for Big School Cuts," 1991). This announcement confirmed the problem acknowledged the previous year by the interim board's vice-president. Since the Chicago Public Schools, by law, could not open with an unbalanced budget, a new frenetic period began.

The new permanent board, which had been impaneled in October 1990, had been warned of its impending deficit during that fall ("Board's Budget Balanced by Smoke and Mirrors," 1990). In a fairly obvious political decision, the superintendent and board had decided to keep the system's fiscal plight out of either the fall gubernatorial or winter mayoral political campaigns. With the issue politically invisible, none of the candidates were pressed to make any campaign promises regarding the impending crisis. Consequently, neither the newly elected governor nor the reelected mayor were constrained to provide any significant assistance in the board's struggle to balance its budget in time to open schools in September 1991.

In addition, LSCs were given no official warning that major cuts might be forthcoming as they went through the spring 1991 budget planning process for the next year ("Board's Fiscal Mismanagement Undermines Long-Term Success," 1991). Only through budget training sessions provided by knowledgeable reform groups did some schools consider the effects of major cutbacks.

Once the deficit was announced, the board attempted to get legislative approval to divert the reallocation of State Chapter I funds targeted to the system's low-income schools, and it sought to intimidate the low-income communities where these schools were located by threatening to close schools in black areas and to terminate leases created to solve overcrowding in Hispanic communities if the funds were not diverted ("Board Passes a Wishful Budget," 1991). The board ignored proffered plans to resolve the budget crisis from a coalition of reform groups ("Reformers Say Schools Deficit Is Overestimate," 1991). When the board's legislative proposals to divert Chapter I funds were overwhelmingly defeated in the face of united opposition by the reform groups ("Senate Kills Bid to Sap Chapter I Funds," 1991), the board suspended the promised employee raises and adopted a series of budget cuts, which, with some unexpected additional property tax revenue, brought the budget into balance. The budget cuts included the elimination of reading improvement programs at the system's 50 lowest-performing schools and the last-minute closing of seven schools, which necessitated a great deal of internal reassignment of teachers and students ("Board Cuts It Close—Schools Will Open," 1991).

The Third Year

Thus the third year of reform implementation was launched in September 1991 amid great chaos. For days, principals found themselves scrambling to find enough teachers to cover their classes, losing faculty members they had come to depend on, and finding unexpected new teachers showing up on their doorstep with different qualifications and capacities ("With Teachers Laid Off, Some Students Are Idle," 1991). Carefully designed school improvement plans were scuttled in the raw effort to match teachers, students, and classrooms. The right of principals to select new staff was trampled under union demands to protect the jobs of displaced teachers from other schools. Regular supplies and educational equipment funds were cut by 90%. Nonteaching union employees were summarily dismissed and then restored when the board's attempted cuts were found to violate employee contracts ("300 School Custodian and Clerical Jobs Restored to Avoid Court Fight," 1991). In line with contingency language included in the original employee contract, the projected 7% raises in the second year were eliminated. In response, the teachers union demanded new negotiations, which eventually led, after an all-night bargaining session in the mayor's office, to an amended agreement granting teachers a 3% increase in 1991–92 and a guaranteed 7% increase the following year ("Daley's Teacher Settlement Has a Familiar Ring," 1991). This contract immediately created a new financial crisis for the system, resulting in a projected $290 million deficit for the following 1992–93 school year.

Amid this chaos, the second set of local school council elections were scheduled to be held. Despite the grave fears of many, most schools found enough candidates to run for open LSC seats, and in most schools the elections were contested for all seats (Designs for Change, 1991). However, voter turnout was only 165,000, half that of 2 years before. But by Thanksgiving, the new councils had begun to function and the school year was beginning to settle down.

The Resources—Reallocated to the School Level

Despite the apparent fiscal chaos and mismanagement at the board and top administrative levels, resources in the system were being redirected. The Chicago School Reform Act required that the Chicago Public Schools reallocate 95% of the State Chapter I funds it received from the state as a result of its enrollment of economically disadvantaged students. At the midway point in reform implementation, 90% of these funds were targeted on the basis of low-income enrollments and more than 60% were available for use at the discretion of the local school councils. During this third year of reform implementation, the average elementary school had about $340,000 in supplementary funding available. Across the system, some 669 teachers had been added to schools, along with 452 professional support staff (counselors, speech therapists, etc.) and 1,916 teacher aides. On average, an elementary school would have added 1 teacher, 1 support staff, and 3.5 teacher aides. (See Appendix B for a full elaboration of financial changes in the Chicago Public Schools during the reform years.)

THE REAL REFORM—CHANGE AT THE SCHOOL LEVEL

But for all the coverage extended to systemwide and state-level activities, the heart of school reform efforts in Chicago is at the local school level. The point of restructuring the Chicago school system is simply to enable and encourage school-level change for the purpose of assuring that Chicago students achieve at levels comparable to those of the national averages. The local school is the essential unit for change in educational governance and improvement. In this section of the chapter, I examine the important actors in reform implementation and the changes they experienced under reform. First, I look at how the local school councils were established and functioned. Then I look at the effect of reform on principals, teachers, and students.

The First LSCs—Learning to Govern

Local school councils, the key structural change under the Chicago School Reform Act, were viewed skeptically by national academic experts and local citizens of Chicago. It was imagined that LSCs would be made up of unintelligent parents incapable of making decisions that would help schools, that they would be largely ineffective, and that they would have little effect in improving schools. The actual operations of LSCs did not fulfill the skeptics' expectations.

Member Qualifications. The first set of council members in the 14 sample schools studied by the Chicago Panel were relatively well educated and had had extensive experience with their schools. Of course, most principals and teachers, in addition to being college graduates, had extensive post-graduate experience. Parents on these LSCs averaged 1 year of college and 5 years of volunteer experience in their schools. High school parents tended to be more educated, averaging 3 years of college. Similarly, community representatives at both types of schools averaged 3 or more years of college experience and, like the high school parents, had been volunteers at their schools for about 3 years. These parent and community LSC members had been active in community volunteer efforts, on average, between 8 and 9 years. Elementary school parents tended to be in their late 30s, while high school parents and most community representatives tended to be in their early to mid-40s. Of course, individual members varied quite widely on these characteristics. Schools also varied significantly; at one school parents had, on average, a tenth grade education, while at several others, they averaged being college graduates. However, as a group, these lay members of LSCs were educated, mature, and experienced. This picture of LSC member characteristics is in sharp contrast to the rhetoric of early critics of the reform legislation that Chicago schools would now be governed by uneducated and ignorant laypeople.

Attendance and Turnover. During their first 2-year term (1989–91), the active participation of individual LSC members was a significant concern, as noted in Chapter 4. During the first year of the LSCs (1989–90), average attendance in the elementary schools had been at 70%, while at the high schools the average had been 78%. During the second year, attendance rates slipped slightly lower, with an average rate of 69.3% for all 14 schools.

During the first year of LSC meetings, three of the sample schools requested that individual members resign as a result of their poor attendance. Some of these nonperforming members did resign, and others resigned for a variety of other reasons (moving out of the area, children graduating from school so parent member no longer eligible, teachers or principals changing jobs). Overall, nearly three-quarters of the original members served out their initial 2-year terms. In individual schools, the experience was quite diverse, from one elementary school in which every original member served the full term to a high school in which less than half the council persisted. When a vacancy occurred, LSCs elected a replacement (frequently the next-highest vote getter in the original election). In four schools, some of these replacements themselves resigned and a second replacement was elected.

Of the 140 elected parents, community, and teacher members of the full group of 14 studied LSCs, 73 (52.1%) chose to run for reelection to a second term during October 1991. Of these, 61 (83.6%) were reelected, meaning that 43.6% of the members of the second-term LSCs (1991–93) were carryovers from the first-term LSCs. Just over half the members in each category stood for reelection, but the results were quite varied. Every incumbent teacher running won reelection, as did 86% of the parent incumbents; but only 60% of the community incumbents were victorious. While systemwide results were similar to those of our sampled schools, more community representatives were reelected citywide (84%) and fewer teachers were reelected (80%) than in the sampled schools (O'Dowd, 1991).

Focus of the Meetings. During the second year of reform, the average LSC scheduled 13 meetings, with most holding monthly meetings and an occasional special meeting. One school held 25 meetings; another held only 9. The average length of meetings was 1.5 hours, with the average at some schools much longer (2.5 hours) and at others quite short (45 minutes).

Acting together, most LSCs adopted school improvement plans, adopted budgets, and selected principals. On an average evening during the first year (LSCs usually met at night), 6 topics would be discussed,

TABLE 5.1. Topics Discussed at LSC Meetings

Categories	Percentage of All Topics	
	Year 1	Year 2
School program	29	27
LSC organization	28	33
Building, security, and safety	13	10
Finance	11	12
Personnel	11	10
Parent and community involvement	4	5
Other	5	4

with school programs most frequently on the agenda. During the second year, LSCs addressed more topics (an average of 10.2), and organizational topics were the leading arena. General arenas of concern remained fairly constant from the first to the second year of reform, but there were some interesting shifts in attention (see Table 5.1).

In both years, the dominant topics of discussion were the organization of the LSC itself and the programs of the school. Nearly three out of every five topics discussed involved one of these arenas. But the focus within each of these arenas shifted during the second year, as might have been expected.

During the first year of the LSCs, the curriculum and instruction provided by the school program was a major focus as LSC members familiarized themselves and debated what the school was actually teaching. During the second year, LSCs paid much less attention to the curriculum but dramatically increased their concern about the way the school programs were being administered. Many of these program administration items were little more than announcements included as part of the monthly principal's report, but other items included the scheduling of classes and special programs, enrollment decisions, and busing concerns.

One school had a heated discussion of promotion and graduation policies that stemmed from the principal's announcement about a letter he intended to send home with eighth-grade students at risk of not graduating that year. Several members asked that these letters be made a full agenda item for consideration. During the later discussion, the debate expanded to consideration of establishing an at-risk program and instituting midyear graduations. The LSC decided to refer the letters and the potential changes in the graduation and promotion policies to its education committee for further review. Thus an item that began as a simple announcement in the principal's report led to a significant discussion and an important proposal to change the way the school approached unsuccessful students.

LSCs were observed to spend more time on their own organization in the second year, up from 28% of all topics discussed in the first year to 33% in the second year (first-year observations were not begun until after LSCs had already organized themselves and therefore a higher number of organizational agenda items may actually have occurred than are reflected in Table 5.1). But within this category, again, the focus shifted. In the first year, nearly a third of the organizational conversations related to securing training for LSC members. With more experience in the second year of their term, members largely stopped talking about training but spent more time on attendance issues and filling vacancies, and on keeping abreast of district activities.

Three practical topics—building/security/safety, finance, and personnel—together occupied about a third of all LSC discussions. During the first year, building/security/safety concerns were slightly more prominent than finance and personnel issues; during the second year, finance topics took precedence among these three. Finance topics included both issues related directly to school budgets and fundraising efforts. Under personnel, discussions of principal selection remained constant for the sample of schools as a whole, though the emphasis in particular schools shifted as nine schools selected principals in the first year while only five did so in the second. All schools participated in mandated annual evaluations of their principals. Finally, parent and community involvement topics increased from 4% to 5% of all topics during the second year.

Different members had different degrees of influence on decisions made by the LSCs. On most topics, about three members were likely to participate. More would be involved on hotly debated issues such as overcrowding; on announcement-type issues, frequently only one person would be talking. As might be expected, principals participated more frequently than any other LSC members. Together, they addressed about two-thirds of all items discussed at LSC meetings (66.3% during the first year, 69.9% during the second). The chairpersons most dramatically increased their participation in discussions (up from 43.4% in the first year to 57.9% in the second). Teachers participated in a third of the topics discussed. Community members spoke about a quarter of the time, and other parents spoke least frequently—to less than one in five of all discussed topics.

Of course, these patterns varied widely in different schools. In one school, during the second year, the principal spoke to 92% of the topics, while at another the principal spoke to less than half of the issues discussed. At one school the LSC chair spoke to nearly three-quarters of all issues (74.2%), while at another the chair addressed only a quarter of the items (28.6%). Generally, if principal participation was high, the participation of the chair was lower, and vice versa. At one school the two teachers spoke to more than half of the agenda topics, while at another the teachers were almost silent, speaking to only one topic in five.

School Improvement Plans. One of the most important discussions conducted by each LSC was around the creation and adoption of a school improvement plan (SIP). Mandated by the reform legislation, each studied LSC adopted an SIP during the first year of reform and discussed changes to the plan during the second year. School improvement plans in the 14 studied schools varied widely, as noted in Chapter 4.

During the second year of the reform effort, SIPs included initiatives in three major arenas: changes in curriculum, changes in school organization, and changes in instructional practice. Other initiatives did not fit into these three categories. Curricular changes included adopting new textbooks or reading programs, adding new art or science programs, refocusing the program emphasis to enhance student esteem (as in the Afro-centric curriculum adopted at one school), or adding curricular labs. Organizational changes included decreasing class sizes, establishing a "walking reading" program (to change student groupings for that subject, allowing heterogeneous grouping for all other subjects), and starting school-within-a-school programs, extended-day offerings, and tutoring. Other initiatives included efforts to improve student attendance, improve discipline in the school, and expand parent and community involvement.

Many of the curricular and organizational initiatives appeared to be add-ons to the regular school program, frequently serving only a segment of a school's student body. Add-on programs were relatively easy to implement, frequently involving little more than using new discretionary funds to hire a new staff person and assigning a space for the program to operate. In most cases these add-ons, while valuable in making progress toward some reform goals, were likely to have little effect on the regular instructional program experienced by most students.

Thus these changes were unlikely to significantly improve student achievement levels, as also called for under the reform act.

Among the 14 observed schools, SIPs included relatively few initiatives aimed at changing instructional practice during the first two years of reform implementation. Only 4 of the 14 schools focused their improvement plans on changing instructional practices in the regular classroom; 3 other schools included instructional change initiatives as part of the SIP. Instructional practices involve *how* things are taught (the way teachers teach) rather than *what* is taught (the curriculum). Some faculties were learning how to use sustained silent reading, writing across the curriculum, or the Socratic method of discussion across all subjects. Hands-on learning in science and math was also emphasized for the entire faculty. At other schools, only teachers in particular departments or at certain grade levels were participating in instructional initiatives. In one school, the primary teachers were adopting a whole-language approach, emphasizing using words in longer passages and stories while deemphasizing worksheets. Team teaching, peer tutoring, and cooperative learning were restricted to individual teachers willing to try out new instructional practices. Teacher leaders indicated that only those teachers who were motivated to improve their own instructional practices pushed themselves to do so. One Professional Personnel Advisory Committee (PPAC) chair commented:

> Some people are willing to change and other people are older and have lived successfully and feel that what they're doing has value, so don't feel the need to change. Those are the people you have to make into believers. (Easton et al., 1991b, p. 33)

Inservice training varied widely in the plans. Some schools used short-term inservices. One PPAC chair described the inservice at her school as one 30-minute session at the beginning of the school year and, later in the year, two 90-minute workshops on the whole-language program. In contrast, teachers at another school attended a continuous staff development program by the Illinois Writing Project for 3 hours every Wednesday afternoon for 10 weeks. Greater instructional change could be expected from a 10-week, 3-hours-per-week staff development program than from two 90-minute workshops.

Interviews with instructional leaders (principals and PPAC chairs) indicated that faculties were making real progress in implementing instructional change initiatives in six of the seven schools with such elements in their SIPs. But they described the implementation as a lengthy and difficult process. They reported that teachers had to be convinced that changing their current practice was worth the commitment of time and effort required. They also had to provide mutual support as they experimented with new strategies and adapted them to meet the needs of their students. These leaders indicated that instructional change initiatives would require an ongoing effort.

It is encouraging to note that more schools included the effort to change instructional practice in their SIPs during the second year than had done so in the first year. However, if student achievement was to improve in Chicago, it was obvious at the midway point that more schools would need to direct a greater focus on this arena.

Across the system, schools were reaching out beyond the borders of the city for assistance. In turn, national school improvement efforts had "marched on Chicago" to assist many schools. In 1988, there had been few national school improvement efforts working in Chicago schools. In 1992, there were more than 170 schools listed under various national reform efforts then working in Chicago. Some of these efforts had a distinctly Chicago flavor, such as the Paideia Program, initiated by Mortimer Adler of the University of Chicago (working with 11 schools). The board's own federally supported desegregation program, Project CANAL, was providing school improvement planning assistance in 71 schools. The Illinois Writing Project, focused in Roosevelt and National Louis Universities, was working with another group. However, other linkages were with major school reformers such as Ted Sizer's Coalition of Essential Schools (11 high schools), Hank Levin's Accelerated Schools Network (4 elementary schools), and James Comer's School Development Program (4 schools). The New Zealand import, Reading Recovery, was being used, with training support from Ohio State University, in 61 schools; the SAGE School Mission Process was assisting 13 schools. These national efforts were providing valuable resources to schools and school staffs as they worked to improve Chicago's schools. These efforts had been largely unavailable to the city's schools prior to school reform.

The Principals—New Roles and Changing Leadership

The Chicago School Reform Act focuses additional authority and responsibility on local school principals in line with findings in the research on effective schools (Brookover & Lezotte, 1979; Edmonds, 1979; Purkey & Smith, 1983). Principals were given new authority to select new members of their faculties without regard for seniority. They were asked to take the initiative in creating the school's improvement plan. Most principals took the lead in proposed spending plans, including the adoption of the local school budget. Principals were expected to play the major role in managing the day-to-day affairs of the school. And, finally, principals were to be held accountable for the successes and failures of the schools. The ultimate form of accountability was that principals could be removed from leadership at the school if councils found their leadership inadequate. Amendments to the reform act adopted in July 1991 also allowed LSCs to dismiss principals during the term of their contracts for direct defiance of LSC directions.

Nine of the 14 sample schools selected incumbent principals to provide continued leadership under reform. At three schools, new principals were selected; at two others, recently appointed interim principals were given 4-year contracts. Thus the proportion of new principals in the sampled schools was similar to the systemwide turnover rate of 38.5%.

While local and national media outlets provided wide coverage to individual schools where principals were not retained, little attention was paid to the evaluation and selection process these schools had undertaken. The process varied from school to school, though most schools followed guidelines proposed originally by the newly created nonprofit agency, Lawyers School Reform Advisory Project; these guidelines were incorporated in official board of education materials. The guidelines carefully separated the evaluation and selection process, suggesting that schools first evaluate the incumbent and decide whether to offer that person a 4-year contract. Six votes were required to retain an incumbent. Only if the retention decision was negative would schools embark on a new selection process. Some schools, however, preferred to test their incumbents against other potential candidates. A supermajority of seven (out of a possible ten votes; principals and students were not allowed to vote on the principal evaluation and selection items) was required to select a new principal. If an LSC could not achieve a supermajority for one candidate, it was to present a list of three acceptable candidates to the district superintendent, who would select a principal for the school. The experiences of three schools during reform's second year exemplify some of the different approaches to principal evaluation and selection taken by LSCs.

At one school, the LSC established a principal evaluation committee that launched the evaluation process at the LSC's first meeting by setting out standards that would be followed. After discussions at several meetings, subcommittees were established to review student progress, staff development, parent and community involvement, and the effectiveness of school programs. Surveys of parents and teachers were designed with input from each LSC constituency (parents, teachers, community

representatives). The LSC met with the principal in three formal evaluation interviews, with members rating each answer on a scale of 1 to 5.
The LSC took public testimony about the principal's performance. The
LSC also received and considered an evaluation of the principal by the
district superintendent. Fairness was a theme throughout the evaluation
process, even to the extent of resurveying the faculty when the original
survey appeared to have been haphazardly distributed. Despite a continuing tension between the principal and some LSC members, including
the chair, at the end of this process the LSC voted to extend a new
4-year contract to the principal, though exercising its right to add several criteria to the performance expected of the principal during the
ensuing 4 years.

At a second school, the evaluation and selection processes were
intermingled. Discussions in LSC meetings elicited ideas about how to
do the principal evaluation, but got little more specific than suggesting
individuals observe the school and report their perceptions to the evaluation committee. Observers suspected that the LSC leaders had already
decided to dismiss the incumbent principal. Before the evaluation was
completed, the LSC chair announced she had advertised the principal's
position in the general superintendent's bulletin. The principal objected;
the district superintendent stepped in to direct the LSC to first complete
its evaluation. The LSC retracted the advertisement and apologized to
the principal. The LSC resumed the evaluation process and conducted a
formal interview with the principal. Although the faculty overwhelmingly voted to retain the principal, the LSC decided not to and opened a
search for a successor. Shortly thereafter, the incumbent took a terminal
leave of absence, leaving the school without day-to-day administrative
leadership.

A principal selection committee was formed with LSC, faculty, and
nonteaching staff represented. The position was readvertised and appli-
cations screened to four finalists, who appeared at a public candidates'
forum. Colleagues of each finalist were interviewed and the results eval-
uated. The faculty favored one candidate; several parents favored another. After an hour-long executive session, the LSC returned to open
meeting to declare itself nearly deadlocked but committed to trying to
come to a decision. A compromise choice of a third candidate finally
won unanimous approval. The successful candidate was then invited to
become the interim principal, a proposal that was accepted. Thus the
new principal actually began work about 2 months prior to the formal
beginning of a new 4-year contract on July 1.

At a third school, the principal selection process eventually reached
the desk of the district superintendent for his choice for a new principal.

The school followed a process similar to that of the first school, except that it also solicited the assistance of a *pro bono* lawyer from the Lawyers School Reform Advisory Project. Although most of the comments made at a public forum on the principal's performance were quite positive, the LSC voted not to extend a new contract to the principal; he was invited to apply for the position to compete with other applicants. The school then followed a selection process similar to the second school's. After a public candidates' forum, the finalists were narrowed to three, not including the incumbent. When, after several attempts, none of the candidates could muster the needed seven votes, the LSC turned the three names over to the district superintendent, who chose one to become the school's new principal.

These three cases show the range of experiences schools underwent as they sought to evaluate and make decisions about their administrative leadership. Of all issues undertaken by local school councils during the first 2 years of reform, it is safe to say principal selection was the single most emotionally charged item on LSC agendas. The selection process would not recur, in a major way, until the first set of principals' 4-year contracts would expire after the third set of LSCs were elected in the fall of 1993. However, some schools would confront the issue prior to that time as current principals retired, left for other positions, died, or became incapacitated.

Of all the actors in the school improvement efforts under Chicago school reform, principals have undoubtedly experienced the greatest change. As just reviewed, they had to undergo a more or less rigorous evaluation and the uncertainty of whether or not they would continue in their present jobs. As noted earlier, about one in six of the principals in office when the reform act was signed into law decided to avoid this stress by taking early retirement, and leaders in the Chicago Principals Association filed suit to avoid their loss of tenure, a suit whose major premise was denied. Some 50 new schools were opened, additional retirements occurred during the first 2 years of reform, and some principals were dismissed by LSCs. Still, some 200 new persons stepped forward to accept the challenge of school leadership under contract to a parent-dominated LSC.

The Teachers—Becoming Increasingly Involved

The constituency that was, perhaps, most ignored in the development of the first 2 years of the Chicago school reform effort is the group that has been the focus of other school-based management experiments across the country—the teachers (see Chapter 3). Though it is obvious that few significant changes could be expected to happen in Chicago's classrooms without the active involvement of teachers, they had been far less the focus of activities in this city's reform efforts. But it appears teachers were quite involved at the school level under reform implementation from its beginnings.

In order to better assess the role and perspective of teachers in the Chicago reform effort, staff from the Chicago Panel were involved in conducting two surveys of teachers across the system. The Panel conducted a small survey of teachers from a stratified, random sample of 12 predominantly minority elementary schools as reform implementation was beginning (Easton, 1989).

Those teachers felt they were well informed about the reform effort, having received most of their information from the school administration and from the news media. They had been discussing reform among themselves and with their colleagues; one-third said they had spent more than 2 hours discussing reform during the previous week, and another one-third had discussed it for at least 1 hour. But they were less likely to see themselves as directly involved in the reform effort. Only one-fifth indicated interest in running for one of the two teacher slots on the LSC (LSCs would include less than 1,100 of the system's more than 24,000 teachers). Less than half thought they would participate on the Professional Personnel Advisory Committee. Teachers who were more knowledgeable about the reform act indicated they would be more likely to be actively involved in reform efforts. On the other hand, more than half had urged parents to run for seats on the LSCs. Teachers were not very optimistic about reform's prospect, expecting little change in student achievement or teacher autonomy and morale.

When teachers were asked, in an open-ended question, to list the strengths and weaknesses of the beginning reform effort, parent involvement led both lists. Teachers were optimistic that parent involvement would help to improve their schools and that more collaborative efforts would develop among parents, teachers, and administrators. On the other hand, teachers were also most fearful of increased parent involvement and particularly worried about the levels of competence parents would bring and about the threat of interference in the classroom. One wrote, "It is difficult to imagine a sudden parental competence or educational interest." Thus teachers saw additional parental involvement as reform's greatest potential strength and, at the same time, its greatest potential weakness.

Panel staff were also involved in a much more extensive survey of all elementary teachers in the system, conducted at the end of the second year of school reform. This survey was sponsored by the Consor-

tium on Chicago School Research (Easton et al., 1991a). The Chicago
Panel's research director, John Easton, led the work group that designed, distributed, and analyzed the results of the teacher survey.

More than 13,000 teachers responded to the survey, a return rate of
over 70%. The high response rate and the time required to complete the
survey (30 to 45 minutes) are indications of how anxious teachers were
to have their voice heard. Sensing this, the work group named the survey "Charting Reform: The Teachers' Turn."

Two years into the reform effort, teachers appeared to be far more
involved in school improvement efforts than they had anticipated when
reform was being launched. More than half of the respondents (53%)
indicated they had been involved in helping to develop the school improvement plan for their school. More than three-quarters (77%) said
they were familiar with the major points in their SIP. More than two-
thirds (68%) indicated they were helping to implement their SIP. A
similar number (66%) thought the SIP would help to make their school
better over the next 5 years. Thus, among elementary school teachers,
there did seem to be a high level of involvement in school improvement
efforts at the school level.

And a majority of teachers were fairly optimistic about how well
the reform effort was working. They believed the principal and LSC
were working well together (71%), that LSCs respected teachers' views
(57%), and that the teacher representatives on the LSCs fairly represented their views (66%). They believed that the Professional Personnel
Advisory Committee was an important voice for teachers in their
schools (68%), that their PPAC represented their views (77%), and that
the PPAC had increased teacher involvement in school policy decisions
(62%).

Interviews with PPAC chairs in the Panel's sample of schools produced a similar picture. Although teacher participation in school improvement planning varied among the 14 schools, teacher leaders indicated that principals and LSCs respected faculty contributions. One
PPAC chair commented, "Last year, [the LSC] took our document and
just about adopted the whole thing as the SIP." Another said, "None of
our suggestions were ever turned down."

When survey responses were compiled into a General Reform Index
for each participating school, teachers at three-quarters of the schools
(303 of 401) felt reform was going well at their schools. In 62 schools
teachers thought reform was doing very well; in another 241, teacher
response was moderately positive. In 89 schools, teachers were somewhat negative, while in only 9 schools were teachers very negative
about reform efforts. The 62 schools in which teachers thought reform

was going very well (the report referred to them as the "lighthouses" of reform) were evenly distributed across the geography of the city but tended to be smaller schools and schools with historically higher levels of student achievement. At three-quarters of the schools, teachers were quite positive about school reform at the end of its second year. But it was also clear that there were some schools in which reform was not working very well at that point.

There were also some troubling findings from the survey. Teachers reported that a serious gap existed in parent–teacher relationships. Teachers thought that their schools reached out to parents (78%), but only half (51%) felt supported by parents and only three in five (59%) felt that parents respected teachers. A majority (54%) felt community members did not make efforts to help their schools.

Disappointingly, only two-thirds (67%) felt their students were capable of learning the material they were supposed to teach. Two-thirds also believed that students' attitudes and habits reduced their chances for success. Meanwhile, teachers claimed to be quite competent in their teaching (93%), to look forward to working each day (77%), and to be certain they were making a difference in their students' lives (90%). Thus the picture once again emerged of teachers who thought they were doing fine; in their opinions, the problems in the school system revolved around lack of parental support, the incapacities of their students, and the habits and attitudes students brought to school with them.

Given this picture, it is not surprising to find that, despite teachers' optimism about the potential of reform, the changes made since reform began had had no effect on their classroom practices (57%). More significantly, a majority (55%) believed their instructional practices would not change as a result of the school improvement plans adopted in their schools, plans that they had had a large share in creating. It appears that teachers believed reform would have an important impact on improving parent involvement and changing student attitudes, which would obviate any necessity for teachers to make any significant changes themselves.

It is unlikely that important changes will be made in the classrooms where Chicago students engage in learning until teachers begin to think seriously about the ways they themselves must change. The relative scarcity of significant efforts to change instructional practice in our sample schools during the first 2 years of reform indicated that teachers had not yet begun to focus on their own responsibility for changing the way Chicago's students experience their schools. Thus, despite the optimism for reform expressed by teachers, a degree of skepticism about their reports seemed warranted.

The Students—Still Too Early to Tell

The ultimate goal of the Chicago School Reform Act is to improve the level of achievement of the city's schoolchildren. There is an emerging debate in the United States about how best to assess student achievement. Some commentators focus on test scores. Others add additional criteria that can also be easily quantified, such as attendance rates, graduation rates, truancy rates, discipline problems, and so forth. Still others suggest that these measures frequently miss important areas of student capabilities and so look to the development of more qualitative assessments of student attainment, such as portfolios and other performance evaluations. These latter efforts are still quite experimental and in the early stages of development. The Chicago School Reform Act, for better or worse, focused more narrowly on quantifiable achievement gains in test scores, attendance and graduation rates, and success after graduation.

After a decade and a half of enrollment declines—partly the result of demographic changes, partly the result of teacher strike disruptions—enrollment had stabilized in the Chicago Public Schools as reform efforts were beginning. Total enrollments were in the vicinity of 405,000 to 408,000 students between the 1988–89 and 1991–92 school years. Attendance patterns through the second year of reform implementation did not change significantly (Easton & Storey, 1990a).

Longitudinal cohort dropout rates continued to vary from year to year, mostly reflecting different promotion and high school entrance policies when the individual class was completing elementary school. Dropout rates generally were about 40% for the classes of 1984 through 1988, but jumped to 48% for the class of 1989 and 46% for the class of 1990 (Chicago Public Schools, 1991, p. 3).

It was unlikely that dropout rates would decline significantly during the 5-year reform implementation effort. As reform was beginning, the Chicago Panel had shown that dropout rates reflect early experiences in school. On the basis of academic grades and attendance records for second, third, and fourth grades for students in the class of 1982, Panel staff had identified, with better than 85% accuracy, which students would eventually graduate from high school and which would drop out (Hess et al., 1989). Thus reform implementation would be unlikely to significantly affect the dropout rate (or obversely, the graduation rate) until primary grade students experiencing restructured schools reached graduation age, some 8 to 10 years later.

The Chicago Panel designed and initiated a major study of student gain scores on standardized tests, using hierarchical linear modeling

(Raudenbush & Bryk, 1986). The study was designed to show whether individual student achievement gains from year to year increased after reform implementation was begun. First results from this study would not be either available or relevant before the completion of the fifth year of the reform implementation period.

Median test score results showed little change during the first 2 years of reform. On the Illinois Goals Assessment Program tests for 1990–91, 77% of all elementary schools fell below state averages; for eleventh-grade reading and math, 92% were below the state average. Since current-year test scores depend on the foundations developed in previous years, it would not be expected that large gains would occur in median test scores from one year to the next. It may be that even 5 years would be too short a time in which to see significant changes. One would expect to see improvement in the early grades more quickly, but 1991 third-grade scores had declined slightly from the previous year. Still, individual-year scores tend to vary widely as cohorts of students vary. It is for this reason that the Panel's study was tracking the same children from year to year over a prolonged period.

THE MIDWAY ASSESSMENT

As the Chicago reform implementation effort reached its midpoint, it would be fair to say that it had not yet significantly impacted student learning. Under the best of circumstances, it would have been too early to have expected much significant change. The first year of implementation was a planning and training year. Second-year tests were taken 8 months into the first year of implementation. That is not much time for major change to have occurred, even if school plans had been quite radical. But, as noted above, school improvement planning at most schools had not yet been very radical.

What had happened was that the basic mechanisms designed in the reform act had been put into place. Local school councils had begun their second 2-year term. In general, these councils seemed to be working quite successfully at most schools, though it was clear there were some for which this was not the case. LSCs had learned how to govern the schools without getting caught up in day-to-day managerial issues. Some had claimed more power, others less. All schools had selected principals, and two out of five had new educational leadership. Principals were developing skills to assume the new roles required under school-based management. Teachers, though largely ignored in the initial training and implementation efforts, had taken increasingly involved roles in planning for school improvement but did not see reform requiring much change in their basic classroom practices. School improvement plans had attacked serious problems in most schools, but in only about a quarter were they likely to significantly alter the way students encountered schools. Thus a foundation for change had been established, but major changes were still over the horizon. The challenge facing Chicago at the midway point in its reform implementation was to bring those major changes into the daily life of the city's schools.

In the following chapter, I look more closely at the school improvement planning process as it was undertaken in two of the schools being studied by the Chicago Panel. The planning process overlapped several years, but it is most closely examined during the third and fourth years of reform implementation.

CHAPTER 6

Years Three and Four: The Struggle with Improvement Planning

The final bell rings at Montgomery Elementary, and students dressed in navy and light-blue uniforms file out of classrooms, making their way to after-school programs. Teachers quickly put their rooms in order and gather their materials for a 2:45 p.m. meeting on school improvement planning. Parent volunteers linger in the halls to exchange tales of the school day. This buzz of activity was [now] common, although [prior to reform] the halls had been empty after 2:30 p.m., the lights turned off, and the doors locked. (Flinspach & Ryan, 1994, p. 293)

During the third year of reform, Panel staff began a more intensive study of two schools that were moving to significantly alter their instructional programs (Flinspach & Ryan, 1992). As a part of this study, we reported on the development of local school councils in their capacity to do concrete planning for school improvement. Those plans resulted in the change described above at Montgomery School (all names in this chapter are pseudonyms).*

EXAMINING SCHOOL IMPROVEMENT PLANNING

In reviewing the school improvement plan revisions in our 14 study schools, we found that different schools took different approaches, primarily depending on the type of leadership provided by the principal. As explained in Chapter 3, it is the responsibility of the principal to present a school improvement plan to the LSC for its consideration, possible amendment, and adoption. The principal is to prepare the SIP in consultation with the LSC, the school staff, parents, and members of

---

*An earlier version of this chapter (Hess, Flinspach, and Ryan, 1993) appeared in *New Directions in Program Evaluation* in September 1993. Reprinted by permission of Jossey-Bass, Inc.

the local community. In just over half our schools, the principal managed the SIP process but involved others, particularly teachers, in designing the proposed plan. In three schools, the SIP was delegated to others to prepare. In two of our schools, principals developed and revised SIPs by themselves, sometimes soliciting input from teachers and others.

Either indirectly or directly, at most schools teachers had significant input into the development of their school's SIP during the third year of reform. They either composed a core group headed by the principal or participated on a series of committees addressing different parts of the plan. Some grade-level meetings and department meetings were focused on SIP revision, and their recommendations were brought to the group compiling the plan. Schools varied widely in the degree of teacher involvement, but our interviews with teacher leaders in each school indicated that teachers had become progressively more involved in the planning process during the first 3 years of reform. These leaders indicated that early on teachers were unwilling to commit extensive time and energy to creating plans they doubted would ever be implemented. However, as teachers found that components of earlier SIPs were being put into place, their attitudes began to change. By the third year, these leaders suggested, teachers generally believed that their voices would be heard and that their suggestions would be backed by the principal and receive adequate funding. This is an important development, given the literature on the crucial importance of teacher involvement in successful instructional innovation (Elmore, 1978; McLaughlin, 1978).

Local school councils continued to be the governing body charged in each school to adopt the school improvement plan. In eight of our schools, the LSC took a formal role in preparing the draft SIP; in six, LSC members had no role until the draft plan was presented to them, and then they routinely adopted the plan presented. Similarly, eight of the 14 schools had conducted some monitoring and evaluation of the previous year's SIP. In half of these, the monitoring was quite informal, with teachers discussing progress in staff meetings and/or the principal reporting achievements to the LSC. Two schools formed monitoring committees, but one of these never met; the other did an end-of-year summative evaluation. The last two schools had a more formalized system, giving regular updates to the LSC. In one school, a self-evaluation instrument was used to gauge the extent of SIP implementation.

As we assessed the evaluation of the SIPs operative during 1991–92, it became obvious that in a third of our schools, the formally adopted SIP had little effect on the regular, daily life of the school. In these schools, the SIP was rarely discussed by anyone; teachers were unaware of its contents; principals could not find a copy of the plan. In most cases, these plans were not realistically related to the life of the school. In another third of the schools, plans were occasionally discussed but were not a regular part of the life of the school. In the final third of the schools, the SIP played a much more vital role; it was regularly discussed in Professional Personnel Advisory Committee meetings, and teachers were actively engaged in revising the plan for 1992–93 implementation.

From our study of the 14 school improvement plans, we found that some SIP initiatives (planned changes) were characterized by vague or generalized descriptions of existing practice, initiatives that sounded good but were unlikely to be implemented, or goal statements without implementing activities or programs. We called such initiatives *symbolic planning*. In contrast, we called initiatives planned by their implementors *pragmatic planning* and found they were more likely to lead to school improvement. Improvement planning at one of the two case-study schools has become increasingly pragmatic over the last 2 years; in the other school, planning has been pragmatic during the entire reform period. A brief description of the planning process in these schools may make the distinction between symbolic and pragmatic planning clearer.

FROM SYMBOLIC TO PRAGMATIC PLANNING
AT MONTGOMERY ELEMENTARY SCHOOL

Montgomery Elementary serves over 500 students in prekindergarten through eighth grade. This neighborhood school is 100% African American and low-income, and it draws most of its students from an adjacent housing project. Although Montgomery has avoided some problems that plague many of the Chicago Public Schools, such as low attendance, high mobility, and overcrowding, it still has its share of troubles. Staff members try to address both the academic and the social needs of their students. They say they must deal with the students' low self-esteem and with corresponding discipline problems on a daily basis. Parents worry about student safety in and around the school. Of particular concern is the constant threat of gang activity in the neighborhood, including the recruitment of the older students into gangs. The challenges that the Montgomery school community face are ones common to many low-achieving, urban schools.

The incumbent principal, obeying the mandate but not the spirit of the reform law, drew up the first school improvement plan by himself. The plan included vague initiatives and perfunctory descriptions of routine operations such as "monitor instruction and pupil progress" and "organize school for instruction next year." He also included items that "sound good" but were not meant to be implemented, such as "utilize computers and calculators in the instructional program" (though no computers were made available to teachers) and "evaluate pupil progress in all subject areas and adjust instruction to meet individual pupil needs as is necessary." His SIP was an example of symbolic planning.

His real attitude toward reform, however, was revealed in this passage from the plan:

> School reform is a paper intensive, meeting oriented, time consuming effort that diminished the energy and creative talents of the staff and parents who are sincerely attempting to meet the demands placed on them. If legislative mandates are all that is needed to correct social conditions and shortcomings there would be no problems with drugs, crime, poverty or the myriad other problems facing society. (Flinspach & Ryan, 1992, p. 13)

During the second year of reform implementation (1990–91), the Montgomery LSC was charged to evaluate the principal and decide on his retention or replacement. The LSC decided a new principal was needed; when the incumbent was not selected, he took a terminal leave. Two days before the second-year SIP had to be adopted, a new principal began her tenure. The outgoing principal had prepared the second-year SIP in the same way he had the first. Although it was too late to completely change the process, the new principal added three of her own initiatives in response to concerns expressed by staff and parents: hiring another teacher to extend the kindergarten classes to a full-day program; devising a male-responsibility after-school program; and hiring a security guard. These three very practical initiatives, characterized in Chapter 5 as add-on planning, were instituted at the beginning of the 1991–92 school year; the rest of the SIP was ignored as irrelevant.

During the third year of reform, these new initiatives were seen to be significant improvements in the life of Montgomery. The full-day kindergarten was seen to be beneficial in better preparing students for the academic challenges of first grade. The after-school program addressed perceived tensions in the social behavior of the school's older boys. The new security guard relieved the feeling of "unsafety" that had pervaded the school previously. More important, the man hired, a moonlighting Chicago policeman, saw his job not only as providing a sense of security in the school, but also as being an adviser to students; he was actively engaged in the effort to improve Montgomery, interacted regularly with the principal, and was very responsive to requests for assistance from individual teachers. These pragmatic add-on initiatives had created a climate in which more fundamental change could be undertaken.

Not surprisingly, when the new principal began the planning process for the SIP to be adopted in the spring of 1992, teachers were much more willing to participate. The principal chaired the 10-week process of developing the plan. She reviewed the record of student achievement in the school and the systemwide goals and objectives of reform adopted by the board of education. She gave a list of suggestions, but she also solicited input from the faculty members. The final plan presented to the local school council was prioritized to reflect the new funds available in the next year's school budget and was focused on the five subject areas included in the system's guide to improvement planning. It was full of very pragmatic plans. We have called this initial level of pragmatic planning *thematic planning*. In our opinion, it represents the first level of realistic planning for school improvement.

Elements of the new improvement plan were implemented the following year (1992–93). A group of teachers initiated a cross-grade whole-language program in the primary grades, working with heterogeneously grouped 5- to 8-year-olds. An African American resource center was opened where classes could work on projects involving African cultures and history. The male-responsibility program was developed further. However, even though these programs grew out of teacher planning, faculty participation was far from unanimous. The new principal expected her teachers to grow professionally, but she would not force participation in staff development activities and did not require teachers to adopt any specific teaching ideology. She said her greatest challenge was persuading these reluctant teachers to change, particularly those who would sign out and leave as soon as the bell rang and their classes were dismissed.

A SHARED VISION LEADS TO DIRECTED PLANNING:
WINKLE ELEMENTARY SCHOOL

Further along in the improvement planning process is a school called Winkle Elementary. Winkle is a neighborhood school housed in a brand-new building. The student body is roughly half Hispanic and half African American. Most families qualify for free or reduced-price lunches for their children. There are about 500 children enrolled from prekindergarten to eighth grade.

During the first 3 years of school reform, Winkle had introduced many new, pragmatic initiatives, implementing Socratic seminars to improve the intellectual content of classroom discussion, beginning extensive use of hands-on learning in mathematics, focusing on experiments in science, and using the Illinois Writing Project to implement a school-wide writing emphasis. Thus the initial focus of school improvement planning at Winkle was on staff development, providing teachers extensive training in new pedagogical techniques and assistance and feedback as they attempted to implement these new approaches to instruction.

Teacher involvement in the planning process had been high in the 1990–91 and 1991–92 SIPs; teachers accepted the idea that they were accountable for plan implementation; they had undertaken changes in the means of instruction for writing, math, and science. Winkle was doing the kind of instructional improvement planning we hoped other schools would emulate. Their planning reflected a vision of a renewed partnership among staff, students, and parents. We call this type of pragmatic planning aimed at achieving a shared vision *directed planning*.

During the 1991–92 school year, with teachers struggling to incorporate the many changes they had already undertaken, the principal decided it was time to shift the focus of improvement planning from staff development to student development, the second leg of what she thought of as a three-sided partnership. In an effort to make upper-grade students "responsible for what they produce in school," the principal proposed establishing stiff minimum eighth-grade graduation requirements, combined with a revamping of the seventh and eighth grade (they called it the junior high) into an ungraded, project-oriented, portfolio-assessed school within the larger school.

The teachers perceived several of these initiatives as needing reworking in order to be practically implemented. They thought of the principal's suggestions as a skeleton for improvement and their job as mediating between these directed plans and real-world classroom embodiment. They retained the existing grade structure and developed a structure of projects similar to that operative in the then current year. By using a more incremental approach to planning, rather than the more radical implementation of the shared vision of student responsibility originally proposed, the teachers accepted only the amount of instructional change with which they were comfortable. Together, the teachers and the principal negotiated the planned changes in the *directed planning* proposals, eventually adopting the higher graduation standards and a project approach to curriculum. The principal, appreciating the crucial importance in the planning process of staff consensus to maintain staff accountability, compromised on the implementation plan for the 1992–93 school year. The negotiated plan was still focused on reaching the shared vision of a reformed school.

The new student responsibility program included several changes in the instructional program for the seventh and eighth grades. Minimal standards were established for passing seventh grade and for graduating from eighth. The project-oriented curricula in math, science, and social studies were designed to foster greater student interest. Teachers began giving students "incompletes" instead of "failures," providing students an opportunity to make up inadequate work before the end of the year. Parents were urged to monitor their children's homework and to help them develop better work habits. The teachers committed to providing extra assistance to students, so that all of them could successfully meet the new requirements. The four junior high teachers reported that the added demands of planning projects, giving individual attention to students, and providing opportunities for students to make up "incompletes" meant that they were at school for 9 or 10 hours each day during the implementation year. In the end, despite significantly higher standards, only three students failed to graduate from eighth grade and only four failed to pass seventh grade.

A MODEL FOR SCHOOL IMPROVEMENT PLANNING

Out of the experiences of these schools we have been studying intensely, we have devised a model of school improvement planning, drawing significantly on the work of Louis and Miles (1990). On one side is the *symbolic planning*, which is largely disconnected from reality whether due to generalized statements, abstract goals without implementation plans, or initiatives that "sound good" but are disconnected from the school's realities. Montgomery School's initial SIP exemplifies this category. In our sample of schools, we found no significant school improvement resulting from symbolic initiatives.

On the other side are initiatives characterized by two major types of *pragmatic planning. Thematic* initiatives introduce major new programs, usually around several different and unrelated themes, some of which may work at cross-purposes with each other. The later development of improvement planning at Montgomery can be characterized as thematic pragmatic planning. *Directed planning* also consists of major innovations, but each is specifically designed to make progress toward fulfilling a shared school vision that emerged from the previous improvement planning efforts of the school community. Thus the components of directed planning are more integrated and complementary.

Entering the fourth year of reform implementation, at least 4 of the 14 schools we were studying were seriously engaged in pragmatic planning about the instructional program of the school. Only 1 of the 4, Winkle Elementary, had reached the point of having a shared vision, and it was the only one that had attempted directed planning. For school reform to be effective in Chicago in the ensuing years, more of the system's 540 schools would have to go about the job of thematic and directed planning in order to improve the instructional program for the city's students.

CHAPTER 7

Nearing the End: Just a Beginning

Restructuring urban schools is a difficult task, even in the best of circumstances. The patterns of American schools have been intransigent for decades. Conceptions of public schools are deeply ingrained in principals, teachers, parents, and community members. Even to imagine a radically different way of educating American youth is beyond most professional educators. The encouraging element of the Chicago school reform effort is that there are principals who have a vision of another way of doing schooling. There are teachers who bring a new passion for interacting with their students, eliciting learning rather than just attempting to instruct in old didactic ways. There are parents and community members who are working hard to reintegrate their schools into their communities and to mobilize the resources of the community to assist in the educational enterprise.

But even the best efforts of local school leaders can be undercut when school administrators, board members, and politicians tolerate fiscal mismanagement, are focused on extraneous issues such as winning reelection, and avoid tax increases needed to provide adequate resources. All these elements have thrown additional obstacles in the path of local school leaders trying to improve the education they offer their youngsters.

As the fifth year of reform implementation was beginning, it seemed as if there were more obstacles than opportunities. The fiscal crises initiated with the 1990 employee contracts hit with double impact during the summer of 1993. In addition to the ongoing imbalance between expenditures and revenues, the 3-year diversion of pension fund revenues came to an end, depriving the board of education of about $75 million in budget-balancing funds. Complicating the picture was the introduction of 1990 census numbers into the state funding scheme: A probable undercount had reduced the number of poor children acknowledged to be living in Chicago by 25,000. The lower census poverty count reduced both federal support for programs for low-income students and State Chapter I funds that had provided additional discretionary programs included in LSC-adopted SIPs. A budget imbalance of more than $200 million prevented schools from starting on time in September 1993.

The interim board of education had launched Chicago school reform successfully, moving a stagnant, stultified school system in a new direction. Its early record led the Chicago Panel to salute the four miracles they had accomplished (see Chapter 3). But it was the interim board that also started down the long road filled with obstacles created by the managers of the system and both state and local political actors. The first misstep was the interim board's selection of the new general superintendent, Ted D. Kimbrough. The second was throwing fiscal caution to the wind to offer employees a 3-year contract providing raises worth 21% plus very expensive bonuses when there was little prospect of additional resources to pay for the contracts.

To many, Kimbrough's leadership was characterized by arrogance toward the public and backbiting intrigue among his own administrative staff. He angered the black community by dismissing black administrators with a long history in the system. He then hired a white, long-time California school buddy from Pasadena to be his deputy superintendent at $140,000 annually. He angered the reform community by fighting every effort to reduce the size of the central administration. He only conceded to further cuts when budget crises forced them on him. Local school leaders were constantly harassed whenever they were willing to risk radical innovation. His leadership threw a chilling blanket over dedicated efforts at school improvement by local school leaders. His administration was characterized by a prolonged fiscal crisis, lack of instructional leadership, and petty infighting. In January 1993, the board of education dismissed Kimbrough and bought out the remaining months of his contract. A national search was launched, with widespread community involvement, including an open forum involving questioning of the two finalists by members of the public. Argie K. Johnson, an administrator in charge of curriculum and instruction in the New York City school system, was selected to replace Kimbrough in August 1993.

But Kimbrough was not primarily responsible for the fiscal crises that dominated his superintendency. As noted in Chapter 5, board vice-president William Singer deserves that blame. He proposed and negotiated the contracts with employees that required a $65 million raid on the teachers' pension fund in the first year and still carried a projected deficit of between $200 and $400 million in the second. The ensuing 3 years of continuing fiscal crisis saw an undercutting of the basic educational program at the school level as everything not required by law was stripped away to save money to pay for the contracts. Even then, the second-year salary increase was reduced to 3% and the third year's raises started a month late.

The constant harassment from the central administration and the cutting away of parts of the basic program as the board scrambled to balance its budget each fall created havoc at the school level. School improvement plans and local school budgets adopted in the spring were worthless by the time school opened each fall. As the terms of the 3-year employee contract could not be met each year, the recurrent threat of strikes discouraged teachers and frustrated LSC members.

Each year the system faced a possible shutdown because it could not balance its budget. The 1990 contract created a financial hole that just kept getting deeper each year. The deficit was so large in the fall of 1993 that a prolonged battle among the board of education, its unions, and the legislature disrupted the opening of school. The board of education adopted a plan of "shared sacrifices" that cut administrative expenditures, lengthened the teaching day (thereby cutting teacher positions), utilized an early retirement program, shifted some medical costs to employees, cut student course schedules, and asked for $150 to $200 million in new revenues from the state legislature.

When the Chicago Teachers Union refused to grant concessions necessary to assume their part of the "shared sacrifice" plan, the governor and the legislature also declined to act; they refused to raise taxes to provide additional revenue. The mayor also strongly opposed raising local property taxes to pay for the higher compensation levels resulting from the 1990 pay raises and the 1991 contract guarantee negotiated under his auspices. Only the intervention of a federal judge, who issued and then extended a temporary restraining order, got the schools open in September. LSC elections scheduled for October were threatened, then postponed, as few candidates could be found to stand for election. Although elections were finally held, the turnout was low. Without new revenues, either through higher taxes or through borrowing via a bond issue, the board was faced with the prospect of cutting expenditures, both by cutting compensation levels (pay cuts) and cutting staff.

In mid-October, the board and its unions reached an agreement. The Chicago Teachers Union was successful in fending off pay cuts, but at the cost of a loss of 1,000 teacher positions. The loss of these positions was made easier for the union by an early retirement option exercised by twice that number of its members. Thus, despite the lost programs in the schools, few union dues-payers lost their jobs, though many were dislocated since vacancies due to retirement rarely matched the positions that were to be eliminated. But the legislative leaders still could not reach agreement on how to keep the Chicago schools open for the rest of the year.

In November, on an appeal by the School Finance Authority to a Federal Court of Appeals, the judge's right to intervene was overruled and schools were once again threatened with closure. A last-minute legislative bailout, based on over $400 million in borrowing, allowed the schools to continue in operation. The borrowing was designed to provide a balanced budget for both 1993–94 and 1994–95, but it created a new deficit of more than $300 million for the 1995–96 school year. This final solution eliminated another 1,000 teachers from the city's schools, thus weakening their basic programs, with the largest effect on the high schools, where student schedules were reduced from seven courses to six.

External forces were working to undermine the most radical experiment in school restructuring embarked on by any major American school system. But at the school level, researchers were finding that reforms were in place that held forth great hope of turning the system around educationally—if it did not collapse financially.

A VIEW FROM THE SCHOOLS

In July 1993, the Consortium on Chicago School Research issued a report (Bryk et al., 1993) that integrated case studies of schools conducted by the Chicago Panel and the Center for School Improvement at the University of Chicago with surveys and original field research on six actively restructuring schools conducted by the Consortium, itself.

This report, *A View from the Elementary Schools: The State of School Reform in Chicago*, described the progress of Chicago Public Schools during the first 4 years of reform. Released during the summer of 1993, prior to the culmination of that summer's financial crisis, the report focused on patterns of school governance and school improvement efforts. The authors examined three new "sites of power" under reform: principals, teachers, and parents/community members.

The study concluded that, though progress was fragile and far from complete, Chicago school reform was generally moving in the right direction. The report examined the 85% of elementary schools performing below national norms. Of these schools, the authors contended, one-third were engaged in significant restructuring, with democratic participation from parents, teachers, and community members. Another third of the schools were making improvements, but had not yet achieved the cohesiveness required to effect lasting changes. In the remaining third, at that point, reform had had little effect.

Types of School Politics

Bryk and his colleagues (1993) identified four types of local school politics.[1] While all schools had increased autonomy from central office control, an estimated 39% to 46% of Chicago's elementary schools still operated under *consolidated principal power* in 1992–93. Parents and teachers in these schools did not broadly participate in decision making, and leadership tended to be either autocratic, with the principal ruling by coercion, or paternal/maternal, with the principal assuming the role of dominant head of a family-like structure.

From 23% to 32% of the schools operated under the politics of *strong democracy*. Principals in these schools actively engaged teachers in school improvement planning and strongly encouraged parent and community involvement. LSCs met regularly and drew on outside participants for information and assistance. While the many members of the school community collaborated extensively, principal leadership was a key attribute of all of these schools.

Between 14% and 24% of schools displayed *mixed politics*, where no single type had yet emerged. Mixed politics usually occurred when parents, teachers, and principals were satisfied with the status quo and were not motivated to change. Most political activity centered on competition for scarce resources.

Adversarial politics dominated only 4% to 9% of elementary schools. Principals, teachers, and parents, in these schools, were engaged in sustained conflict over control of the school. The principal had been unable to establish leadership, and the school community tended to be factionalized.

Types of School Improvement Efforts

Five types of improvement initiatives were identified by the research team (Bryk et al., 1993). Early in reform, the authors contended,

---

1. The following summary of the consortium study draws heavily on an article entitled "A View from the Schools: Reform Gains Real—But Fragile" in the Chicago Panel's newsletter, *Panel Update, 8*(5), Summer 1993. Andrew Wade was then editor of the newsletter.

most schools had focused on *environmental order* issues, especially concentrating on security and safety. Schools used discretionary funds to purchase supplies, repair the physical plant, and implement new discipline and attendance programs. Virtually all schools had moved beyond these initiatives to institute at least *some* academic changes by the end of the fourth year of reform.

Peripheral academic change occurred when no clear improvement plan was developed. In schools in this condition, funds were used to add programs and staff in a haphazard manner; the authors suggested that such changes were unlikely to trigger lasting improvement.

Christmas tree schools also lacked cohesive planning, but their efforts were more expansive. These schools added programs that "looked good" but did little to enhance instruction and may have impeded one another's success.

A number of schools had taken a more focused, systemic approach, however. *Emergent restructuring schools* spent time discussing major issues, tried out new ideas, and encouraged parent and teacher participation. In these schools, teacher groups organized professional development activities and reevaluated the instructional program.

Sustained system activity occurred when restructuring efforts had time to develop, essentially forming a changed school. Heightened levels of professional activity, changed roles for principals and teachers, and strong parent and community ties characterized these schools. A common direction was emerging to guide improvement efforts.

Unfocused reform approaches (peripheral academic change and Christmas tree) were taken by 26% to 35% of Chicago's elementary schools. These schools added programs without rethinking core instruction or encouraging substantive teacher and parent involvement. Schools with unfocused initiatives were often characterized by unsupportive (either autocratic or excessively tentative) principal leadership, limited community involvement, and isolated faculties. Teachers in these schools more often reported that they believed students were incapable of learning, that student attitudes prevented them from succeeding, and that reform had had no effect on their teaching practices.

In contrast, the authors estimated that 36% to 45% of schools were engaged in systemic restructuring (emergent restructuring and sustained system activity); these schools reported wide participation and increased collaboration among teachers, parents, and principals. Planning was a strategic matter to these schools, with many people participating in the development of the school improvement plan, broad engagement by faculties, and close attention given to implementation and evaluation of plan components. Relationships between school professionals and parents/community members tended to be positive and informal. Teachers were collegial and demonstrated a commitment to students and the neighborhood, as well as a willingness to embrace change.

Of the remaining schools, 15% to 25% showed features of both unfocused and systemic approaches, while another 11% to 13% could not be classified.

School Characteristics

All of the types of school politics and improvement approaches were distributed in schools throughout the city. Characteristics such as school size, ethnicity, and percentage of low-income students affected their occurrence to some degree. Hispanic-dominated and less poverty-impacted schools tended to have more strongly democratic governance patterns.

School size was the most significant characteristic. Small schools (less than 350 students) were much more likely to pursue a systemic approach to restructuring than were large schools. Since it is easier to maintain informal interaction in small schools, adversarial politics tended to be rare in these schools. Small schools seemed to facilitate the emergence of strong democratic practices.

Politics and School Improvement

Strong democracy schools were most likely to attempt systemic improvement. Sixty-six percent were engaged in systemic improvement efforts, and another 16% displayed at least some features of systemic improvement. Only 9% of democratic schools had a predominance of unfocused initiatives.

Mixed politics schools also tended toward systemic restructuring. Almost half were taking a systemic approach to restructuring, while many others reported at least some features of systemic change. This trend might indicate that mixed politics schools were moving toward greater democracy.

Not surprisingly, consolidated principal power and adversarial schools infrequently engaged in systemic restructuring. Over 80% of adversarial schools reported unfocused improvement efforts. In schools where the principal "ran the show," teachers and parents remained largely uninvolved in school reform; less than 30% of these schools reported systemic improvement efforts.

EXPERIENCES OF ACTIVELY RESTRUCTURING SCHOOLS

To further identify the characteristics of successfully improving schools, six schools were studied extensively by Bryk and his colleagues (1993). The six schools studied by the Consortium were recommended by organizations working directly with them (not by random or objective selection). They represented a broad geographic, ethnic, and economic range. The research team entitled this part of their report "Experiences of Actively Restructuring Schools." Hence, the schools began to be called "EARS schools."

The Role of LSCs in EARS Schools

Clearly the most significant decision made by the LSC at each EARS site was selecting or retaining the principal. Councils selected candidates strongly committed to the local community, and the Consortium researchers reported the LSCs were actively working to support that person. Councils at EARS schools also actively promoted parent and community involvement, took action to improve the physical condition of the school, and worked to improve safety and discipline both inside and outside of school. The general focus of these successful LSCs was on local needs. EARS councils actively participated in school improvement planning and budgeting, but it was principals and teachers who offered direction. Cooperative relationships, strong principal leadership, and open dialogue with professional staff have made these LSCs integral parts of their school communities, the authors reported.

Principal Leadership

Strong leadership was common to all six EARS schools. Principals had developed solid working relationships with their LSCs, grounded in sensitivity to local needs and good communication. Prior to reform, principals had been considered successful if they "kept the lid on" their schools and followed the directions dictated by the central office. With decentralization and democratic decision making, new leadership styles seem to have evolved.

Adjectives such as *inclusive, committed,* and *compassionate* were used by the school community to describe the EARS principals. These leaders conveyed a clear vision of what they wanted their schools to become and encouraged open communication, group ownership, and commitment to make the vision a reality. EARS principals were reported to be strong in their core beliefs and persistent in their efforts, though none used domination as a tool to lead their schools.

Strategic First Actions

Each school took a series of key first steps to convey an image of renewal to their communities. Principals were highly visible and accessible to the local community, promoting their school vision and learning about local issues. Symbols such as T-shirts, logos, and business cards for teachers were used to create excitement for school renewal and promote the attitude that "things are different now." Principals and LSCs promoted a wider mission for their schools, encouraging expanded parent presence and wider responsibility for children beyond classroom instruction.

Improving the faculty was the primary means principals pursued for instructional change. With reform came greater principal authority over staff selection. EARS principals actively recruited quality teachers, checking references and interviewing extensively to find professionals committed to the total development of their students.

Weak teachers received a clear message from EARS principals to either improve their performance or leave. By maintaining high classroom visibility and clear expectations, principals gave teachers notice that hiding behind closed classroom doors was no longer acceptable. Some teachers had been reassigned to less desirable positions and if they failed to improve their performance, EARS principals were willing to begin formal termination proceedings, though they complained the process was cumbersome and slow.

EARS principals also devoted considerable discretionary resources to staff development, encouraging teachers to attend workshops and providing substitutes to cover classes. While the authors noted that professional development activities are most effective when they reach segments of the faculty as a group (e.g., all primary teachers, all mathematics teachers, etc.), most retraining had not yet reached this level of coherence. EARS schools, however, were taking steps to develop the concept of "professional community" among their faculties.

Committees had been formed to involve teachers with organizational matters, and discretionary funds were used to partially compensate teachers for weekend efforts. Most teachers in the EARS schools were participating in some manner. Much of the participation related to curriculum and instruction, spurring higher teacher interest in improving classroom practices.

Each EARS school also actively pursued partnerships with outside agencies, developing links with universities, businesses, service agencies, and other schools. Principals frequently acted as entrepreneurs for their schools, using their networks of contacts to secure resources, training, and new ideas. Reform has made public schools much more accessible to the outside world, the authors contended, and EARS schools had capitalized on the opportunities made available.

Strategic Use of Discretionary Money

One of the most significant changes in school finance under reform is the transfer of increasing amounts of State Chapter I money to local control, providing principals the opportunity to strategically support school improvement plans (see Appendix B). The amount of money each school received varied considerably; EARS schools received between 10% and 40% of their total school budgets in discretionary funds (combining state and federal resources), yielding between $400 and $1,600 per pupil. EARS schools tied discretionary spending closely to their school improvement plans, ensuring that the educational priorities were reflected in the budget. Initially funds were used to improve environmental conditions, replenish supplies, and add some beneficial programs. As reform progressed, a greater proportion has been allocated to improving instruction, primarily through professional development. However, the report noted, due to the inadequacy of overall funding, schools were frequently forced to dip into discretionary funds to cover what had previously been basic educational costs.

WAS REFORM WORKING?

Bryk and his colleagues announced that, after 4 years of reform implementation, Chicago's schools were restructuring in ways that could lead to major improvements in student learning. Of the schools most in need of change—schools where student achievement had been well below national norms—one-third had developed strong democratic support and participation within their school communities; these schools were following a systemic approach toward reform. Another third displayed some of these characteristics but were not as far along in implementing change.

The authors suggested that it was still too early to use standardized achievement scores to evaluate school reform. While the Chicago School Reform Act called for all Chicago schools to reach national norms within 5 years, in the authors' assessment, this was unlikely to occur. They warned that a fixation on achievement scores could do a serious disservice to the thousands of teachers, parents, and principals who had abandoned the notion of a "magic wand" and instead had devoted years of hard work toward changing the ways schools operated in Chicago.

The authors of the study expressed concern about the effects of "inadequate financial support," and their concern proved to be entirely appropriate. As has already been indicated, the 1993–94 school year was begun only under a temporary restraining order issued by a federal judge. The board's budget was at least $200 million out of balance, with an even higher deficit projected for 1994–95. The ensuing fiscal settlement cut 1,000 teachers out of local schools and chopped high school schedules from seven courses to six for each student. The school year was constantly interrupted, and a feeling of crisis dominated the schools until Thanksgiving. Teacher morale was severely strained.

The fifth year of school reform lurched along; the chaos engendered by the fiscal instability undermined much of the progress made during the previous 4 years of reform. This was particularly true for the system's high schools, where reform had been less successful all along. There was less disruption in the elementary schools, and the prospects there continued to be brighter.

Part II

Challenging the Accepted Assumptions

Virtually all citizens living in the United States share a set of assumptions about public schooling in this country that are deep-seated and usually unexamined. These assumptions are based on images of public schools rooted in childhood experiences and in portrayals of schools in books, films, and the news media. Most adults consider themselves experienced observers of the public schools because they spent 13 years in them. Many of these assumptions are reflected in the ways colleges of education prepare future teachers, provide graduate training to existing teachers, and equip future school administrators.

The Chicago School Reform Act was designed to challenge many of these accepted assumptions and to provide an opportunity for local school actors to challenge other assumptions that the framers of the act had not considered. It is hard for many adults to conceive of public schools that do not start at some specified early morning time and end at some specified time in mid-afternoon, or schools that do not have a summer vacation of about 10 weeks. They cannot imagine schools that do not divide their students into groups of about 25 (more or less), most of whom are within a few months of being the same age and to whom a teacher is assigned. They do not understand a school that is not run by a principal; they have no experience with a building that houses several different schools, each of which is quite different from the others. But the assumptions that lie behind each of these images of public schooling are not written in stone. They were forged earlier in this nation's history, when schools served primarily agricultural communities or, later, urban areas involved in mass production. As we move out of an industrial century and into an information age (Avishai, 1994; Carroll, 1992), new assumptions should be examined and entertained.

One major assumption in American public education, already discussed in Chapter 2, is that "at-risk" students are spread evenly throughout the student population and can be identified for special, individualized attention. This is clearly not true in large urban school systems. When 80% of a high school's entering freshmen are reading at least 2 years below the ninth-grade level and more than half are at least 1 year overage, indicating that they probably repeated a grade at some point during their elementary school careers, it is not rational to think that these students will be adequately served by programs that assume only a few of them are "at-risk." A different approach is required, and the Chicago school reform effort is a different way of attempting to meet the needs of these students.

The chapters in this section examine some other assumptions directly challenged by the Chicago school reform effort. The popular conception of a large urban school system setting policies for all schools, recruiting staffs from across a metropolitan area, and forcing all students from a specific neighborhood to attend a specific school is well established. But desegregation and magnet schools have both worked to send students out of their home neighborhoods. Such practices disconnect schools from the communities within which they are physically located. By contrast, suburban and small-town schools are closely identified with their individual communities. Why should urban schools be disconnected from their local communities if there is value in that connection in suburban and rural areas? Why should it be assumed that more centralized decisions and those made at higher levels of government will be fairer to students in individual schools than those made in the community? Why is it safe to assume that persons whose jobs are connected to the present assumptions about public education are better equipped to decide what is good for students than the parents of those students? And why should we assume that the world of the twenty-first century will be similar to the world of the beginning of the twentieth century, and that an educational structure designed to serve the beginning of the twentieth century is the best structure for the twenty-first century? Chapter 8 examines the connection between decentralization of school systems and the reempowerment of urban communities.

During the twentieth century, our nation has made efforts to improve significantly the opportunities for members of minority groups. In the middle of the century, advocates for civil rights focused their efforts on the federal government to redress local discrimination. It became a cardinal principle that centralized policy setting would be fairer than local prejudice. But toward the end of the century, as the federal government was controlled by persons less committed to equity concerns and as larger governmental bureaucracies, such as school systems, were seen to be failing the most disadvantaged members of our society, this assumption began to be challenged. Strategies of racial justice that focused on individual rights, rather than opportunities for racial, linguistic, and economic groups, are now open to question. In Chapter 9, I explore some of these issues.

A key arena for improving the learning of inner-city students is the kind and quality of instruction they receive and the curriculum to which they are exposed. The framers of the Chicago School Reform Act made no pretense of knowing what the best form of instruction was for inner-city students or what the best curriculum for diverse groups of students would be. Philosophically, the framers were committed to the notion that there would be no one best system (cf. Tyack, 1974) and that different schools might quite successfully adopt different approaches to curriculum and instruction. But maintaining the status quo was the easiest path for any school staff. The struggle to encourage instructional and curricular change by enlisting the assistance of reformers from across the nation and local experts, without dictating the specific changes any school should adopt, is described in Chapter 10.

However, convinced of the shortcomings of the curriculum and instructional practices of even the best public schools today, many academic educators overlook the issue of resources available to restructure public schools. Touted by leaders seeking to preserve their competitive advantage and pass it on to their children, some academics have sought to show that differences in resources available for a child's education are unrelated to that child's chance of educational success (Hanushek, 1986; Walberg & Fowler, 1988). By ignoring the processes by which academic work is chosen for publication and by using simplistic counting procedures, these scholars convinced many in the academic community that money does not matter. More recent, more sophisticated academic examinations of these data (Hedges, Laine, & Greenwald, 1994) have shown the opposite to be true. Meanwhile, state courts across the country were never fooled by the intellectuals' statistics; frequently their testimony was declared "not credible" (*Committee* v. *Missouri*, 1993). In state after state, the courts have found that money does matter. In Chapter 11, I examine the changes in basic assumptions about the operations and finance of public school systems from the perspective of a decentralized urban school district.

The chapters in this part examine the taken-for-granted assumptions of public schooling in the United States and show how the Chicago school reform effort challenged many of them. Since the current national debate about reforming this nation's public schools is being carried on largely without examining these assumptions, though at times proposing changes that defy some of them, it may be valuable to look at them more closely.

CHAPTER 8

Decentralization and Community Control

The last two decades of the twentieth century have seen extraordinary interest in public education, both in the United States and in countries around the world.* Two competing themes have been present in many of the efforts to change public schooling: greater centralization and greater decentralization. Not infrequently, these two themes have both been advanced at the same time. Thus, in both Great Britain and the United States, there has been a movement toward the establishment of national goals and objectives, national standards of what children should be able to know and do when they complete public schools, national certification of acceptable teaching practice, and national means of holding school people accountable. At the same time, in both nations, there is a concerted effort to move decision making down to the school level, to decentralize practical decision making. Under both themes, the traditional loci of control, states and local school districts in the United States and local education agencies in England, are losing authority both upwards and downwards along the "chain of command." (For a more detailed account of similarities and differences in school reform in Great Britain and the United States, see Hess, 1992a.)

After a decade of fits and starts in educational reform, with a number of divergent directions undertaken by various reform advocates and a clear bias toward diversity of approaches and decentralization of authority, a countermovement emerged at the beginning of the 1990s that is oriented toward bringing attempts at improvement in the various levels of education into a common alignment. This countermovement is being spurred by leaders in the Consortium for Policy Research in Education (CPRE), which involves scholars from Harvard, Rutgers, Michigan

*An earlier version of this chapter appeared in Stephen L. Jacobsen & Robert Berne (Eds.), *Reforming Education: The Emerging Systemic Approach*, Corwin Press, 1993, pp. 66–86. © 1993 by the American Education Finance Association. Reprinted by permission of Corwin Press, Inc.

State, Stanford, and the University of Southern California (Olson, 1992). This countermovement, making references to the proclaimed success of the educational systems in several European countries, seeks to create coherence among national goals and objectives for education, the patterns of teacher training, the criteria for certifying teacher competency, the educational curricula offered in schools, and the programs of testing and accountability by which we can judge both student and school achievement (Smith & O'Day, 1991). The salience of this countermovement was vastly increased when key members of the CPRE team assumed important positions in the U.S. Department of Education in early 1993.

At least at first blush, this "systemic reform" effort is sharply contrasted to the decentralization efforts that marked the 1980s. The early efforts toward decentralization were rooted in two research traditions. During the 1970s and 1980s, a series of researchers were identifying individual schools that could be considered "effective," particularly those that were effective with socially and economically disadvantaged young people. The best summary of this research is still to be found in Purkey and Smith (1983). The scholars involved in this research were identifying the characteristics that set "effective schools" apart from those that were ineffective, with the presumption that if schools could change their behavior such that they matched the lists of "effective school" characteristics, they would be equally successful with their students.

A second research strain examined the conditions under which educational innovations were successfully implemented (cf. Elmore, 1979; Mann, 1978). This innovation research emphasized the necessity of "teacher buy-in" if real change was to occur in public schools. It is important to note that several members of the CPRE team had provided some of the most important analyses of earlier reform implementation efforts.

The 1980s decentralization movement was initially given impetus by actions of local teachers unions affiliated with the American Federation of Teachers (AFT). In 1983, the Hammond (Indiana) Teachers Union proposed to rewrite its contract with the school system to create, in every school, improvement teams who would share decision making with the principal in seeking to improve that city's public schools. A key element was the agreement to waive either union contract provisions or bureaucratic regulations that would hinder reform efforts. This initiative gained much higher visibility when adopted by the Dade County Public Schools, the nation's fourth-largest school system (Hanson et al., 1992). It has since been copied in several other school systems where teachers are affiliated with the AFT. Toward the end of the decade, the AFT's competitor, the National Education Association, launched its own shared decision-making program, Schools for the 21st Century (Etheridge & Collins, 1992).

The effort to reform the Chicago Public Schools took a more radical form of the decentralization approach. Richard Elmore (1991) has described why he thinks the Chicago reform effort stands apart from others of the 1980s:

> First, it originated from a grass roots political movement, formed around a nucleus of business, philanthropic, and community organizations, in response to increasing evidence of chronic failure of schools to educate children. Most other reforms have originated from the action of policy makers, legislatures and governors, at the state level; and, at the local level, coalitions of superintendents, union leaders, and board members.
>
> Second, the Chicago reform is, more than any other, based mainly on the theory that schools can be improved by strengthening democratic control at the school-community level. Most other reforms have been based either on theories of regulatory control—increased standards for teachers and students—or professional control—investments in the improvement of teachers' competence and increased decision making authority at the school site. While the Chicago reform has elements of both regulatory and professional control, it is mainly based on a theory of democratic control.
>
> Third, the Chicago reform is probably more ambitious—some would say radical—than any other current reform in its departure from the established structure of school organization. The creation of 542 Local School Councils with significant decision making authority for schools is, by itself, an enormous departure from established patterns of school organization. The departure is even greater when democratic control is coupled with the other elements of the reform—commitments to reduce central administration, reallocation of resources to the school level, changes in school principals' roles and responsibilities, and the like. (p. vii)

Chicago's reform effort has frequently been characterized as a change in governance, but that change was intended to provide the opportunity for changes to take place in the educational programs in schools. There are exciting instances of such changes, as the chapters in Part I indicate, but more schools need to be focused in that direction. Whatever success is created by the Chicago reform effort, the emphasis on school-by-school change has raised questions about the normal assumptions of the operations of public school systems in the United States.

In Chicago, school reform is being advanced by shifting the locus of power away from a central school system bureaucracy and governing board to democratically elected councils at the local school level. Contrary to the professionalization forms of shared decision making, which primarily change the relationships of principals and teachers in exercising the power already located at the school site, significant powers have been devolved to the schools, and nonprofessionals predominate in the membership of the new governing councils. These councils have real power over real resources and real jobs. Whether they will be successful in improving the achievement of the real students attending the city's schools is yet to be seen. It is also not clear that the changes introduced under this reform effort will alter the way schools are organized and create structures radically different enough to lead the way into the information age (Carroll, 1992). What are the issues raised by the adoption of such a dramatic reform plan, and why has such a concerted centralizing countermovement toward systemic alignment emerged in opposition?

FOUR ARENAS OF CHANGE IN CONCEPTIONS OF SCHOOLS

There are at least four arenas in which major changes in the way we conceptualize public schools are taking place. These arenas are the battleground on which the forces of decentralization and the forces of a new, more aligned centralization are contesting. They include the locus of control of schools, which types of people will control schools, the functions schools undertake, and the images of what schools are.

Locus of Control

The Chicago reform effort represents the most radical form of school system restructuring that has devolved power and authority away from the local district board of education and its central bureaucracy downwards to local schools. As indicated above, earlier efforts at decentralization had been initiated by teacher unions as a vehicle for their members to share in managerial power that already existed at the school site; only infrequently did schools gain additional powers under these plans. Only in Chicago was significant new authority vested at the school site. One distinctive feature of the Chicago reform effort was to shift the locus of school control from the district to the school itself.

In theory, central authority in Chicago was reduced to goal setting, monitoring, and contract negotiations. Although central administrators fought a bitter delaying action, even purchasing and staff development resources were to be vested in the schools under the Systemwide Goals and Objectives reform plan formally adopted by the board of education for 1992–93. Unfortunately, by the end of the 1993–94 school year, little in this plan had been implemented, though a systemwide restructuring project was then being undertaken.

With control shifted to more than 540 local schools, great diversity could be expected to emerge, since school councils are charged to meet the specific needs of their enrolled students. However, with greater diversity, a more open enrollment procedure is required to allow students to escape newly adopted program emphases that are not congenial to already enrolled students. An analysis of fall 1991 enrollment data, when an open enrollment plan was originally mandated by the reform act, showed that, through desegregation plans and informal agreements, 28% of elementary students and 54% of high school students in Chicago did not attend their neighborhood schools. The General Assembly had delayed this mandate earlier in 1991, and the first stage of a formal open enrollment policy was not implemented until the 1994–95 school year. Thus Chicago-style decentralization is more attuned to community control of school programming than to systemic alignment.

But at the same time, centralization at the national level has been gaining wide attention. For the first time, national goals for education have been advocated by both Presidents Bush and Clinton and approved by the governors of the various states; in 1994, Congress adopted the America 2000 goals. A former secretary of education, William Bennett, proposed a model school curriculum. Commissions have been established to develop common standards for teacher certification and national achievement assessments. Although quickly sidetracked, legislation was introduced in Congress to force equalization of funding among school districts within individual states. Reputable scholars such as Michael Kirst and Allan Odden are questioning the rationale for the continued existence of local boards of education. Thus authority is moving away from the local school district in two directions: downward to the school level, and upward, first to the state in added regulations introduced as part of statewide reform packages in the middle 1980s and more recently to the federal level through goals, curricula, certification standards, and testing.

Predictably, school district officials have reacted negatively to both these efforts to usurp their previous authority. They have also reacted defensively to efforts to move control *outside* the system of public schools. Although there has been a tradition of home-schooling in the United States that dates to pioneer days, recent publicity about the practice has led to regional superintendents' attempting to use truancy laws to force children being home-schooled to return to the structured school monopoly. In one sense an extension of home-school privileges, which are now guaranteed by law in many states, vouchers have received even more intense opposition from public school advocates. Fearing that vouchers will primarily divert scarce resources from public schools to private ones, public school leaders are also leery of any related developments, such as greater enrollment choice among public schools, contracted management of schools and school systems, or the new for-profit Edison Project schools being developed by Whittle Communications.

Thus public school officials have resisted every effort to remove students from their control and give control over students' futures to their parents, with one major exception. The irony is that while some primarily suburban regional and state officials try to compel home-schooled children back into structured schools, inner-city and rural school officials have done little to overcome, or have even welcomed and encouraged, the absence of chronic truants and other troublesome students from their schools. From this evidence, it would appear that school officials are more worried about losing their monopoly over the more affluent middle-class students than they are about exercising their responsibility toward lower-class inner-city and rural children.

Another irony of this moment in school restructuring, with its unprecedented support from the business community in the United States, is that the value of community control is lost on many business advocates. Instead, they see only the "inefficiency" of the existence of so many small school districts. They focus their whole effort on reducing local control by forcing district consolidation in the name of saving tax dollars. They do not even consider the loss in effectiveness as control is moved further and further from the home and school site. In this sense, the business community, despite its commitment to decentralized decision making as touted by various business gurus (cf. Deming, 1982; Peters & Waterman, 1982), has been a much closer ally of the centralizers than of the decentralizers.

The question, then, is where the locus of control of public education should be in the twenty-first century. Should the federal government control all schools in the United States, as is the case in many other, usually more homogeneous, nations? Should control continue to reside in the traditional sites of authority: states and local districts? Or should control shift to local communities? If control shifts to local communities, diversity and discontinuity will be encouraged in contrast to the homogeneity that could be expected from a systemic alignment of schools controlled at the federal level. A consequence of community control, then, is enrollment choice, for it seems wrong to force students to go to a particular kind of educational program unless all schools are monotonously the same. Today, under more centralized control, many schools are monotonous, but the quality of schools is obviously not the same across individual states or across the nation.

Political, Professional, or Democratic Control?
Alternatives to Bureaucratic Management

As Elmore (1991) has suggested, there are at least three competing theories about who should control what happens at local schools. One group of scholars and activists has focused on greater regulatory control. Thus the 1980s saw the development of wider systems of accountability with the development of statewide report cards on each school and the U.S. Department of Education's infamous "wall chart" comparing public educational statistics from the 50 states. In a different vein, the efforts of the teachers unions and the Carnegie Task Force on Teaching have emphasized professional control at the school site, with teachers sharing in the managerial decision making. Lastly, the Chicago reform effort, the various enrollment-choice programs, and home-schooling have all emphasized parent control of schools and schooling. All these movements have sought to wrest control away from school district bureaucrats, board members, the union, and the political *patrones* related to those districts.

During the nineteenth-century era of the common school, schools were the reflections of their communities. They embodied the community's cultural values and mores, which were generally quite homogeneous. As communities became diverse and the country urbanized, the nation's more than 40,000 school districts were consolidated into the 15,000 that now exist. A century ago, there were 51 different systems controlling the 540 public schools that now are governed by the Chicago Board of Education (Herrick, 1984). But the 15,000 districts across the United States use very different ways of controlling schools. In some states, school districts are still quite synonymous with local communities; in Illinois in 1990, exclusive of Chicago, the average size of the state's more than 900 school districts was about 1,350 students. Other states, particularly in the South, organize districts along county lines, and these districts share the bureaucratic structures of the nation's large urban systems. As these bureaucratic school systems developed in the early twentieth century, control was removed from local communities and vested in the hands of "rational managers." Education was to be removed from the hands of the politicians and given its own profession-alized leadership (Katz, 1992). Schools were also to be removed from the parochial concerns of communities dominated by divisive ethnic traditions so that their children could be blended together, could be Americanized. This was an integrationist philosophy focused on ethnic and national background rather than race. It was the failure of that philosophy in the face of racist intransigence that led racial and ethnic minority leaders during the 1950s and 1960s to reject the melting pot image of America in favor of the image of a tapestry of diversity that is interconnected and whose beauty depends on the interwoven connec-tions. Not surprisingly, leaders of diverse communities had little confi-dence that centrist leaders could move beyond the melting pot image to foster diversity. Thus a movement toward community control began to reemerge in the late 1960s, highlighted by the events in Ocean Hill–Brownsville that led to the establishment of 32 community boards of education to govern New York City's elementary schools (Rogers, 1968).

But a second trend was occurring at the same time. With huge post–World War II federal subsidies for mortgage guarantees, road construc-tion, commuter rail development, and sewer and water extensions, sub-urbs were established and the white middle class abandoned the central cities. Gradually the political and administrative leadership of cities and their governmental services was assumed by minorities. Many thought that when minorities controlled these governments, including school boards, that minority city residents and students would be better served. But conditions in cities and in city schools did not markedly improve as newly ascendant minority bureaucrats found they faced even tougher problems to solve than those that had confronted their white bureau-cratic predecessors. And like bureaucrats everywhere, of whatever color, these bureaucrats were no more willing to tolerate diversity than had those who had gone before them.

Thus a new dimension of the "Who Controls?" controversy emerged. It was one thing for progressive local leaders to oppose the oppressive regimes that resisted desegregation of urban schools and in-stead funneled resources into schools still mostly attended by whites. But what was one to do when the white leaders were finally replaced—and the oppression was not relaxed? What was one to do if the first black superintendent in a city like Chicago sought to "teacher-proof" the curriculum and thereby reduced schooling to filling in blanks on a worksheet under the guise of a "mastery-learning" abomination that was repudiated by the guru in that field? What was one to do if the second black superintendent used the same "blaming-the-victim" rhetoric as had his embattled racist predecessors to excuse ridiculously low student achievement levels? What was one to do if the newly emerging black political and civic leadership articulated a "service" philosophy that also turned inner-city children into "victims," victims needing the paid professional services of the newly emerging black middle class? This social service approach disempowered students just as certainly as had the "blaming-the-victim" rhetoric. Central office bureaucrats, whether malevolent seekers of political and economic privilege, or benevolent service providers meeting presumed student needs, were both incapable of meeting the diverse needs of a student body composed of at least four major racial/ethnic groups and multiple economic levels.

Decentralization, whether in schools or public housing, was a strategy for wrenching power away from those who would impose singular solutions, whether of the political Right or Left, on diverse and divergent needs of students. Community control was now being offered to inner-city neighborhoods similar to that which had continued unabated in suburban and rural communities throughout the twentieth century in states like Illinois.

However, it should be noted that neither the rural communities nor the urban ones had the resources to fully exercise local choices. Thus the rise of a new round of equity law suits was a means of regaining greater "local control." Ironically, state governments and rich suburban districts regularly used "local control" through property taxes as the rational goal of states that justified currently existing inequities.

It is for these reasons that the decentralizers look askance, in ways very similar to those of their local bureaucratic antagonists, at politicians' proposals to divert resources away from their schools (vouchers) and at political and academic proposals for centralizing national goals, curricula, teacher preparation, and testing.

For many in the inner city and in rural areas, public education could easily be understood as a massive colonial enterprise, with schools as colonial outposts of a foreign and oppressive regime. Schools were regulated by distant state governments not responsive to the concerns and funding needs of inner-city and rural areas; these state governments were controlled by populations quite different from those living in inner-city and rural communities. The schools were staffed with professionals who drove in from outside the community and who left the area as soon as possible after completing their contracted labor. The only local residents granted jobs in these institutions held more menial positions, and even the best of these jobs, such as building engineer or head custodian, were reserved through union control for the lower levels of the colonial elite. Even when members of their own kind succeeded, through education in the colonial institutions of higher education, and assumed professional positions in inner-city and rural schools, and later were granted administrative leadership, they frequently expressed the same derision for the native children and excused their inability to improve these schools by asking, "What do you expect us to do when we have so many poor children enrolled in our schools?"

Community control, on the other hand, starts from a different premise: the empowerment of local, nonprofessional actors. Instead of focusing on the deficits of the disadvantaged, it emphasizes their capacities, some of which are frequently not valued in the larger cultural society. As Don Moore (1992), one of the architects of the Chicago reform effort, has argued, empowering parents establishes a different agenda than that established when school professionals are in uncontested control. By placing parents in control of the decision-making process, school professionals must convince parents that proposals they are making will benefit the school's students, not just its staff. Only by assuming that all children have similar needs can centrists, whether at the national, state, or school district level, claim a similar focus on the needs of students. At the same time it must be acknowledged that simply establishing parent or community control does not guarantee that local actors will, in fact, put the needs of students foremost. Still, it is self-evident that it is more likely that the needs of these students will be foremost if it is their parents who are making the basic decisions.

One of the issues faced in the Chicago reform effort was how to give parents real financial control. In the past, when new general purpose funds were made available to the school system, they tended to be absorbed in giving current employees higher levels of compensation. Without debating whether these higher levels of compensation are appropriate or not, one other important question is how to make additional assistance available to students under the decision making of parents. The vehicle for doing that in Chicago was the use of State Chapter I funds. As pointed out in Chapter 3, these funds were partially targeted to schools prior to reform on the basis of enrolled disadvantaged students, but they were utilized in such a manner as to supplant regular local funding efforts. Thus their compensatory effect was being negated. As a result of the reform act, by the fifth year of its implementation, the average elementary school had $491,000 in supplemental funding whose use was entirely at the discretion of local school councils dominated by parents. These funds were no longer general purpose funds accessible to union negotiations for compensation increases, though their use was diminished somewhat by program cuts adopted by the central board of education to accommodate pay raises.

A related issue in parent–teacher relationships is the class status of each group (Michelle Fine, personal communication, 1992). While it is tempting to think of teachers as insiders and parents as outsiders, thus having less power, economic class has a powerful effect on relationships between the two groups. The Chicago School Reform Act recognized the potential for professionals to co-opt parents in the school-decision making process (cf. Malen & Ogawa, 1988). Therefore parents were given a majority of seats on the LSCs, and school professionals between them were given only three (two teachers and the principal). In inner-city systems, lower-class parents tend to look up to teachers. On Chicago LSCs, parents were astounded to realize that teachers are just regular people, with the same faults and blemishes they themselves have. On the other hand, more affluent parents, particularly in the suburbs, frequently look down on teachers as less educated, politically protected, and financially impotent (not working at any important work). Affluent parents expect teachers to accommodate their desires for their children. Affluent parents have waged stiff battles (e.g., over censorship) among themselves to gain control over educators. Not infrequently, suburban school superintendents feel inordinately victorious when they are able to fend off the superordinate power of such parents.

To this point, the argument has been conducted as if school control were only in the hands of one group or another and the question was which group should have the control. In fact, none of the various advocates argue for sole-party control. All see the necessity of involving all stakeholders in the decision-making process. During the past century of primarily professional control, the role of parent participation has been consciously reduced and very nearly eliminated, to the point where one former state education commissioner could entitle a book about expanding parent participation *Beyond the Bake Sale* (Henderson, Marburger, & Ooms, 1986). In this context, it was more likely that parents would be the stakeholders left out of decision making rather than teachers, principals, administrators, or politicians. Thus, for inner-city schools, it is the decentralizers who are most radically changing the answer to the question: Who should control the public schools?

Shift in Function

As with the efforts to shift control away from local districts in two different directions, there are two quite different proposals about what functions should be carried on in schools. On the one hand, there is an effort to return to the basics as the sole function of schooling. Under several different guises, this effort focuses on the instructional role of schools and suggests that other services provided by schools are either diversionary or simply "waste." For example, Bruce Cooper (Cooper, Sarrel, & Tetenbaum, 1990; see also Hess, 1992d, in rebuttal) defined anything not directly contributing to the interaction of teachers and students in direct instruction in regular classrooms as waste and a candidate for elimination in future school budgets. In some cases, the "return to the basics" movement is simply a cover for eliminating some portion of the school's program with which a number of parents or citizens disagree, for example, sex education. In other cases, the claim is made that the school's program, both educationally and in terms of other services, has become so broad that there is no central focus; this diverts students from learning what they really need to know and be able to do. The controlling imagery behind these related efforts is a return to the "common school" of the nineteenth century.

The trend in the opposite direction is to build on the gradual accretion of services provided at the school site, from specialized and compensatory education programs and federally supported free and reduced-price meal programs, to social work geared to assure the best learning context for students, to nursing services, which have begun to turn into health clinics. This trend is now merging with efforts to treat families more holistically in terms of all government-provided services. From this perspective, schooling is only one of the many services being provided to families, services that frequently occur in a disconnected and overlapping way. Instead of seeing families through the narrow lens of various social service categories (unemployment, housing, welfare, health, nutrition, education), holistic advocates suggest governments should treat families as "wholes" with interconnected problems. Schools are a logical site for bringing these various services together, since public education is the one government service that reaches nearly every family, particularly those extensively using governmental social services (Payzant & Pendleton, 1993).

This emphasis on holistic treatment of families is complemented by those who would like to reintegrate schools into efforts at community building. The nineteenth-century common school was frequently at the center of the community. In many twentieth-century suburbs and rural small towns, schools still play that role. But in urban school systems, the schools are frequently closed 5 minutes after the last student leaves and they sit idle until school opens the next morning. The emphasis on decentralization in urban school systems and bureaucratically organized county systems and on more extensive use of school facilities also intersects nicely with efforts at revitalizing inner-city and rural communities.

Shifts in the Image of Schools

As Carroll (1992), Avishai (1994), and many others have noted, the primary image underlying the present organization of schools in the United States is that of the efficient factory. Schools are places where large numbers of young people can be sorted and separated into appropriate batches using some convenient criterion such as age or test scores, manipulated by different persons with different specializations, and emerge as products about which the workers can be proud. Unfortunately, in rural and inner-city areas, the "product" is not measuring up. When that happens, the workers throw up their hands, claim they have done their tasks as they have been trained to do, and blame the raw material as deficient. Less charitable critics and parents in the inner city have claimed that their children are being herded into "factories for failure."

Some reformers have proposed changes that could best be described as efforts to improve the current inefficiencies in these factories. Some suggest narrowing the focus to the "essentials" so that schools may focus on what is really important and, thereby, be more successful. Others have sought to correct the deficiencies in the raw materials by emphasizing early childhood education and even infant intervention through parenting training. Still others have simply sought to replace ineffective characteristics of schools with those that have proven to be associated with effective schools. Albert Shanker, the president of the American Federation of Teachers, once called this "goosing up the old structure to make it work a little better." He went on to suggest, at the inauguration of the Chicago Teachers Union's Center for Restructuring Schools, that more radical change would be required for schools to meet the challenges of the twenty-first century (remarks delivered January 1992).

Other reformers, sensing the long-awaited demise of the Thorndyckian model of efficient schools, which defeated the more individualistic approaches advocated by John Dewey at the beginning of this century, have emphasized developing communities of learners in which each student is given special attention and concern. Thus Philip Schlechty (1990) can suggest:

> One need not be an admirer of America's corporate leaders . . . to understand that in the information-based society, commitment to human development and creating the conditions of freedom, growth,

and respect in the workplace are not simply ethical choices. Investing in people is simply good business, for in the information society, knowledge and the ability to use it are power. And those who have knowledge are the employees. (p. 40)

Still, one suspects that the demise of the Thorndyckian factory model of schooling will not be accompanied by a return to early-twentieth-century personalization, though education in the information age will undoubtedly deal with more individualized instruction than factory-model schools were able to provide. The long-awaited triumph of Dewey is still not likely, because the efficiencies developed during the twentieth century will still be required in the new information age. Instead of turning back the clock, it is more likely that a new synthesis will emerge that still sees schools as efficient organizations but focuses much more on individualized instruction and uses far more advanced technology than the books, blackboards, and chalk that are still the staples of many late-twentieth-century public schools.

DECENTRALIZATION OR CENTRALIZATION: HOW TO MOVE FORWARD?

Decentralization, shared decision making, and school-based management emerged as central themes in the reform movement of the 1980s. That movement provided a powerful critique of the rigid and stultified institution public schooling has become. It opened the way for an advocacy for individuals and for diversity as an alternative to standardized tests, measures, and curricula. It fits into a movement for community reempowerment.

But even before decentralization had time to demonstrate whether or not it could be a vehicle for improving student learning, it was challenged by a new centralism, strangely supported by both the political Left and the political Right. Centrists of both the Left and the Right recognize the challenge posed by those who would take authority away from the center and vest it in local control. Their counterattack is founded in the experience of other, smaller, less heterogeneous, and more centralized nations. It appeals to the logic of alignment: If we expect students to meet certain national goals and to do well on assessments (whether standardized tests as we now know them or other, more sophisticated measures developed in the future), it makes sense to assure that students are studying the materials to be covered in the tests and are taught by professionals who were trained in the same material and in methods of pedagogy appropriate to reaching those goals. This is a powerful position. Implicitly, it assumes a more continuous, incremental approach to school improvement than the potentially more radical changes required to meet the needs of an information age.

The problems to be addressed in the last decade of the twentieth century are whether this new centralism can accommodate the diversity affirmed by the decentralizers and whether the decentralizers can assure that the diversity they value can still be incorporated within a framework adequate to produce graduates capable of living and working in a common social milieu. This latter concern has heightened value in the decade that has seen political decentralization in Europe result in widespread chaos and bloodshed. But the greater question is whether, out of the struggle between the centralizers and the decentralizers, a new image of schooling can emerge that will result in a new way of organizing schools appropriate to the emerging information age.

CHAPTER 9

Race and the Liberal Perspective in Chicago School Reform

With a few exceptional periods, the first eight decades of the twentieth century were marked by policies reflecting the liberal perspective, particularly in the realm of public education.* Matching the development of rationalized and depoliticized public management that saw the rise of town managers, public education developed a professionalized school bureaucracy, and correspondingly universities developed departments of educational administration (Katz, 1992). Later, at midcentury, school desegregation dominated the social issues of the 1950s and 1960s, as "separate but equal" was overturned by *Brown* v. *Topeka Board of Education*. In the later 1960s, in line with the philosophy of the federal government's war on poverty, compensatory funding to offset the disadvantages of poverty or special conditions of children became an accepted mechanism to broaden access to equality of educational opportunity. The emphasis on rational management was reflected in hierarchial bureaucratic organizations at all levels of governmental organization, as discussed in Chapter 8.

One of the central precepts of the liberal political strategies of the middle of the twentieth century was that local interests regularly denied to minorities civil rights and equality of opportunity. From this perspective, perhaps founded in the perception that racial bias was far more virulent in the South than in other regions of the United States, it was a logical strategy to rely on the imposition of directives (judicial, legislative, and executive) from higher, more centralized jurisdictions to overcome local prejudices. From this perception grew a massive civil rights strategy, rooted in the U.S. Supreme Court decision in *Brown* v. *Board of Education*, elements of which are still relevant in arenas such as securing finance equity among school districts in a state. But, as the extent of northern racial bias was revealed in Chicago and other cities in

---

*An earlier version of this chapter appeared in Catherine Marshall (Ed.), *The New Politics of Race and Gender*, Falmer Press, Washington, DC, 1993, pp. 85–96.

the late 1960s and as the national reins of power were assumed by political conservatives with less concern for equality for all Americans, the understanding that "centralized" meant "more progressive" and "local" meant "more unequal" was discarded by many who worked in America's cities.

The 1980s witnessed a turning of the political tide, as more conservative forces took control of federal policy making in reaction against the perceived failures of the liberal social agenda. The conservative agenda focused on reducing the role of government, which implied both fewer services to those who were economically disadvantaged and a reduced attention to assuring the civil rights of minorities and the handicapped. At the same time, minorities claimed political control of many large cities, including Chicago.

The efficacy of public education was also being called into question. The National Commission on Excellence in Education (1983) said we were *A Nation at Risk* and bemoaned the "rising tide of mediocrity" in our schools. But the attack on the failures of the midcentury liberal strategies did not come just from the Right. By the end of the decade, Jonathan Kozol, one of the dramatists of school failure in the 1960s (Kozol, 1968), was again investigating schools across the country and being startled by "the remarkable degree of racial segregation that persisted almost everywhere" (1991, p. 2). Kozol was particularly concerned that the nation seemed to have abandoned the moral implications of *Brown* in favor of seeking equal, if separate, education for minorities. He then went on to describe the *Savage Inequalities* that give the lie to any claims of achieving equity.

School desegregation efforts in America's major cities have not met with great success. Urban geography, demographic changes, and court decisions, such as *Milliken I & II* in Detroit, have effectively eliminated the possibility of interdistrict school desegregation for most urban areas (Monti, 1986; Tatel, Lanigan, & Sneed, 1986). While some scholars continue to document the benefits of individual student integration, where that can be accomplished (cf. Crain & Strauss, 1985; Rosenbaum, Kulieke, & Rubinowitz, 1987), the vast majority of urban minority students are more likely to be left in the racially isolated settings Kozol encountered (Monti, 1986; Tatel et al., 1986). This was clearly the case in Chicago.

I first became aware of the disillusionment of community activists with the "centralized" strategies for achieving equity as the Chicago Public Schools sought to adopt a plan for the desegregation of its schools in 1980–81. For Chicagoans, who had successfully resisted the efforts of the 1960s and 1970s, desegregation in the 1980s had quite different connotations than it would have had two decades earlier. By 1980, only 18% of the city's public school students were white, and these white students overwhelmingly attended a few predominantly white schools. Similarly, three of five black students attended all-minority schools, and another 25% attended schools with less than 30% white student enrollment.

But when the newly installed minority-dominated board of education sought to fashion a desegregation plan, it had much more difficulty than it had anticipated. Black community leaders were reluctant to take visible positions on the desegregation issue, and the five black board members eventually voted against the plan, which was adopted. At one set of public hearings during the planning process, only one black leader forthrightly advocated busing. "If it means my kids have to get on a bus to guarantee our civil rights, then my kids will be on the bus," he said (Hess, 1984, p. 138). But no others echoed his sentiments. Based on their testimony, black parents were far more interested in improving the quality of their neighborhood schools than in sending their kids off to other parts of the city to attend better schools or to attend schools with white kids.

Pierre van den Berghe's (1973) typology of pluralism provided insight into these events. To better describe the racial conditions in urban America, I renamed his three categories "stratified pluralism" (with caste-like characteristics), "egalitarian pluralism" (a consociative model reflective of the Swiss cantons), and "uniform incorporation" of diverse peoples in a "color-blind" society (Hess, 1984, p. 132). The advent of the Black Power movement of the 1960s and 1970s had revealed a disenchantment with pursuing "individual integration" (uniform incorporation) in favor of seeking "equal access to power and economic resources" (egalitarian pluralism). To eliminate caste-like stratified pluralism in Chicago, minority leaders in 1980, I suggested, were pursuing strategies that would produce a society based on egalitarian pluralism rather than one built on uniform incorporation. But the desegregation effort was being driven by a legal interpretation more consistent with a society of individual integration. One lawyer from the Department of Justice, commenting on the board's public hearings, complained, "They weren't supposed to be running a referendum on the Constitution!" (Hess, 1984, p. 138). It appeared that, by the late 1970s, many black leaders, while reluctant to openly break with the traditions and history of the civil rights movement of the 1950s and 1960s, were pursuing objectives of equal access rather than those of individual integration. Their silence on the desegregation plan was indicative of their awareness of the difficulty of explaining that their goals had not changed, but their strategies had. It was this shift away from a strategy of individualized integration and toward egalitarian pluralism that was to puzzle Kozol only a few years later.

CHICAGO SCHOOL REFORM:
LEFT-OVER LIBERALISM OR NEO-CONSERVATIVE CONSPIRACY?

Kozol (1991), among others, is suspicious that reform efforts focused on restructuring are little more than the creation of "a more 'efficient' ghetto school" (p. 4). Other critics have other complaints. In fact, the Chicago School Reform Act has been lionized and vilified by commentators from both the Right and the Left. Chester Finn (Finn & Clements, 1990) and Harold Howe (1988) have both lauded it as one of the most radical efforts to reform America's schools. Meanwhile, Myron Lieberman (1989) and Gary Orfield (1991) deride it as not radical enough. Does the Chicago effort represent a rejection of liberalism and an embracing of more parochial neo-conservative approaches of community control? Is it one more frantic effort to patch up the failed massive bureaucratic solutions of the War on Poverty that Chubb and Moe (1990) say is doomed to equal failure because it still relies on democratic control? Are the architects of the reform effort "left-over liberals of the 1960s," as Bruce Cooper (1990) has suggested? Or are they misguided neo-conservatives in liberal clothes, as Orfield has implied? Does it make any difference what label they wear?

In this chapter, I attempt to describe the conditions that led reform advocates in one major American city to champion the elements of the legislation enacted in 1988 and to examine the challenges to traditional liberal strategies this reform effort poses. As one of the several "architects" to whom Cooper referred, I would assert that the intellectual roots of the reform effort in Chicago are clearly in the egalitarian and compassionate soil of the traditional liberal perspective. But the solutions were fashioned more pragmatically than ideologically. They were directly connected to the analysis of the problems being experienced in the Chicago Public Schools during the 1980s. In that sense, perhaps it is fair to say the Chicago approach embodies a rejection of the failed, centralized strategies earlier liberals had designed to solve the problems of schooling for low-income and minority students. However, I would maintain that it is the *strategies* of midcentury liberalism that had been unsuccessful in Chicago, not the philosophical perspective. The Chicago school reform effort was not an abandoning of the effort to assure equality of opportunity to all of the city's students; it was an assertion that, under the then reigning liberal paradigm, such opportunity was still being systematically denied.

THE FAILURE OF THE LIBERAL AGENDA IN CHICAGO

When the outcomes of the 1981 desegregation plan were later examined (Easton & Hess, 1990; Hess & Warden, 1988), the results were disappointing from the perspective of disadvantaged minority youth. By 1986 the system had successfully eliminated all predominantly white (above 70%) schools, and only a third of white students then attended majority white schools. But for minority students, there was little benefit, as only 3% more minority students attended desegregated schools in 1986 than had done so in 1981. Dollars and staff were disproportionately focused on new and continuing magnet schools, and white students were disproportionately enrolled in magnet schools. By the 1988–89 school year (the year in which reform legislation was finally enacted), white students made up only 12% of the public school enrollment, and the percentage of minority students attending predominantly (above 85%) minority schools had actually increased from 58% to 63%! After a decade of centrally directed desegregation, minority students were no better off than they had been at the beginning of the effort, even though an increasing proportion of desegregation resources was devoted to predominantly minority schools in the later part of the 1980s.

In addition to the continuing and intensifying racial isolation, minority students were attending schools in which student achievement was very low. In 1985–86, as noted in Chapter 2, eighth-grade students attending magnet or desegregated schools (those with enrollments above 30% white) were achieving at the national norms or above on the Iowa Test of Basic Skills, while those in the 300 racially identifiable or racially isolated schools were from 8 months to more than a year behind the norm. In high schools, all students did less well. In desegregated and selective-entrance schools, median students performed at the 42nd percentile (norm = 50th percentile), while in segregated schools the median was at the 24th percentile.

Our study of the dropout phenomenon in Chicago (Hess & Lauber, 1985) showed that 43% of entering ninth-graders never graduated from a Chicago high school. Once again, as noted in Chapter 2, segregated inner-city schools (in aggregate, less than 6% white) had a cumulative dropout rate of 56%, while the mostly desegregated and selective high schools (together 34% white) had an aggregated dropout rate of 25%, slightly below the national average. We called this a system of educational triage (Hess, 1986). A study by Designs for Change (1985b), another key organization in the Chicago school reform effort, came to similar conclusions about achievement and dropout rates. But we noted that some high schools, despite receiving high proportions of ill-prepared students, were more successful than others with similar enrollments. Our follow-up study (Hess et al., 1986) had findings similar to other effective schools research (cf. Purkey & Smith, 1983)—that the quality of the principal, the type discipline maintained, the clarity of the educational philosophy, and the degree of direct and interactive instruction in the classroom were all associated with schools with lower dropout rates. The Designs for Change study had also emphasized the findings of the effective schools literature. An earlier Designs study, led by Donald Moore, who was to become the chief of the "architects" of the reform legislation, had shown that Chicago was engaged in a pattern of racial steering in special education classifications (Moore & Radford-Hill, 1982).

In addition, we were also documenting the failures of the centralized administration of the school system to efficiently manage the system or to provide equitable resources to disadvantaged students, even when the system's chief administrators themselves were minorities. Our 1986 study was called *"Where's Room 185?"* because it documented a widespread practice of shortchanging Chicago high school students of their instructional opportunities by scheduling them for excessive study halls that were either chaotic or, frequently, nonexistent. Students at one high school with "Room 185" (a supply closet) on their schedules knew they were to come to school late or leave early for that period. In Appendix B, I have outlined the fiscal mismanagement and skewed priorities of the school system prior to enactment of the reform legislation.

By 1987, the failures of rationalized, central bureaucratic management and court-ordered desegregation to meet federal guidelines to produce adequate and equal opportunities for educational success for economically disadvantaged and minority students were obvious to all in Chicago. Minority control of the school bureaucracy and the city government produced no new opportunities for black and Hispanic students; desegregation had been ineffective in improving the lot of 97% of the previously racially isolated Chicago public school children. The time had arrived for a wide-ranging and more radical reform.

THE REFORM RESPONSE

The school reform movement in Chicago, the solutions embodied in the agreements of the second year of the mayor's education summit, and the Chicago School Reform Act (P.A. 85-1418) that developed out of these efforts, were responses to the perceived failures of the Chicago Public Schools and of the strategies embodied in educational policies being enacted by the school system and the state. The reform movement was shaped by the acknowledged failures of the preceding decade, including the unwillingness and inability of the federal government to initiate metropolitan solutions to segregated schools, housing, and job opportunities, as promised in the 1980 consent decree agreement between the Justice Department and the Chicago Board of Education. School activists dismissed the possibility of changing the whole of society before attempting to improve the city's schools. The focus was on Chicago and its schools, not the whole society and its problems. Reform leaders, supported by the effective schools literature and similar local studies, were convinced that schools in Chicago could do a *better* job of educating the city's children, no matter what disadvantages they brought with them to school.

This is a distinctly different conviction about the educability of disadvantaged inner-city youth than that embodied in typical metropolitan desegregation approaches, which spread out low-achieving students into schools dominated by higher-achieving majority students. In those schools, minority students frequently achieve no better than they did in their inner-city schools, but desegregation advocates suggest these students' goals are higher and their later life opportunities are enhanced (Orfield, 1986). Such advocates focus on the "escape opportunities" for a few minority students while consigning the much larger number of minority students who remain behind to continued failure. This paternalistic posture has preempted other approaches under the liberal perspective but seems harshly at variance with ensuring equality of opportunity for all. It, too, represents a posture of educational triage: escape for some, intentional neglect for the majority who cannot be rescued.

In line with the conviction that Chicago could offer better educational opportunities to all its disadvantaged students, the goals of the reform act, as noted in Chapter 3, were designed to equalize opportunity in the city's schools and lift student achievement levels to the national norms. The law envisioned accomplishing a normal distribution of scores on standardized achievement tests within 5 years. Reformers recognized that this was a terribly optimistic goal, but they felt that it was necessary to make it explicit in order to engender the required changes immediately, rather than "with all deliberate speed." Further, the effective schools literature had emphasized that one of the critical elements was a widespread conviction among a school's faculty that "all kids can learn" (Brookover, 1991; Designs for Change, 1985a).

The second major component of the legislation is a mandate to reallocate the system's resources to remedy the inappropriate allocation and supplanting of state compensatory funds. This provision forced the closing of many positions in the central administration and the shifting of resources to the schools for their discretionary purposes. By the fifth budget year, the percentage of staff working in nonschool locations had dropped from 12% to 8%, while discretionary spending had reached an average of $491,000 per elementary school. Base-level funding had begun to level out, and total expenditures per pupil were more clearly correlated with the proportion of low-income students enrolled (see Appendix B). This accomplishment is in line with the traditional liberal equity goal in school finance circles of treating equals equally (horizontal equity) and unequals unequally (vertical equity) (cf. Berne & Stiefel, 1984).

Still, it was the making of the "individual local school the essential unit for educational governance and improvement" (P.A. 85-1418, Sec 34.1.01B) that raises the greatest controversy about the Chicago School Reform Act.

Responsibility is placed in the hands of actors at each school site. This is contrary to the mistaken characterization of the act as focused on "community control" (Mirel, 1990) in the sense of that notion as used in New York (Rogers & Chung, 1983) and Detroit (Glass & Sanders, 1978). In those cities, authority was devolved to large community subdistricts with populations of hundreds of thousands. Such a plan was introduced by Republican legislators in Illinois as a competitor of the Chicago School Reform Act but lost in the House as the current school-site-focused reform was enacted. In Chicago, authority is vested directly at the school site, which has important implications for community (in the sense of neighborhood) impact, as noted in Chapter 8.

As noted in the introduction to Part I, there are two separate types of authority shifts that have been propounded under the image of school-based decision making or school-based management: the shifting of who is involved in decision making and the actual devolution of authority from higher levels of the school system bureaucracy to the school level. The Chicago School Reform Act uses both types of authority shift, expanding the categories of persons making decisions at the school site and significantly expanding the arenas about which decisions can be made. In the Chicago case, decision making is shared among parents, community residents, teachers, and the principal.

Principals are given the primary responsibility to develop a school improvement plan and a school budget. Teachers have significant input in fashioning the SIP. Principals can select new staff. But both the SIP and the budget must be approved by the whole LSC, which also determines who will be the principal. Parents comprise the majority of the LSC, but it takes seven votes to select a principal, so parents alone cannot select a school's educational leader. In our study of 14 representative schools, we found few examples of decisions made solely by the votes of parents. But the potential for parent dominance is always present; parents make up a majority of the LSC, the chair of the LSC must be a parent, and they have the potential to dominate principal selection. In our sample of schools, we found at least two cases in which the faculty recommended retention of the incumbent principal but the LSC voted to select someone else.

The reform community did split apart over addressing the *Savage Inequalities* Kozol (1991) so powerfully described. In April 1992, the Coalition for Educational Rights, which I served as president and whose membership included the Chicago Urban League, the Chicago Panel, and the state League of Women Voters, worked with Senators Arthur Berman (Democrat of Chicago) and John Maitland (Republican of downstate Bloomington) to fashion an amendment to the Illinois Constitution that would have made education a fundamental right in this state. The amendment was approved by a 60% majority in each house and put on the November ballot for adoption by the citizens of Illinois. While most of the community and school-based reform advocates strongly supported the amendment, business leaders who had previously supported Chicago school reform, such as the executive director of the Civic Committee of the Commercial Club and the chairman of CNA Insurance (a board member of the business-dominated reform group, Leadership for Quality Education), led the opposition. This effort to create a binding mandate on the state to more adequately fund its schools and to assure greater equity in the levels of funding between districts fell 3 percentage points short of the 60% majority needed for adoption in the general election.

DIFFERENT STRATEGIES TO CREATE MORE EQUAL OPPORTUNITIES

In this chapter I have attempted to correct some widely held misapprehensions about what the Chicago program is. As noted earlier, it is not an effort at the type of community control manifested in the decentralization efforts in New York and Detroit, though it does devolve authority away from centralized control and contributes to the empowerment of local neighborhoods. Local control in the Chicago effort is far more localized than in those cities. It is not an abandonment of efforts to provide an equal opportunity for all students to succeed. It is not an abandonment of the traditional liberal goals of integration (the limited success of the board's desegregation plan is protected in the legislation), though it recognizes the current legal restrictions on addressing the city–suburban racial segregation currently typical of metropolitan areas in the United States. Rather, it is an attempt to improve the education offered to the vast majority of minority students who continue in segregated or racially isolated settings in the nation's third-largest school system, students frequently ignored by rationally managed public education systems and liberally inspired desegregation plans. Further, the reform act significantly extends the compensatory approach that had been diluted and corrupted by both state and local policy makers of the 1970s and 1980s, even though many of those officials were themselves black or Hispanic. And the educationally activist members of the reform movement were leaders in the effort to change the way state funding is provided to schools in Illinois. Reform in Chicago is an effort to deal with the failures of traditional liberal strategies in the changed demographic and political context of the end of the twentieth century, while still pursuing statewide remedies where available.

The Chicago reform effort does call into question the logic of the connection between the liberal philosophical perspective and the strategies adopted by liberals in the 1950s and 1960s, which were linked to the professionalized, rational governance strategies of the early decades of this century. From the Chicago perspective, the midcentury liberal solutions simply were not working for the city's disadvantaged young people. Chicago reformers were unwilling to allow those students' needs to go unmet for the sake of allegiance to ineffective "traditional liberal strategies," and they were not willing to settle for providing a triage strategy of escape for a few while the needs of the majority were ignored.

Thus, in Chicago, the strategies were changed. In many ways, school reform was just one focus for the broader changes in the society. Predating the school reform movement, Chicago's community leaders had abandoned an effort to create an integrated society of uniform incorporation in favor of establishing an egalitarian pluralism of equal access to power and resources. I have already described this change during the desegregation planning period. Similar changes were occurring in the fields of politics, housing, and job development. To this extent, Kozol's (1991) concern that we may be returning to the "separate but equal" strategies of *Plessy* v. *Ferguson* may have some relevance.

However, the fundamental mistake of midcentury liberals may have been in focusing on school segregation rather than residential segregation as the target for civil rights activity in the North. Segregated schools were an obvious target in the South, where government-run services were segregated but blacks and whites lived in close proximity to each other. But in the North, where the institutions were not segregated by law but reflected the segregation of neighborhoods, it may be that the advocates of civil rights chose the wrong target. Implicitly, the Chicago desegregation consent decree recognized the limits of school desegregation when only 18% of the students were white and therefore included a pledge, never fulfilled, by the federal government to seek to address the interrelated issues of housing, employment, and economic development. "Controlled enrollment" was easier to implement than "controlled residence," but its effectiveness for the vast majority of minority students was nil. Having a desegregation decree in place has been more satisfying to Chicago's civil rights advocates than to the students it sought to benefit. The Chicago school reform effort was designed more for effect on these students than for satisfying liberal sensibilities.

While maintaining as many desegregated settings as possible, the school reform effort built on the strategy of egalitarian pluralism. It added to that communitarian notion the "traditional liberal" approach of providing compensatory resources to the most disadvantaged in order to equalize educational opportunities. At the same time, it recognized the legal and political constraints to creating metropolitanwide solutions. "Traditional" (i.e., 1960s style) liberals such as Orfield and Kozol have criticized the Chicago reform effort for being willing to work within these constraints rather than focusing exclusively on a quixotic attack on those windmills. For critics such as Orfield (1991), any effort operating within the recognition of existing constraints is "preposterous" (p. 10) and doomed to failure. In this stance, he comes to a position identical to that of his conservative protagonists, Chubb and Moe (1990), who equally consign the Chicago reform effort to inevitable failure because it retains democratic control of the schools. But as the educational amendment campaign showed, many of these Chicago reformers were also willing to take on the statewide inequities about which Orfield worries.

Reformers in Chicago were simply unwilling to wait for a midcentury-type liberal political resurgence, a new civil rights movement, or a new War on Poverty to fix our whole society before trying to improve the educational opportunities available to the city's disadvantaged students. To agree, as most Chicago reformers do, that school reform cannot deal with all the disadvantages young people bring to the schools, is not the same thing as saying there is nothing the schools can do to improve the educational opportunities they are now providing students. The either/or perspective adopted by Orfield and some defenders of liberal political correctness alienates others with a liberal perspective who have to deal with the failed results of the midcentury liberal "so-called" solutions. If "liberals" are unwilling to recognize the failures of their own attempts at solutions, how liberal are they?

However, there is another dimension to the Chicago reform effort that is outside the purview of the typical liberal–conservative debate. The Chicago school reform effort shifts the boundaries of what is traditionally thought of as "schooling" (Stanley Hallett, personal communication, 1992). Under this reform effort, schooling in urban centers is reestablished in the context of local community, from which it had been extracted as part of the rationalizing, bureaucratic reforms of the early decades of this century.

In most communities in America, schools represent at least half of the local political life through elections to the school board and referenda votes on educational resources. School funding typically represents more than 60% of the tax bills of Illinois' property owners. Schools represent one of the major foci for discussions about the nature and future of local communities. In urban America, this discussion has been stripped away from city residents and neighborhood organizations. Under Chicago school reform, with biannual elections of local school council members, this political discussion is reemerging. Designs for Change (1991) reported that the number of elected black and Hispanic school board members nationally nearly doubled after the first LSC elections. A new level of political leadership is being developed, the ramifications of which are not yet fully clear (cf. Poinsett, 1990).

Further, neither traditional liberals nor traditional conservatives take seriously the energy that is released when local communities are empowered to address their own identified problems. As Don Moore (1992) has pointed out, when parents are involved in school improvement planning, the problems that are identified are frequently very different from the problems identified by school professionals. Consequently, the resources available to address problems are also far broader. When schools are part of an inaccessible, encapsulated system, they are both protected from, and unable to utilize, the vitality of the communities in which they are located. Parents and community LSC representatives have proven to be important resources when schools have been threatened or their programs cut under Chicago school reform (Flinspach & Ryan, 1994).

Finally, by loosening the bureaucratic control, the opportunities for school-level innovation are multiplied. Innovation ceases to be a top-down policy initiative accompanying each change in superintendent; such innovations have been notorious for their ineffective implementation. Instead, each local entity becomes a potential innovation site. Already in Chicago, more than 170 schools have been identified (Hess, 1992e) where new national reform efforts have been established, ranging from curricular innovation such as the Algebra Project or the Illinois Writing Project, to pedagogical changes implicit in the Accelerated Schools approach or cooperative learning, to organizational reorientation through projects in Total Quality Management.

Still, it is not clear that the Chicago reforms will be successful. Toward the end of the initial 5-year focus of the reform act (1989–1994), progress has been quite significant from an organizational development perspective. The system's resources have been redirected. Authority has begun to shift. New leadership has been installed in more than half of the newly semi-autonomous subunits of the system. Plans for improvement have been adopted at all units, with varying likelihood of producing significant change.

But from the perspective of whether the changes that have occurred will impact the way students learn in Chicago's schools, and therefore have a significant effect on student achievement levels, the picture is less clear (Bryk, Deabster, Easton, Lupescu, & Thum, 1994). As critics of the Left (Sizer, 1988) and Right (Finn & Clements, 1990) have noted, unless really radical change is undertaken, it may not be enough. The question for Chicago is whether the school councils—which have attacked important noninstructional problems such as overcrowding, gang influences and disruption, discipline, deteriorating facilities, and low attendance—can focus on the instructional programs of the schools in their next stage of development. For it is only then that we might expect to see the new strategy at the heart of this city's school reform effort produce the radical change called for by the critics of both Left and Right.

CHAPTER 10

Struggling to Change
Teaching and Learning

There is little hope that student achievement will rise in urban schools unless the basic interaction between teachers and students changes. There are many components to that interaction, and many strategies exist for changing the teacher–learner relationship. One of the fundamental premises of the authors of the Chicago School Reform Act was that no one "silver bullet" existed to change the relationships between teachers and students in Chicago. Instead, the philosophy was more, "Let 1,000 flowers bloom." By encouraging diverse approaches selected by individual schools, we hoped that teacher buy-in at the school level would be higher and the most successful strategies would be more easily identified later in the process.

Clearly, a fundamental finding in the effective schools research, raising teacher expectations about students, was a key element in our thinking. Reformers had also looked carefully at the systemwide approach taken to retrain all teachers in the Pittsburgh Public Schools (Johnston, Bickel, & Wallace, 1990) but had been uneasy about imposing a single style on all Chicago teachers (Pittsburgh had adopted the Madeline Hunter approach for its systemwide retraining approach). A systemwide staff development effort had been a component of the agreements in the mayor's educational summit. But instead of prescribing a single approach, reformers repeatedly proclaimed the need for extensive staff development, although they reserved to faculty at each school the right to decide what assistance they needed.

One likely reason we were reluctant to dictate strategies for changing teaching and learning in schools is that few of us providing the momentum and leadership to change the Chicago Public Schools considered ourselves to be experts in curriculum or pedagogy. Further, reformers had little confidence that educational leaders in Illinois, whether in the school system, the union, or the universities, knew much more about these issues. The Chicago school reform movement came from outside what Michael Katz (1992) calls the synergistic relationship between public schools and schools of education. In fact, many reformers, myself included, were deeply skeptical about that school–university relationship, which I would more likely then have characterized as a "conspiracy." Leaders in the area schools of education were amazingly quiet during the movement to launch reform of the Chicago schools, seeming to reinforce the attitude articulated by Superintendent Byrd when he asked, "What can you expect when we have so many poor kids?" ("Byrd Defends School Anti-Dropout Role," 1987).

However, our lack of expertise did not blind us to the importance of changing the kind of teaching occurring in Chicago schools. In our matched-pairs ethnographic study of eight Chicago high schools (Hess et al., 1986), Chicago Panel staff had identified more direct instruction and more interactive instruction as two of the characteristics that distinguished schools with lower dropout rates from those with higher percentages of students dropping out. But we were reluctant to dictate how schools should move to encourage teachers to engage in more active classroom leadership (rather than extensive use of worksheets) and how we could promote more interactive pedagogy that engaged students in the learning process (rather than the much more prevalent one-way exchanges we saw in many prereform classrooms). We knew some of the things we wanted, but we were not confident that we knew all the ways to get there; we were convinced there was more than one way to be successful.

STRATEGIES FOR CHANGING TEACHING AND LEARNING

As I write about the efforts to change teaching and learning in Chicago, I find myself in dialogue with two persons I consider close colleagues and mentors, Bill Ayers and Michelle Fine. For the past year, I have been reading recent books they have produced: Ayers's *To Teach: The Journey of a Teacher* (1993) and Fine's edited volume *Chartering Urban School Reform: Reflections on Public High Schools in the Midst of Change* (1994). And I am conscious that this book will appear in a series co-edited by one of the foremost experts in the field, Ann Lieberman. In this company, I am very conscious of my limitations. But I am also conscious that there must be a dialogue between policy advocates like myself and instructional experts like Ayers and Lieberman and the colleagues Fine drew around herself in Philadelphia.

Much is happening in the whole arena of changing teaching and learning in American schools, and others have more carefully described these efforts than can I (cf. Fullan, 1991; Hargreaves, 1989, 1994; A.

Lieberman, 1988). Some efforts focus on raising the quality of the teacher force nationwide by shifting the nature of teacher preparation and establishing a national certification for master teachers (Carnegie Forum, 1986). Others, like those described by Ayers and Fine, focus more on changing what teachers are actually doing in urban classrooms. In seeking to change Chicago schools, I find myself more in dialogue with Ayers and Fine than with the national teacher upgrading movement, though I am not unsympathetic to that work.

One of the reasons I am intimidated by Ayers and Fine is that I have little experience with teaching in public schools. I did spend 14 years doing extensive adult teaching in intensive, life-changing, short-duration seminars. Some of that work was in seminars designed for high school young people. I also have experience teaching in university classrooms. But I am aware that these experiences do not translate directly to public school classrooms.

When I sit down with Ayers's book and read about classroom incidents that demonstrate changed approaches to inner-city student learning, I am filled with hope but also overawed with the difficulty of translating those experiences into 23,000 classrooms across Chicago. When I read of the efforts of Fine and her colleagues to build the capacity of Philadelphia high school teachers to change the nature of teaching in that city's comprehensive high schools, I am thrilled by the early successes but devastated by the silencing on issues of race, gender, and class that they expose. I wonder whether Chicago schools, with their informally segregated seating patterns in faculty lunchrooms, are any different, and whether we can hope to dramatically change student achievement without addressing the silent subplots of racism, sexism, and patronizing classism. But I also wonder if we can get there, one group of teachers at a time.

The Chicago reform effort is postulated on the need to improve the capacity of city teachers as they struggle with teaching students who bring significantly different strengths into our city's classrooms than those of more affluent suburban young people. But as reform was being considered and debated, and as the reform effort has been implemented, a second strand has been prevalent as well: getting rid of nonperforming or low-performing teachers. Disgusted critics of the Chicago schools frequently cite the statistic that only 6 of 25,000 teachers are dismissed for incompetence in any given year. Restrictions in the teachers union contract are the next most frequent complaint. How are these conflicting approaches, capacity building and sanctions, to be balanced? How can they be made complementary?

To date, the Chicago effort has been primarily focused on providing the opportunities for change and improving capacity in the city's teachers. There are impressive efforts underway, which I describe in the next two sections. But there is also an awareness that, under the present approaches, capacity building is limited to those who recognize the need for change and who are willing to enter into the change process. As noted in Chapter 6, principals like the one at Montgomery School continue to struggle with what to do about the teachers who do not want to change and who slip out the door as quickly as the students at the end of the day.

Interestingly, this is a problem that was first addressed by the Chicago Teachers Union during reform discussions. The CTU had long advocated adopting the Toledo Plan of peer review by teachers (Chicago Teachers Union, 1986). Aware of the untenableness of publicly defending poor teachers, the CTU also quietly stopped providing counsel to every teacher charged with incompetence by the school system, while continuing to insist on protecting their members' due process rights. The CTU recognized the need to put pressure on low-performing teachers to improve, not simply to provide opportunities for improvement. While a watered-down version of the peer review process was included in 1985 statewide reform legislation that made it somewhat easier to remove poorly performing teachers after a remediation period, the school system never took advantage of this offer by the teachers to cooperate in breaking the culture of silence about the performance of colleagues. The CTU was left to launch its own initiative in teacher retraining through its Quest Center, described below.

By contrast, the effectiveness of sanctions in changing teacher behavior is beginning to be seen in Kentucky. Recent research by the Appalachia Educational Laboratory (AEL) (1994) indicates that teachers are changing their practices, dramatically increasing the amount of writing they require of students, to match the new expectations embodied in the state's new assessment and accountability system. In the process, teachers are finding how they have been shortchanging their students through lower than realistic expectations. One teacher told AEL researchers:

> I had a kid last year who couldn't write a sentence . . . not "The dog bit," nothing. . . . I read a short story in his portfolio the other day and it was almost five pages long. . . . I look at him and I think, "What if all I had stressed had been grammar skills and punctuation skills but he had never transferred that?" Last year he was the slowest kid I had, and I thought, "I'll never get a portfolio out of him." We had no problem. He's the first one to hand his portfolio in. (Appalachia Educational Laboratory, 1994, p. 46)

In light of the one-third of Chicago schools that have made little effort to improve since the inception of the Chicago School Reform Act, I believe we need to look closely at using powerful sanctions on schools and faculties that have failed to take the opportunity to improve their capacity or to plan for change and providing rewards for those that are successful. Still, what has been attempted in building capacity deserves attention.

USING NATIONAL REFORM EFFORTS TO CHANGE TEACHING AND LEARNING IN CHICAGO CLASSROOMS

Historically, the Chicago Public Schools has not welcomed the interference of outside experts "messing about" in its schools. Prior to the passage of the Chicago School Reform Act, outsiders had to secure the permission of the general superintendent (through recommendation from the Department of Research and Evaluation) to work in any Chicago school. As Dick Elmore commented during a 1990 advisory panel meeting at the initiation of the Chicago Panel's reform monitoring project, big-city school systems are frequently ignored in research and reform efforts nationwide simply because it is so difficult and time-consuming to secure entrance into their schools. As he pointed out, most funded research projects are of relatively short duration (under 18 months from funding until the report due date), which requires site entry proceedings that are not cumbersome or time-consuming.

With the passage of the reform act, the central office no longer had control over who was providing assistance or doing research in individual schools in the system. Thus national reformers had a readily accessible market of urban school sites in Chicago, if they were willing to reach out to individual schools to secure entry. It was the hope of the framers of the reform act that exactly that kind of assistance would be requested by Chicago schools and would be made available, if requested.

For example, the Chicago Panel began publishing a monthly (during the school year) journal, *Reform Report*, dedicated to describing different national reform efforts and highlighting in each issue a Chicago school that was implementing the ideas from the featured reform effort. The Panel has produced 3 years' worth of such issues. Now, having served the purpose of calling attention to opportunities available to Chicago schools, the journal will shift gears to focus on the schools that have been most successful in improving student achievement and outcomes and to report on the causes of their success. In Chapter 5, I have described some of these outside reform efforts. Here I would like to focus on three more comprehensive efforts and three more focused efforts.

Schoolwide Reform Efforts

In 1984, Ted Sizer published *Horace's Compromise: The Dilemma of the American High School*. Shortly thereafter, he began to articulate the principles that would describe a refocused secondary school. With colleagues from schools not too distant from Brown University, he began to develop the Coalition of Essential Schools (Muncey & McQuillan, 1992; Sizer, 1989). As the Chicago reforms were getting underway, Sizer was establishing a relationship with the Education Commission of the States to dramatically expand his work nationwide through a project called Re:Learning. Illinois was to be one of the cooperating Re:Learning states, and in the fall of 1990, 10 Illinois "Essential High Schools," including 2 from Chicago, began planning their restructuring efforts. The MacArthur Foundation provided funding for 9 additional Chicago high schools to join the network. Each school would get $50,000 per year for 3 years to receive training and support from the Coalition in its effort to restructure along the lines of Sizer's nine principles. One of the key principles most frequently emphasized by Coalition schools is number four on Sizer's list: "Teaching and learning should be personalized to the maximum feasible extent" (Muncey & McQuillan, 1992, p. 50). The fifth is: "The governing practical metaphor of the school should be student-as-worker rather than the more familiar metaphor of teacher-as-deliverer-of-instructional-services." The seventh principle encourages higher student performance without high pressure: "The tone of the school should explicitly and self-consciously stress values of unanxious expectation." The approach of the Coalition is to provide staff development assistance to school faculties as they seek to design methods of implementing the nine principles and to facilitate exchanges among Coalition schools so that teachers may act as "critical friends" to one another as they seek to change their schools (Watkins, 1992).

It is easy to see that this approach is strongly focused on changing the nature of teaching and learning in Chicago's inner-city high schools. Early experiences, however, led me to think that the participating Chicago schools had little commitment to Sizer's nine principles and were just "taking the money and running." Now it appears that some Coalition schools do seem to be implementing some fairly radical restructuring, such as Chicago Vocational High School's restructuring into seven or more schools-within-a-school.

An elementary-level counterpart to Sizer's effort is Henry Levin's Accelerated Schools Network (Hopfenberg, Levin, Meister, & Rogers, 1991). Levin, of Stanford University, started from the premise that the traditional practice of slowing down the curriculum for students who were falling behind simply condemned these students to never catching up. He argued that the only way to help students who were falling behind was to develop a curriculum that would accelerate their learning. Thus the principles behind his approach are to speed up the curriculum and to develop higher expectations by teachers of students who had fallen behind. While the introduction of four Chicago schools into the Accelerated Schools Network was widely touted, administrative conflicts at the state level led to the establishment of a state network of accelerated schools that was not directly tied to Levin's movement. A number of Chicago schools now are part of this Illinois network.

The third schoolwide approach is less directly focused on teaching and learning; instead it directs teachers and other school staff to focus more directly on the individual students they are teaching and the problems they may be encountering as they seek to be successful in school. The Comer Development Process began work in 1991–92 in four schools through the intermediary efforts of Youth Guidance, a member organization of the Chicago Panel. The Comer Process has since expanded to 14 schools. It focuses on creating a healthy mental environment within which schooling might take place. Comer has had remarkable success in raising student achievement in other inner-city contexts, but the evidence in Chicago is still inconclusive.

Subject-Based Reform Efforts

In a more focused effort, the Algebra Project has identified that subject as the gatekeeper that high school staffs use in determining math tracking decisions. Failing to pass (or take) algebra frequently consigns inner-city students to general education or vocational education programs. The project's primary advocate, Robert Moses, has developed approaches to make algebra and pre-algebra more relevant to inner-city kids, for example using distances and times between mass transit "L" stops as the context for problem solving. The project combines an emphasis on adding algebra and pre-algebra to elementary and middle schools' curricula and changing the pedagogical methods through which inner-city intermediate-grade teachers approach math. In Chicago, organizers from the Algebra Project have developed an extensive citywide network and infrastructure for staff development and teacher sharing. By 1994, it was active in more than a tenth of the city's schools.

Another widely used, but more narrowly focused, program is Reading Recovery. Originally developed in New Zealand and then marketed in the Midwest through Ohio State University, Reading Recovery focuses on extensive intervention in first grade to assure that every student leaves first grade reading adequately. The program has a heavy emphasis on tutoring, requires changes in classroom management and scheduling for early primary teachers, and encourages changes in both expectations and pedagogy by participating teachers. The program relies on intensive training for a core group of teachers who then become the trainers of other teachers, thereby spreading the program more widely and more quickly than could otherwise be possible. The Chicago Public Schools provided active support in securing training for teachers from a number of Chicago elementary schools. More than 100 Chicago elementary schools have participated in the Reading Recovery training process.

Another more focused program, though one with comprehensive, cross-school implications, is the Illinois Writing Project, an outgrowth of the movement that sprang from the Bay Area Writing Project (Gomez, 1988; McCarthey, 1992). In Chapter 6, I described Winkle School as one that was furtherest along in directed planning for school improvement. The Writing Project emphasizes modeling the writing process for children by helping teachers to learn to be good writers. The use of a 10-week, 3-hours-per-session staff development course conducted by the Illinois Writing Project, with subsequent coaching and counseling by project staff, was a key element in the development of Winkle Elementary. The action-oriented staff development process (also highlighted in Fine's Philadelphia volume in Lytle et al., 1994), which is central to the nationwide strategy of the Writing Project, raises for self-reflection and struggle the critical issues of individual teachers' pedagogies. The stories of teachers in Winkle School as they struggled to change their own teaching practices were poignantly presented in video form for wider audiences, making clear how difficult is the process of teacher change and changing the interaction in which teaching and learning happen. Teachers talked about leaving school crying in frustration at their own inability to implement the different strategies to which they had committed themselves, but their struggles and eventual success became the foundation for the dramatic success of the school. Writing scores rose from the lowest quartile to exceed the state median in about 4 years. Success in changing the way writing was taught and the extent to which it was used across the curriculum then translated into other efforts, as described in the junior high programs in Chapter 6. The Illinois Writing Project is now working with more than a tenth of Chicago elementary schools.

There are a number of other initiatives used by Chicago schools that have resulted in changes in teaching and learning. Some, like the Paideia Program (Adler, 1982), have Chicago roots but interact with national efforts; Paideia school leaders are trained in multiweek intensive summer sessions at St. John's College in New Mexico. Teachers are trained in using Socratic questioning approaches in seminars focused on great literature, both classical and contemporary. A local Paideia center has been established to provide support to Chicago Paideia schools, headed by one of the original Paideia school principals (Brazil, 1988). Other projects are more localized and less well known outside of Chicago. I turn next to describe some of these.

CHICAGO-BASED EFFORTS TO ENGAGE TEACHERS IN CHANGE

Teachers were widely viewed as the forgotten element in Chicago school reform. And teachers initially viewed the reform effort as not having a lot to do with what they were doing in classrooms. Elsewhere (Hess, 1994a) I have described the shift in perspective of teachers, from being interested spectators to partners in the serious effort to improve many Chicago schools. But there were some who, from the very beginning, saw the opportunity the reform act provided.

At the same time that the Citywide Coalition for School Reform was being organized, during the first year of reform implementation, a group of teachers, who generally subscribed to the tenets of progressive education and had chafed under the mechanized approaches to instruction that characterized most prereform Chicago schools, organized themselves into the Teachers Task Force. The Teachers Task Force acted as an arm of the Citywide Coalition, bringing a teachers' viewpoint to the collaborative discussions of reform activists. Initially they received much support from Bill Ayers at the University of Illinois at Chicago and from Mary Lewis at Roosevelt University. Roosevelt became the home of the Teachers Task Force and the location for a foundation-funded "teacher-in-residence" staff person. The task force supports efforts to implement more student-centered teaching practices and fosters exchanges, both in its periodicals and in teacher exchange meetings within individual schools and across several school sites. The hopes of some reformers that the task force would become a powerful voice for teachers in opposition to more restrictive positions of the Chicago Teachers Union were never realized. Five years later, the task force continues as a fairly loose-knit network helping individuals or small groups of teachers to change and to reflect on the changes they are attempting. It does not appear to be the harbinger of a sea change among the city's faculties.

However, in a development that surprised many, particularly those who had had such high hopes for the Teacher Task Force, the union itself became a major actor in encouraging schools to restructure and helping teachers change their methods and focus of instruction. In early 1992, the Chicago Teachers Union Quest Center was formally launched, with a governing board that had representation from the area schools of education and a number of reform groups to complement the majority who were classroom teachers. I am privileged to have served on the Quest Center board since its inception. The Quest Center received a 3-year grant of $1 million from the MacArthur Foundation to support its efforts to assist groups of teachers in 45 schools (about 8% of Chicago schools) in bringing about teacher-led restructuring. The CTU has provided extensive graduate-level coursework (credit granted through the University of Illinois at Chicago) in school restructuring and instructional change. School teams seeking acceptance into the Quest Center network (roughly 15 have been accepted in each of the initial 3 years) agreed to go through an initial training process, then submitted applications that had to include the agreement to their plan by both the principal and the LSC president. Once accepted into the network, school faculty members were encouraged to partake of the extensive faculty training designed by the union staff and had a facilitator assigned to assist them in their restructuring efforts. These facilitators were outstanding classroom teachers who were recruited to take leaves of absence to help in this restructuring effort. While many of the initial restructuring plans focused on schoolwide change, a clear trend toward more focused, smaller efforts at creating schools-within-a-school has emerged. The Quest Center has now received national attention and commendation (Bradley, 1994).

The Quest Center was the brainchild of the CTU's Assistant to the President for Education Reform, John Kotsakis. Deborah Walsh, who had assisted Kotsakis in planning the center, was recruited from the national staff of the American Federation of Teachers to return to Chicago to be the center's director. Kotsakis was also involved in many other reform initiatives, for example, sitting on the steering committee of the Consortium for Chicago School Research and helping to design, interpret, and write the first report of the Consortium's surveys of teachers. The Chicago reform effort lost a key actor when Kotsakis suffered a massive heart attack and died in September 1994.

Recognizing that there must be top-down support for bottom-up change, the Quest Center, in cooperation with the Department of Instructional Services of the Chicago Public Schools and the Council for Basic Education, developed a wall chart of benchmark learning outcomes for the fourth, eighth, and twelfth grades. Those outcomes have now been reviewed by the faculties of every Chicago school and have been correspondingly adjusted to reflect teacher responses and adopted by the school system; Quest Center schools are now developing new, teacher-designed assessments for use in local schools to help teachers understand the progress their students are making toward reaching the adopted outcomes. The Consortium on Chicago School Research has replaced the Council for Basic Education in the ongoing partnership, which is now seeking to create a new systemwide assessment system and professional development activities aligned with the new outcomes.

There are a number of other, smaller initiatives that have developed in partnership with the school system to help build the capacity and abilities of individual Chicago teachers. Predating reform, a Chicago entrepreneur, Martin Koldyke, had established a teacher award program, in conjunction with the local Public Broadcasting Station, WTTW, Channel 11. It presents "Golden Apples" to outstanding teachers from across the metropolitan area and provides them a sabbatical semester at Northwestern University. As reform was beginning, Koldyke's Golden Apple Foundation launched two new initiatives. The first brought together previous award winners in an Academy of Educators who made their expertise available to other teachers. The academy also suggested, and the foundation implemented, a scholarship program for inner-city Chicago high school students to attend college to train to become Chicago teachers. In 1992 Koldyke was appointed chair of the Chicago School Finance Authority, the agency responsible to the state legislature for overseeing the system's finances and reform efforts.

Another outgrowth of the Golden Apple Foundation is a program initiated in concert with several area schools of education, the Chicago Teachers Union, and the Chicago Public Schools called "Teachers for Chicago." The program is designed to recruit experienced adults or younger college graduates with nonteaching majors to teach in Chicago while they earn a master's in education and gain their teaching certificates.

An important dynamic in the process of teacher change is the work of outside groups to facilitate that change. For example, the Chicago Foundation for Education, led by Joyce Rumsfeld, wife of the former U.S. Secretary of Defense, makes small grants to teachers to enable and support their efforts at innovative instructional projects. A smaller but similar effort more focused on reading is the Rochelle Lee Fund, led by and honoring a former outstanding Chicago teacher.

Another notable effort is the "Links to Learning" campaign, initiated prior to the passage of the reform act by Designs for Change at Dumas Elementary School, but now operating with corporate support at more than 100 elementary schools. Paper chains are created and strung down school corridors, with each link representing a completed book read by a student in the school. This motivational program nicely complements shifts to whole-language instruction in participating schools.

Finally, there are a number of efforts more broadly construed under the image of staff development. While some members of the mayor's education summit had hoped that reform would include a Chicago version of Pittsburgh's Schenley Training Center, the cost of that program had prohibited its inclusion in the reform act. However, others reached out to try to fill the void of such a systemic staff development effort.

Perhaps the most ambitious project was designed by Leon Ledderman, a nationally recognized physicist at Argonne National Laboratories in the Chicago suburbs. Ledderman had been instrumental in establishing the Illinois Math and Science Academy, an elite residential high school for tenth- through twelfth-grade students who are particularly gifted in those subjects. The school is fully funded by the state of Illinois. Ledderman recognized the need to dramatically alter the way in which math and science were being taught in Chicago schools, particularly in the elementary schools. Therefore he helped to establish a training academy, using some of the techniques of the Schenley Center; teachers would be freed from their classrooms for a period of training in math and science instruction while their schools were provided substitute teachers to cover their classrooms. In the Chicago academy, teachers were only out of their classrooms one day a week, but the training extended for the full year. Unfortunately, the academy was never adequately funded by the state, as Ledderman had envisioned, and foundered after several years. While its financial health has been restored, the academy has not regained its former prominence.

The schools of education in the Chicago area, which had not been in the forefront of national efforts to restructure teacher education, responded to the passage of the Chicago reform act by increasing their efforts to provide staff development to the city's teachers. For example, the Teachers Center of Northeastern Illinois University began to sponsor a series of workshops for teachers on the implications of reform for their teaching. The universities also began to examine and change their own graduate programs in curriculum, pedagogy, and administration to provide teachers and future administrators with the skills and knowledge they would need to foster school improvement and work in a school-based management environment. Loyola University and Roosevelt University have developed a new joint administrative certificate program focused for Chicago teachers.

Thus there are numerous efforts to reach out to individual teachers and small groups of teachers to encourage them to change their pedagogical approaches and curricular offerings. But we must recognize that there is a major difference between a systemic staff development effort and diffuse efforts to enhance the capacities of individual teachers who are then returned to schools where the culture emphasizes maintaining the status quo. Even if the diverse efforts in Chicago were as successful in reaching every teacher as were the efforts in Pittsburgh, there can be little doubt that the effect would not be as significant as the systemic, focused professional development strategy employed in that city. In Chicago, staff development is an important tool to be exercised as part of a local school's plan for improvement; it is not *the* strategy for reforming the school system.

CREATING SMALLER CONTEXTS TO CHANGE AND PERSONALIZE TEACHING AND LEARNING

A development attracting national attention is the focus on creating smaller school communities of learning in which students and teachers can shed the anonymity of large urban schools. National attention had been drawn to this strategy through the work of Anthony Alvarado and his colleagues in District 4 in East Harlem (cf. Fliegel, 1989; Harrington & Cookson, 1992). Most prominent among the many small schools developed in District 4 are the schools that make up the Central Park East complex, led by Deborah Meier. Farther down the East Coast, the Philadelphia Schools Collaborative developed the schools-within-a-school approach described by Fine (1994). A small schools movement has been developing in Chicago and now has the backing of the new general superintendent, who endorsed an exploratory systemwide workshop for interested school staffs.

It has been obvious for some time that the anonymity of large urban schools presents peculiar problems for improving inner-city schools, particularly high schools. But the issue of school size flew in the face of the industrial-efficiency models of the early part of this century and the consolidation efforts that focused on the inadequate programs of very small rural high schools. The issue was also clouded by the fact that many of the "lighthouse" elite suburban schools and highly successful, though highly selective, urban schools were among the largest schools in a state.

But during the 1980s, research began to focus on the advantages of smaller school size. Our research at the Chicago Panel had identified smaller size as one of the important variables in the prereform success of some of the city's elementary schools (Hess & Greer, 1987). A special edition of *Education and Urban Society* (Cienkus, 1989) focused on the issue of school size and its importance for success. And the Consortium for Chicago School Research's teacher survey found school size to be one of the important variables associated with a higher success rating on the reform index (Easton et al., 1991a). Thus the stage had been set for an effort to encourage the development of small schools in Chicago.

Two different groups have led the small schools movement in Chicago. Businessmen and Professionals in the Public Interest (BPI), a public interest law firm famous for winning a landmark public housing suit that has resulted in the relocation of thousands of inner-city public housing residents to rent-supported housing in the suburbs, began its interest in small schools after Alex Polikoff, the head of the firm, visited the Central Park East schools. Shortly thereafter, Polikoff and BPI brought administrator John Falco to Chicago to tell the District 4 story to Chicagoans. BPI has pushed the small schools notion, supported several schools trying to develop the small school concept, and sponsored a small schools task force to engage the interest and effort of other reform groups. Polikoff has been a key factor in securing the commitment of Superintendent Argie Johnson to fostering the development of small schools in Chicago. This is in marked contrast to the actions of the previous superintendent, who spent more time trying to shut down small schools to save money.

The second effort to promote small schools is located at the University of Illinois at Chicago. Bill Ayers was able to secure foundation support to create a Small Schools Workshop at the university, providing seminars on the development of schools-within-schools and developing a small staff to provide technical assistance to groups of teachers attempting to develop such schools. The Small Schools Workshop and BPI work collaboratively, though maintaining parallel activities, to foster the development of small schools in the city. Their efforts frequently overlap as well with the school-within-a-school efforts of the CTU Quest Center.

One example of the efforts of all of these groups to help the development of small schools is their involvement with the Foundation School. This nationally recognized innovative school (Ruenzel, 1993), led by Lynn Cherkasky-Davis, started as an effort by the reform-minded principal of Dumas Elementary School, Sylvia Peters, to leaven and alter the teaching style of her school's faculty toward a more progressive education approach. When Peters left to join the initiating think-tank of the Edison Project, the LSC chose as her replacement the assistant principal who had been more closely aligned with the more traditional teacher faction. Cherkasky-Davis and her colleagues were pressured to leave Dumas. Rather than leaving individually and scattering to schools across the system, they decided to seek a home where they could create a school-within-a-school; with assistance from the aforementioned groups, they found a home at Price Elementary School. During the next 2 years, the relationships among Foundation and the principal and LSC of the host school encountered many tensions and began to deteriorate. The innovative school was forced to move and is now located in an unused wing of Wendell Phillips High School. The school is small by design (about 200 students), keeps class sizes small and heterogeneous, and uses extensive grouping and regrouping to facilitate team teaching and cooperative learning.

The difficulties of this school indicate the problems of nontraditional entities within the still largely traditional mindset of the Chicago school system. Schools-within-a-school (SWAS) create several institutional problems not anticipated in the reform legislation and beyond the experience of school system bureaucrats. Does each SWAS have to have its own principal and LSC? Does it have a separate budget? Can its budget be segregated within a total school budget? Does the school LSC have final say over the SWAS budget? Are there separate discipline policies for each SWAS within the same building?

But the experience of the Foundation School also indicates the dissonance created by a largely teacher-dominated experimental school in a system emphasizing parental control of school governance. Foundation school is a teacher-led experiment in reestablishing the principles of progressive education in more personalized classrooms. The faculty is self-recruited and very cohesive. Parents are valued as educational assistants, both in the school and at home. Still, the faculty has been apprehensive about subjecting their ideas to the control of an LSC, preferring to negotiate their tenure in a host school rather than establishing their own governing council. However, the leadership of the school has not always been adept at negotiating the boundaries between their vision of the school they want to create and more traditional host schools within a system in the midst of its own governance-oriented reform. Amid all these uncertainties, the Foundation School has been assisted by all three of the school-within-a-school advocacy groups.

A final note about the creation of small schools is suggested by experiences in New York City. Frustrated by the inability to successfully restructure many of the large, failing urban high schools described so tellingly by Michelle Fine (1991a), the school system has embarked on a process of closing down two of them, replacing each of them with six independent schools. The replacement schools are developing by adding classes each year for the next 4 years, drawing heavily from the students who would have enrolled in the schools being closed. When the last seniors graduate from the old buildings, the independent schools will be invited to share the space in the now vacated buildings. In this manner, nonfunctional inner-city schools are being phased out and replaced by new, smaller, theme-oriented high schools. While this experiment is being closely observed by some Chicagoans, there has not yet been an effort to replicate this strategy in our city.

CONCLUDING THOUGHTS ON CHANGING TEACHING AND LEARNING

While not explicitly the focus of the Chicago School Reform Act, changing teaching and learning is the ultimate goal of the city's reform effort. True to the context of the reform act, there is no single directional strategy for changing teaching and learning in Chicago such as there was in Pittsburgh. However, that does not mean that there has not been an effort to change the nature of instruction in the city. In fact, there have been many efforts, with great differences in effect. To date, there has been little systematic effort to examine the differential success of these various approaches. This is an effort the Chicago Panel would like to assume, if resources can be found to support the enterprise.

Dick Elmore (1990), in the conclusion to his edited book on *Restructuring Schools*, suggests that the most likely of three scenarios for the next generation of educational reform will be a scenario very similar to that playing out in Chicago: states becoming the focus of funding and power decentralized from the school district to the local school. Elmore then suggests the two problems with this scenario are that localism at the school level will lead to incoherence in programs and that the resulting adaptive realignment of school programs is not likely to produce change in the basic conditions of teaching and schooling. At the present writing in late 1994, conditions in Chicago appear to confirm Elmore's concerns. There are many different approaches being taken in Chicago, with little clear coherence between the approaches. Elmore sees this as a problem. The framers of the Chicago reforms see this as fertile ground for the new directions that will be successful to take root. At present, there is little evidence to suggest which perspective is more correct. Relative to Elmore's second concern, that there is little guarantee of basic change, few Chicago examples could be mustered of schools that are radically changing. The Foundation School may be the most radically different school to yet emerge.

The Chicago reforms have been criticized as primarily being all about governance and power, who will control the local schools. Thus it was interesting for me to read of tales of reforming classrooms in Philadelphia that kept coming back to the theme of power. The Philadelphia reformers kept confronting the issue of who has and who exercises power in inner-city public schools. At some points, their concerns were with the central administration; at other points, with the teachers union. But in a fascinating way, they were more focused on the exercise of power within schools and within classrooms, on conflicts between charter teachers and a principal, between charter leaders and other teachers in a school, among the teachers within a charter, and even more poignantly, between teacher and students within a classroom.

One charter teacher leader described his own experience this way:

> Yet a teacher such as myself . . . must also confront questions of practice and theory that revolve around the ways my students construct their understandings of language and power, and how they interrelate. Additionally, for a teacher involved in a massive restructuring of an urban school, issues of language and power percolate to the surface with increasing frequency. Subsequent decisions about those issues have repercussions not only within one classroom, but throughout the school as a whole. Concerns about whose voice gets preference, what role language plays in all classrooms, and what access to power education provides [to students] get considered, defined, and acted on as teachers work in groups to rethink the conception of their school. (Fecho, 1994, pp. 180f)

There are many efforts in Chicago to give teachers the opportunity to lead in the movement for school change. Numerous movements have been recruited or have grown up independently in the Chicago schools to provide assistance to teachers, principals, and LSCs as they seek to change their schools. There are a number of heart-warming examples of principals and teacher leaders who are working diligently to change the way teachers interact with their students. One teacher union leader recently reaffirmed the importance of the Quest Center, but then went on to ask if a discernible movement could be detected among the union's rank and file pushing for more significant reforms. She noted there is little pressure from the membership on the union's officers to lead the movement for reform. She worried more about her classroom colleagues' complacency, acceptance, and helplessness about the status quo. Teachers have to see themselves as part of the solution if teaching and learning in Chicago classrooms are to change. That is happening in some schools, but not in enough. It is for this reason that I will examine the Kentucky system of rewards and sanctions more fully in the next chapter.

Perhaps all school restructuring is about changing the distribution and use of power. The governance reforms in Chicago focus on the distribution of power between the school district and the individual school, and, at the school level, among the principal, teachers, parents, and community. Students occupy only a small role in the Chicago reform act, filling one position on high school LSCs. To date in Chicago, we have little evidence of extensive discussions about the distribution of power among teachers and between teachers and students. The discussions of voice and silencing that characterize the writings of those active in the Philadelphia Schools Collaborative have been missing in Chicago. Perhaps we in Chicago have something to learn from our Philadelphia colleagues on this point. Perhaps we will not see real changes in the interactions between teachers and learners until the conversations in Chicago schools start to examine the difficult issues of race, class, and empowerment in the learning process and the unacknowledged biases about the learning capacity of inner-city minority students are exposed and contravened. There are still many miles to go before we in Chicago can rest from our efforts to change teaching and learning in this city's schools.

CHAPTER 11

Changing Assumptions About
School Operations and Finance

During the 1980s and 1990s, a debate has raged about how schools should be financed and operated. Professional educators regularly call for additional funding. Taxpayer advocates call for increased efficiency in the operation of schools to hold down costs. And some, both school employees and outside critics, have questioned whether money makes a difference anyway, particularly in large urban school systems.

Some scholars have contended that the funding level of public schools is not connected to the effectiveness of their educational efforts, particularly as measured through student achievement (cf. Hanushek, 1986; Walberg & Fowler, 1988). However, most of the efforts to disconnect funding and student achievement have begged the question. They have relied on comparisons of districts with different funding levels and different student outcomes in a given year rather than on tracing changes in funding in the same district over time. By limiting themselves to cross-district comparisons, these fiscal skeptics ignore many confounding variables in coming to their conclusion that money does not matter, and they illogically project a static-in-time comparison *between* districts to predict the effects of changes in funding over time *within* any individual district. More critically, they simply ignore the moral question of whether educational opportunities should be equally available to all students.

Recently, studies like these have come under sharp intellectual attack (cf. Hedges et al., 1994). Hedges and his colleagues at the University of Chicago have criticized both the logic utilized by Hanushek and the correctness of his analysis of his data. Hanushek examined more than 100 studies of school funding and achievement and claimed that "there is no strong or systematic relationship between school expenditures and student performance" (Hanushek, 1989, p. 47). Therefore, he asserted, money does not make a difference in public schooling.

Hedges and his colleagues pointed out the logical mistake of using a null hypothesis (no consistent proof that money matters) to assert the opposite conclusion (that money therefore does not matter). The lack of current, consistent proof that money matters would not prove that money does not matter! But more important, using more sophisticated statistical techniques than those used by Hanushek, Hedges and his colleagues demonstrated that the overwhelming evidence of the studies Hanushek chose to examine is that *money does make a difference*. In fact, Hanushek came to exactly the opposite conclusion than that supported by his evidence. "The question of whether more resources are needed to produce real improvement in our nation's schools can no longer be ignored. Relying on the data most often used to deny that resources are related to achievement, we find that money *does* matter after all" (Hedges et al., 1994, p. 13).

The studies of Hanushek and his colleagues have been unconvincing to non-academics as well. They have also been rejected by the courts in several states as "not credible." For example, in September 1992, the issue was brought before the Missouri Circuit Court of Cole County, in the state capital of Jefferson City, in a suit challenging the constitutionality of that state's school funding system. In ruling for the plaintiffs, Judge Byron L. Kinder wrote:

> The Court finds and concludes that the amount of money available for schools can and does make a difference in the educational opportunities that can be provided to Missouri children. The present Missouri school system does not provide an "equal opportunity" for each Missouri child as guaranteed by the Missouri Constitution. Vast disparities exist in the funding and resources available . . . [which] are not because of differing student needs, but instead are associated with local property wealth or are simply irrational. (*Committee for Educational Equality et al.* v. *State of Missouri et al.*, 1993, p. 2)

After noting that he found credible the testimony as to the negative effects of inequitable and inadequate funding of schools provided by experts from Missouri and school finance experts such as Kern Alexander, John Augenblick, Van Mueller, and myself, Judge Kinder noted:

> The Defendants . . . presented evidence through Dr. Eric Hanushek, Dr. Herbert Walberg, Dr. John Alspaugh and Dr. Robert Jewell—the general gist of which was that monies do not make a difference in providing an education; hence it does not matter whether there are inequities or inadequacies in public school funding. This . . . is directly contrary to the real positions of the Intervenor-Defendants [wealthy school districts who hired these "expert" witnesses] herein for they would have no interest in this litigation nor would they be

paying for litigation costs if it were not for the purpose of preserving the larger amount of school funds on a per pupil basis. . . . The Court finds the testimony and evidence presented through Dr. Hanushek, Dr. Walberg, Dr. Jewell and Dr. Alspaugh to the effect that inequalities and/or inadequacies of funding of public schools do not make a difference in educational opportunities and educational output not to be credible. (*Committee for Educational Opportunity et al.* v. *State of Missouri et al.*, 1993, pp. 21f, G3f)

Without even appealing the circuit court's judgment, the Missouri legislature adopted a new school finance scheme that seeks to overcome differences in property wealth between school districts by providing state support to give each school district the resources available in the district at the 95th percentile in property wealth per pupil. In addition, the state has dramatically increased its support of the costs of public schools.

During the late 1980s and early 1990s, the courts in a number of other states also were overturning their school finance systems and asserting that money does make a difference. In New Jersey, in a case dating back almost 20 years, the state supreme court required that schools in the 29 poorest urban districts should have resources equal to those of the richest districts; in a follow-up decision, the court mandated that students graduating from those districts should not only have equal educational opportunity, but should be economically competitive with students graduating from the richest districts. In Texas the state supreme court has required a new state school finance system, with several interim judgments on the unacceptability of proposed solutions, that has now led to a system of revenue sharing between rich and poor districts. In Kentucky (see below) the state supreme court determined that the entire school system was unconstitutional, not just the finance system, leading to a comprehensive educational reform act adopted in 1990. In Alabama a circuit court declared that the school finance system was unconstitutional because it did not provide enough resources for an adequate education in the state's schools. A projected bipartisan agreement to solve the Alabama problem has since fallen apart, and litigation to the state supreme court is now likely (see Verstegan, 1994, for a review of these cases and litigation in other states).

However, it is also clear that the mere presence of more funds will not automatically assure a more productive and effective school district. While it is evident that the absence of funds imposes severe constraints on schools and school districts, the presence of adequate levels of funding does not guarantee that the funds are used either appropriately or effectively. *How* funds are used is as important as *how much* money is available. Hedges and his colleagues emphasize that funds spent on reducing class size and hiring teachers with higher abilities have the greatest impact on student achievement. "We do not argue that money is everything. It is how we spend the money, and the incentives we create for children and teachers that matter most" (Greenwald & Hedges, 1994, p. 18). But the decision about how funds will be used frequently depends on conceptions the decision makers have about public schools.

However, these basic assumptions about the system of public education in the United States in the latter half of the twentieth century are largely unexamined. One by one, these assumptions have been challenged during the past 25 years. In this chapter, I look at a key set of assumptions about the organization and financing of public schools, the challenges that have been mounted against these assumptions, the new assumptions that are replacing the traditional ones, and their implications for designing a new system of operations and finance for states such as Illinois.

TRADITIONAL ASSUMPTIONS ABOUT THE ORGANIZATION OF PUBLIC EDUCATION IN THE UNITED STATES

There are eight assumptions that are particularly important to examine, all of which have been challenged during the past quarter century. Undoubtedly, there are additional assumptions worth examining when addressing specific problems in school improvement. I have focused on these eight because they seem to be at the heart of the current organization of school finance and operations.

1. States provide basic support for school districts in a relatively fair way through a combination of state and local resources.

Prior to the early years of the twentieth century, public schools were almost entirely supported by local taxes, with minimal support, through grants in aid, from state governments. Early in this century, Cubberley (1906) and others began to demonstrate the unfairness of such a system and to advocate that states equalize funding among school districts. In 1927 Illinois, like other states, adopted a foundation formula approach to shared state and local funding of schools advocated by two school finance experts, Strayer and Haig (1923). Under a Strayer–Haig formula, the state legislature establishes for each student a foundation level of support necessary to provide an efficient system of public schools across the state. Local school districts are required to raise a part of that foundation amount through local taxes, using at least a minimal tax rate. The state government would then provide whatever a local district could not raise, on a per-pupil basis. In its simplest form, the foundation formula is:

Foundation Level (per pupil) = Local Taxes + State Support

The required state contribution can be calculated by reversing the formula:

State Support = Foundation Level − Local Taxes

This system works well as long as the foundation amount relates to the actual cost of education and is established at a level above or close to what most districts can raise in local taxes, on a per-pupil basis, with the minimally required tax rate.

There are a number of other ways of combining state and local resources to support public schools and many refinements to address particular priorities and emphases in different states, but this foundation approach most directly embodies the assumption that state and local resources should be combined to provide a fair funding system.

2. Local control is important to allow school districts in diverse communities to make different decisions about the importance of education.

In most states, the foundation formula is established in a manner that allows individual school boards who want to provide an enriched educational program in their schools to tax their citizens more heavily than the minimum required to reach the foundation level with state support. With the added resources, these districts might add extra programs, might have smaller class sizes, or might attract better educated and more experienced teachers through higher salaries. In the early years of this century, this local control was thought to be important in allowing cities that needed a more highly educated work force to spend more on their children than might rural areas, where education was not seen as being as important to adult success. In some states, the state would guarantee a similar resource yield when districts raised their tax rates by similar amounts, thereby effectively raising the foundation level for districts who taxed themselves more highly.

3. The way to assure quality education across a state is to mandate high-quality standards in teachers, programs, and buildings.

By controlling the *inputs* of public schools, the state would assure that schools across the state would all meet at least minimally acceptable levels of performance. Teacher certification standards have been established to assure that all those educating our young would be, at least, minimally competent. School programs also had to meet state standards, with carefully specified minimums in years of English, math, science, history, and other subjects that students must pass before they could be declared high school graduates. Over time, these program standards came to include mandated units on the state constitution, on citizenship, and on other valued arenas such as the Jewish Holocaust in Nazi Germany. Minimal standards were also established for buildings (fire and safety) and for facilities such as gymnasiums and libraries. School districts were accountable to assure that all their schools met state standards and mandates. In line with the early-twentieth-century understanding of industrial efficiency, school districts were expected to be organized hierarchically and to exercise command and bureaucratic control over their individual schools.

One outgrowth of these minimum standards was that if all teachers were at least minimally equally educated, then they could be interchanged with minimal impact on the program of a school, at least within the standards for each developing specialty (e.g., primary grade teachers or high school math teachers). Similarly, if teachers are interchangeable, then their compensation should be largely undifferentiated, reflecting only differences in training and years of experience. With such an understanding of interchangeability, teachers began to argue that they should be able to select the schools in a district at which they would teach, based on their seniority in the district. Thus school staffing became reduced to hiring the appropriate mix of teacher certificates while establishing placement procedures designed to satisfy worker desires, not student needs.

4. Students vary in ability, and the job of teachers is to allow each to reach his or her full potential.

Teachers have always understood that some students are "brighter" than others and that different students will shine in different subjects. The student who does well in math may not write nearly as creatively as others; the facile readers may be real "klutzes" in auto mechanics or music. Teachers know that their responsibility is to bring out the best in their students, whatever that is.

Psychometricians and test makers built on that knowledge to design tests that would distribute students along a predetermined "normal" curve that took a bell shape. With a focus on reading and math (a bias toward more "academic" subjects) and using multiple-choice questions that were easy to score (thus reducing testing costs), these tests were designed to help teachers see the weaknesses and strengths of their students when compared to the rest of the nation on various subcomponents of the tested subject. By design, students taking these tests would always end up in categories like "the bright" (top 23%), "the average" (middle 54%), and "those falling behind" (the bottom 23%). Students achieving their full potential would end up in their appropriate place on the bell curve. While implicit in the design of these tests were assumptions about what average students should know at each grade level, by design these tests would never assure that all students met certain prescribed levels of achievement.

5. Districts fund all their schools equitably, except as necessary to provide extra resources to specialty schools designed to meet the special needs of their students.

Most larger school districts established formulas to allocate resources among schools in a fair way. Frequently, during the second half of the century, contracts with employee unions included agreements on many of these formulas: how many children per classroom, for how many square feet each janitor would be responsible. These contract provisions regularly recognized that higher costs were appropriate for high schools, due to the departmentalization of teachers into subject specialties. Larger school systems frequently established specialty schools for students with particular needs or behavior problems. Elite schools were also supported, frequently with enriched programs for more limited student populations than could be provided at every school.

6. Larger schools and larger school districts are more efficient because they can use economies of scale and provide greater specialization.

The drive for industrial efficiency in the first half of the twentieth century convinced educators that small schools and small school districts do not use their staff efficiently (do not reach maximum class sizes and cannot support a broad enough program) and have duplicative staffing at the administrative level. Thus the number of schools and school districts were dramatically reduced during the first half of the century. In Illinois, the more than 15,000 school districts were reduced to fewer than 1,000 by 1986, though that figure is still very high compared to the number of districts in many other states. It was also assumed that large school districts, by aggregating purchases and buying in volume, could derive significantly lower prices for commodities.

7. *The role of the federal government in public education (nonexistent prior to* Sputnik) *is to protect the rights of students and to provide compensatory aid to special needs students.*

Throughout the first half of the century, the federal government had virtually no role in public education in the United States. Its first significant involvement, ensuring the civil rights of students, followed the Supreme Court's 1954 decision outlawing segregation in public education in *Brown* v. *Topeka Board of Education.* Following the launching of *Sputnik* by the Soviet Union in the late 1950s, the federal government began to support the development of math and science education. As part of the Johnson administration's War on Poverty (Moynihan, 1969), and in response to the Coleman Report's (1966) emphasis on the importance of the social and economic status of children for their educational success, the federal government began to provide assistance to students with special needs. Title I funds were provided to assist economically disadvantaged students. In the 1970s, additional assistance was provided to physically and mentally handicapped children and to those with a limited proficiency in English.

8. *Withdrawal of financial support for programs is the appropriate sanction on districts that mismanage their use of funds.*

In line with a grant-making mentality, the federal government adopted a sanctioning process that operated by withdrawing funds from school districts that misused or inefficiently managed federal funds. If school districts were unwilling or unable to document how federal funds were being used or that they were reaching the students for whom they were intended, then the appropriate action of federal officials was to refuse further grants-in-aid and, on occasion, to seek to recover funds that had been inappropriately used. During the past decade, some, particularly in the business community, have sought to extend this assumption about appropriate sanctions to include reducing funding for school districts whose students are not learning adequately.

CHALLENGING THE TRADITIONAL ASSUMPTIONS

The traditional assumptions about the organization and funding of public schools began to be challenged in California when the state was sued for inequitably funding its schools (*Serranno* v. *Priest*, 1970). More than half the states have been similarly sued during the past quarter of a century, and one case found its way, unsuccessfully, to the U.S. Supreme

Court. Most of these suits have sought to show that public education is a fundamental right of children in these states (under the education articles of their state constitutions) and that, therefore, children should enjoy the equal protection of the law to be treated substantially the same.

These cases basically argued that, because of differing access to property wealth in districts across the relevant state, local districts were unable to provide substantially equivalent educations to their children and existing state equalizing efforts were inadequate to compensate for those differences (Verstegan, 1994). Frequently these suits also argued that poor school districts were deprived of local control of educational programs because they did not have enough resources to meet all the standards and programs mandated by state governments, that only the wealthy school districts were able to exercise local control. As the assumption that state funding was relatively fair was challenged, many states sought to improve the fairness of their funding systems, including states not challenged in court.

In 1974 the U.S. Supreme Court, in *Rodriguez* v. *Edgebrook* (a case originating in the federal courts in Texas), declared that education was essentially a state, not a federal, function, and therefore the equal protection clause of the 14th Amendment to the U.S. Constitution did not apply to state school finance laws. The Texas system was allowed to stand, until it was finally overturned by its own state supreme court as part of the round of new litigation brought in a number of states in the 1980s.

Illinois, however, is one state that has withstood several constitutional challenges. Currently, another case, *Committee* v. *Edgar*, is wending its way toward the state supreme court. The 74 school district plaintiffs comprising the Committee for Educational Rights are strongly supported by the Coalition for Educational Rights; I served the Coalition as board president from 1991 to 1994.

As already noted several times, the effective schools research has challenged the assumption that mandating high standards for educational inputs (teachers, programs, buildings, resources, etc.) would result in schools of uniformly high quality, so that differences in student achievement could be explained by differences in student family backgrounds or student effort. Similarly, *A Nation at Risk* (National Commission on Excellence in Education, 1983) challenged the focus on controlling the inputs of public education, insisting instead that we should focus on the results, in terms of student learning.

As noted in Chapter 3, Edmonds and his colleagues in the investigation of effective schools showed that teacher expectations play a critical role in the performance of students. In short, teacher expectations became self-fulfilling prophecies for their students. Schools that were effective in having low-income students achieve at high rates were characterized by teachers with high expectations for their students. Schools that were ineffective in achieving high levels of student performance in inner cities were dominated by teachers who had low expectations for their students. The students seemed to live down to their teachers' expectations in ineffective schools. This research called into question the assumption that there would always be some who were falling behind and could not be expected to do normal work. It particularly called into question the assumption that low-income students could not meet high expectations. It asserted that schools could make a difference in the achievement levels of their students. It also called into question the interchangeability of teachers. Teachers with the same credentials differ in ways that can have important effects on student outcomes.

In addition to focusing on the results of schooling, the release of *A Nation at Risk* also began to foster a new role for the federal government. The U.S. Department of Education began to be aggressive in monitoring changes in the achievement and abilities of American students, widely distributing the results of the National Assessment of Educational Progress (NAEP). The federal government, recognizing the importance of the effective schools research, was a catalyst in the development of a new set of expectations for what American students should know and be able to do.

Another effort, in the early 1990s, also called into question the compensatory aid assumption about the federal government's role. The Commission on Chapter I (1992) issued a report highly critical of the ability of the federal government to provide compensatory aid to economically disadvantaged and special needs students when the basic level of funding provided by states and local districts was so inequitable, both within and between states. The commission argued that poverty-impacted students received so much less in basic support in their schools that federal aid did not even equalize funding, let alone create a compensatory extra.

Our research on the Chicago Public Schools that contributed to the adoption of the Chicago School Reform Act of 1988 challenged the assumption that large urban school districts were more efficient than smaller districts through economies of scale. This research (e.g., Chicago Panel, 1988) demonstrated the inexorable tendency to siphon resources away from schools to the administrative bureaucracy and questioned the presumed economies of scale that resulted in limiting contract bidding to a few large purveyors who could rig higher, not lower, prices and required a massive warehousing and distribution system, diluting the cost savings of mass purchasing and resulting in frequently delayed delivery.

As noted in Appendix B, funding was not equitably distributed among individual Chicago schools. We found huge differences in funding among schools, particularly related to differences in teacher experience. Teachers with the most experience were concentrated in schools with the fewest low-income students (Hess & Greer, 1987), and basic expenditures per pupil were consequently higher in these schools (Chicago Panel, 1988). In fact, schools with students with some of the most severe educational needs (e.g., those with between 90% and 99% low-income students) received $350 less per pupil than did those with few economically disadvantaged students. The assumption that large school districts funded their schools more equitably than states funded their school districts was not true in Chicago prior to the 1988 reform act.

The Chicago reform effort also challenged the assumption that resources should be primarily directed to the school district rather than to the individual schools. School-based budgeting was a primary strategy in the school improvement effort under Chicago school reform. At about the same time, the Thatcher government in Great Britain was also challenging the assumption that local education agencies (LEAs, the equivalent of school districts) should be the focus of funding public education. Under the 1986 and 1988 reform acts, Great Britain provided an opportunity for local schools to opt out of their LEA in favor of being "grant maintained" directly by the national government and mandated that 85% of all LEA funds must be passed on directly to local schools (Hess, 1992a).

In 1989, in response to a *Serranno*-like law suit, the Kentucky supreme court declared that the whole system of public education in that state violated the state constitution by providing students with an inequitable and inadequate education. The "adequacy" standard was important in that the court noted the state was not providing enough resources for students to receive an education that would enable them to meet the high standards of achievement needed for the twenty-first century. The Alabama courts would use a similar adequacy standard in declaring that state's school funding system unconstitutional.

The Kentucky Education Reform Act of 1990 (KERA) explicitly challenges the assumption that mandating and monitoring educational inputs is an adequate approach and that the local school district should be the primary focus of state accountability and support. KERA focuses on student outcomes, adequate state-provided resources, a shift of authority to the school level, and the holding of individual schools accountable for improving the achievement of their students. The adequacy of resources includes both funding and support for teachers, who are expected to change both *what* and *how* they teach. KERA also challenges the notion that students should be deprived of educational opportunities because of the misbehavior of adults by focusing the law's sanctions on the adults themselves.

Finally, reforms in Michigan are emblematic of challenges to the assumption that state and local resources should be combined to provide a foundation level of school support. While the particular components of the Michigan reforms do maintain the form of combined state and local support, the effect of the legislation is to establish a high foundation level fully funded by the resources of the state, though using a virtually mandated local property tax on nonhomestead property. Other states that have moved to primarily state support of basic education include California, New Mexico, and Florida (Guthrie, Garms, & Pierce, 1988). Hawaii, which has no local school districts, provides full state funding for all school purposes. The Michigan finance reform reflects a problem that gave new salience to the 1980s round of litigation: Property wealth in most states has become dramatically more disparate, undermining state efforts to equalize between school districts.

Indeed, in Illinois in 1980 about two-thirds of all property wealth in the state ($50 billion) was located in the six-county Chicago metropolitan area, while only one-third ($30 billion) was located in the state's other 96 counties. However, by 1991 property wealth in the metropolitan area had about doubled to $100 billion, while values downstate had actually declined (to $29 billion), meaning the metropolitan area now comprised almost 80% of all property wealth in the state. This disparity in wealth has given rise to the new advocacy position that "all the wealth of the state belongs to all the children of the state."

NEW SYSTEM ASSUMPTIONS

The challenges to the traditional assumptions about the organization and funding of public education have led to the emergence of a new set of assumptions. These assumptions have not yet gained universal acceptance, particularly among experienced teachers and administrators who entered the profession under the traditional assumptions. But they are gaining widespread support among those committed to accomplishing dramatic improvement in the nation's schools. Some of these new assumptions are more controversial than others.

1. The focus should be on outcomes, not inputs.

The single most important shift in thinking about the public education system is the shift from a focus on assuring the standardization of educational inputs to assuring a high level of achievement by students. In 1994 Congress adopted into law the framework of Goals 2000 agreements reached in 1989 between President Bush and the governors of the various states, then led by the future president, Bill Clinton of Arkansas. These goals hold high expectations for the achievement of all students, and schools are to be held accountable for the success of their students in reaching these expectations. In turn, schools should be given the flexibility to change what they are currently doing, because current ways of operating are not now resulting in the desired higher levels of student achievement. Early efforts to shift away from a preoccupation with educational inputs focused on providing schools or school districts with waivers from state mandates, district regulations, and employee contract provisions. More widespread deregulation through charter schools, private management of public schools or school districts, and learning zones (areas granted automatic freedom from mandates) is now being considered. Some observers fear such deregulation could lead to increasing the inequity in educational opportunities that now exists in American public education. Others suggest the inequities are already so extreme, both across states and within large metropolitan areas, that the threat is minimal. Some monitoring of equity effects on student outcomes seems appropriate.

2. All students can learn at high levels, and our society needs them to do so.

This assumption is the one many teachers, school administrators, and policy makers find most difficult to accept. They have lived their entire professional lives under the assumptions of the bell curve and find it impossible to believe that students on the bottom end can be brought up to acceptable levels. They also do not believe that the whole distribution of students can be moved to higher levels of performance. Correspondingly, such teachers reject suggestions that they are responsible for seeing to it that these students reach high levels of achievement. Widespread skepticism about this assumption is one of the major obstacles to dramatic school improvement.

Yet this assumption is at the heart of reform efforts like Chicago's or the Kentucky Education Reform Act. Teachers who do not believe that all students can learn at higher levels than they now do find it difficult to question the effectiveness of their current efforts, whether they work in low-achieving inner-city or rural schools or high-achieving suburban schools.

There are also some who doubt that our society needs all students to achieve at higher levels. One of the arguments made for improving schools is that our national economy is becoming less competitive when compared with those of other industrialized nations. Some argue that improving the productivity of all adults is critical to improving our competitive position. But others (e.g., Andy Hargreaves, personal communication, 1994) have questioned whether our society really values all workers or whether we are developing a job structure shaped like an hourglass, in which half the jobs have requirements that are higher than ever but the other half are significantly "dumbed down." Educators who are convinced that the bottom half of the class will never have jobs that make significant demands on their capabilities would be less inclined to dramatically alter their current pedagogical practices for these students, with whom it is much more difficult to be successful. Yet, under KERA, one criterion of school accountability is improving the performance of the lowest-achieving students in each school.

3. Individual schools are accountable for the successful achievement of their students.

Following the release of *A Nation at Risk*, states across the country began to develop means of higher accountability. In some states, such as Arkansas, the effort focused on raising the input standards through measures such as testing the basic competence of classroom teachers. Many other states turned more explicitly to focus on outcomes, establishing school report cards that detail student achievement levels and relevant characteristics of students and staff at individual schools.

In Illinois, school report cards and a state-run assessment program (Illinois Goal Assessment Program, IGAP) were mandated by the state school reform act of 1985. Starting with reading and math, the IGAPs now include social studies, science, and writing as well. Report card scores are released to the media, and listings for every Chicago school and most suburban schools are carried in the metropolitan newspapers each fall. These report cards helped establish the need for reform in the Chicago public schools.

This accountability assumption is most extensively applied in Kentucky (cf. Guskey, 1994), where statewide expectations of proficiency have been adopted as the criteria for school accountability. Although still in a transitional period, the state has established a baseline of student achievement for each school and adopted benchmarks for biennial improvement for each school, designed to assure that all schools have all students reach the level of proficiency over 20 years. These higher expectations for student achievement are accompanied by an extensive program of teacher retraining, a shift toward a multi-aged, nongraded primary program, and additional support for families of low-income students. In this sense, the Kentucky reforms address the three components of an integrated reform context advocated by Milbrey McLaughlin and Joan Talbert (1993)—improving content, enabling teachers' learning, and supporting students.

Against a goal of universal student proficiency, the baseline indicated that only 15% of Kentucky students achieved at proficient or better levels in 1993–94. Schools that exceed their biennial benchmarks receive rewards, equal to about $3,500 per teacher, that might be pocketed by the staff or used for school program enrichment. Schools that fall below their baseline receive sanctions and additional funds to support change. A distinguished educator is appointed by the state to work with each of these schools to establish a program of improvement. In schools declining by more than 5%, the distinguished educator would take control of the school and could dismiss low-performing staff; students would be allowed to transfer to another school not in decline. The implementation of this most severe set of sanctions has been delayed until 1996–97, though distinguished educators and planning grants were scheduled to be assigned to districts in 1995.

It is not yet clear whether Kentucky's combination of rewards for improvement, moderate sanctions in the form of an outside-appointed improvement coach with planning assistance funds, and ultimate sanctions that include mandated changes, loss of tenure, and student rights to transfer out will combine to foster the kind of school improvement necessary for student achievement to dramatically improve. Alone, this system would not seem to mobilize the support for reform that experts on teacher change tout as necessary (A. Lieberman & McLaughlin, 1992; Little, 1993; McLaughlin & Talbert, 1993). But in combination with the extensive teacher training offered across the state in cooperation with the state department of education and the family resource centers, which provide support to families in poverty, this approach may provide part of the answer advocated by McLaughlin (1987), who says that one "lesson learned is that successful implementation generally requires a combination of pressure and support from policy" (p. 173). However, she continues:

> But pressure alone cannot effect those changes in attitudes, beliefs, and routine practices typically assumed by reform policies. . . . Support, alone, also is a limited strategy for significant change because of competing priorities and demands that operate with the implementing system. (p. 173)

However this demand for accountability is implemented, there is a growing acceptance of the assumption that schools are responsible for the achievement of their students. This is a dramatic reversal from the post–Coleman Report era when educators could claim, with general acceptance, that there was little that could be expected of them when their students were poor or lazy.

4. Local control should move from the district level to individual schools.

School-based management (SBM) is a component of reform strategies articulated both by decentralizers such as Chicago reformers and by advocates of coherent systemic reform as a bow to the innovation and implementation studies conducted a decade previously by their colleagues and counterparts. Charter schools are a more radical version of granting individual public schools more local control and at the same time freeing them from many, if not most, mandates and input standards.

Less widely accepted by bureaucrats and policy makers is a corollary emphasis on moving school funding from the district to the school level. The Chicago reform effort began to move funding to the school level, conceptually through the notion of "lump-sum budgeting" contained in the reform act, but practically in a more circumscribed way through the discretionary funding that might provide as much as a quarter of a school's budget. As indicated above, in Great Britain this greater focus on funneling funds directly to schools is accomplished by a mandatory 85% pass-through and the delegation of far more spending authority to schools than is currently the case in Chicago.

Allan Odden (1994) has suggested that the school finance system of the future will be based on directly funding individual schools, giving them complete control of their budgets. This budget flexibility is a logical component of a system that shifts from controlling inputs to one that focuses on outcomes at the school level. He also suggests that compensation schedules will need to become more differentiated as specific skillsets are identified to round out a more diversely conceived faculty than that of the industrial model of interchangeable staffing.

5. All schools must be provided with adequate and equitable funding.

If schools are to be held accountable for the outcomes of their students, they must all operate on a level playing field. Having exposed the fallacy of assuming the field is currently level, reform advocates are now focused on new methods to create equitable finance systems. Given the awareness of the increased disparity in school district wealth, there is a new attention being given to making the state responsible for providing the primary support of individual schools. This trend is clearly seen in the Midwest, where a number of states have recently changed their school funding mechanisms. In addition to Michigan (described above) and Kentucky (where a higher state-supported foundation level was established and a guaranteed yield option for additional funding has been used by virtually every district in the state), Kansas recently adopted a statewide property tax to broaden access to the state's property wealth, and Missouri has significantly changed its funding approach. Meanwhile, the disparity in school funding has grown greater in Illinois.

As the federal government takes a larger role in defining what American students should know and be able to do and in establishing national curriculum-setting practices and national achievement assessments, it is reasonable to suppose that a heightened federal role in assuring equitable and adequate funding of schools might be forthcoming. In fact, the reauthorization of the Elementary and Secondary Education Act in 1994 contained some provisions designed to pressure states to more equitably fund their own schools.

6. Sanctions should be applied against adults when students are not adequately educated, not result in the removal of resources from underachieving students.

The obviousness of this assumption is matched only by the difficulty in implementing it in a reasonable fashion. Of course, criminal sanctions against individual employees have long been the pattern in public education. But short of criminal action or fiscal collapse, major efforts to implement this assumption have been only recently attempted.

The state of New Jersey adopted an educational bankruptcy law in the mid-1980s. Under that provision, the state may declare a school district to be educationally bankrupt after demonstrating that certain conditions exist. The state may then appoint a superintendent who would act like a "receiver" in financial bankruptcy situations, with the power to suspend board rules and contracts and restructure the operations of the school district. Thus the sanctions apply against the job security and contract patronage of the system's previous managers. The Chicago School Reform Act included an educational bankruptcy component, but its provisions were so narrowly drawn that it had not yet been invoked after 5 years of reform implementation.

The Kentucky sanctions are an example of a more sophisticated effort to embody this assumption in the regular operations of a state's system of public schools. In a less dramatic way, the New York City

Public Schools, while nurturing networks of teachers seeking to develop new patterns of inner-city pedagogy (A. Lieberman, in press), has also moved to phase out two low-performing high schools, replacing them for classes entering after 1994 with multiple small schools staffed by faculties congenial to these innovative practices. Originally dispersed across the community served by each school, the smaller alternatives will eventually become co-tenants in the prior high school buildings after their last classes graduates in 1997.

The common thread that is now gaining acceptance in these diverse and often clumsy approaches is that the students do not deserve to be sanctioned when schools are not succeeding. However it is to be accomplished, the sanctions should be focused on adults and should not result in the removal of program resources available to the victims of these failing schools.

7. School system management, whether at the state or district level, must shift from a pattern of command and control to one of monitoring and support.

This assumption, a corollary to the assumption about shifting from regulating inputs to monitoring outcomes, has proven to be most difficult to implement in Chicago and elsewhere around the country. Administrators in established bureaucracies have become adept in the turf battles through which they extend their scope of control—and thereby assure higher levels of compensation. All the current reward incentives focus on the accumulation of control and the ability to command obedience. Resistance to changing this assumption is deep-seated and not amenable to compromise. But there are beginning to be signs of success.

In Edmonton, Alberta, under former superintendent Michael Strembitsky, a series of administrative functions were reconceptualized to be purchasable services by individual schools. The resources formerly supporting those aspects of the administration were redirected to the schools through school-based budgeting. Employee positions to provide these services exist only to the extent that schools are willing to contract to have these services provided by central office staff rather than by some other supplier.

Similarly, the mandatory pass-through of LEA funds in Great Britain has led some LEA staff to become quite entrepreneurial in "fees-for-services" arrangements, both with their own schools and with schools that have left LEAs to assume "grant-maintained" status (personal communication, Christopher Trinick, Director of Education for the Solihull Education Department, 1994).

In Kentucky, KERA mandated the elimination of the previous state department of education and virtually eliminated the elected state super-intendent of schools (constitutionally mandated, the office could not be eliminated; but its responsibilities were shifted to the newly created appointive position of commissioner of education and the superintendent's salary was reduced to a token amount). But, 4 years later, the new state department, though taking on a range of new responsibilities, particularly in support of the implementation of KERA, continues to manifest command and control attributes.

In Chicago, a 5-year battle first to emasculate the central administration and more recently to begin to redefine its functions with the assistance of the nation's preeminent "corporate reengineering" consultants still left central office employees frustrated at being understaffed and schools chafing at unreasonable administrator efforts at command and control as 1994 was coming to a close. But new efforts were being launched to provide ongoing support for schools most in need of improvement. Self-assessment guides were prepared to help schools understand where they need help and where they might be able to provide assistance to other schools. Some central office staff were being set aside as a tactical support team to focus on the schools most in need of remediation. And outside reform groups collaborated with the system to win a $50-million grant from the Annenburg Foundation to link outside partners with schools seeking to improve.

There is no clear picture yet of what a monitoring and supportive district office would look like, but it is clear that that is what must emerge in the years ahead. It is becoming clear that this support must be quite different from the traditional staff development of half-day workshops, school-year opening lectures, and credit-gaining university courses. Ann Lieberman (in press) talks about "staff development in a new key" that focuses on making teachers into learners, both within school and outside of school. This kind of support must continue over longer durations and promote risk taking that requires supportive relationships and protected environments. How it can develop in a context that also involves monitoring is still problematic.

8. The primary federal role in public education will be to set standards for the achievement of all students, to monitor their performance, and to assure that the standards are met.

This assumption about the emerging role of the federal government in education is not one that is enthusiastically embraced by many in the education profession. As noted in Chapters 8 and 9, there is suspicion about the beneficence with which the federal government might implement this assumption. Yet the political trends in this direction are quite persuasive. In 1994 Congress both adopted the Goals 2000 standards and granted the U.S. Department of Education new powers to influence state funding schemes. The department continued support for efforts to develop new curriculum standards and new assessment practices.

DEVELOPING A NEW STATE SYSTEM OF FUNDING AND OPERATIONS BASED ON THE NEW ASSUMPTIONS

Activists seeking to see schools improve the achievement levels of their students struggle at both the macro-policy level and the micro level of school-site change. The Chicago School Reform Act was a major effort to change the macro-policy context for schools in the city of Chicago. As we have seen, different schools have responded in different ways to the new opportunities, resources, and independence made possible since 1988. Some schools have seized on the new opportunities to make extensive changes in the way teachers and students interact with one another. In other schools, various actors have degenerated into unproductive conflict. In too many schools, very little has changed. The Chicago reformers recognized the disconnection between macro-policy mandates and the school-level actors responsible for implementing the mandates. Therefore, the *what* to do was left up to school-level actors to decide. We now face the problem of what to do when some school-level actors simply decide to do nothing. What has been lacking in Chicago, to date, is the pressure McLaughlin (1987) describes as the necessary counterpoint to support. In Chapter 10, I described the various networks that have been developing among schools and teachers in Chicago. In what follows, I propose macro policies designed to provide the pressure for change for those schools that have not yet taken advantage of the opportunities provided. But because these proposals are statewide proposals, a statewide set of networks must also be developed to complement the pressure for change, and the resources and flexibility must also be provided. The macro policies that I advocate may be crude policy instruments at first but can be refined as they are implemented during a transition period, just as the Kentucky reforms have been evolving since the general directions were established in law. An evolutionary transition is preferable in order to minimize unforeseen dislocations and to allow schools the opportunities to plot their own course toward improvement before the system of rewards and sanctions is operative.

An effort to develop a new state system of school funding and operations based on the new assumptions just articulated would require a legislative program with four interrelated parts. There must be a performance-based student assessment and school accountability system that includes both extensive support to teachers seeking to undertake change and sanctions for adults in low-performing schools who refuse or are incapable of change. There must be a different distribution scheme that moves funding to the school level. There must be initiatives that encourage innovation that is more than just incremental. There must be an altered finance package based on the entire wealth of the state to assure that all schools have a level playing field in seeking to improve student achievement.

In the paragraphs that follow, I use Illinois, the state I know best, as the example. However, the principles behind the specific recommendations are more widely applicable and frequently draw on policies being implemented in other states.

A Performance-Based Student Assessment and Accountability System

Currently, the most well-developed state system of assessment, support for change, and accountability is that in operation in Kentucky. I would propose adopting a similar state system. It would require the State Board of Education to adopt a set of learning outcomes that would define the proficient performance expected of every student. The state would then ask a private contractor to develop a set of assessments, similar to those developed in Kentucky, that incorporate open-ended questions designed to test both basic skills and higher-order reasoning. These tests would be supplemented by portfolios maintained and assessed at the school level, except for a sampling from every school that would be scored at the state level to assure statewide quality control. Each type of assessment would be designed to demonstrate levels of progress toward proficiency or, for a few, their achievement of a standard of excellence well beyond proficiency. In Kentucky, the levels are described as novice (little or rudimentary knowledge and mastery), apprentice (a developing knowledge and skill base), proficient (meeting state expectations), and distinguished (significantly exceeding state expectations). The existing state assessment system can be used to provide a baseline and transitional accountability system while the contractor is developing the final assessment system.

While the new assessment system is being developed, and a transitional baseline of school performance is being established, the new resources and flexibility in the following recommendations should be put in place. Just as in the Chicago experiment, schools would be given a new opportunity to develop plans for improvement. And, as in Chicago (see Chapter 10), networks of support for change must be encouraged to develop, particularly working with the schools with the lowest existing levels of performance.

Using aggregated student assessment ratings, each school in the state could then be held accountable for steadily increasing the proportion of its students who have achieved proficiency in each assessed arena (e.g., reading, math, writing, social sciences, physical sciences, the arts, etc.). A set of rewards and sanctions should be established appropriate to meeting or failing to meet reasonable progress toward universal student proficiency. In Kentucky, a 20-year time frame for achieving universal student proficiency was adopted, with schools expected to reduce the number of students not now proficient by 10% during the first 2-year period after baseline data were collected. Schools exceeding their benchmark improvement by at least 1% earned rewards equivalent to $3,500 per teacher. Schools not meeting their improvement benchmarks or declining would receive various levels of sanctions, including the appointment of a consulting distinguished educator who could make recommendations for school improvement. Schools failing to meet their benchmarks for 3 years or declining by 5% from their baselines would be required to implement the distinguished educator's recommendations, their faculty would lose tenure protection, and their students would be free to enroll elsewhere.

A School-Based Distribution System

Ideally, a statewide school-based distribution system would provide state support directly to individual schools and would allow site-based management councils to exercise local liberty options for additional revenues. Currently in Illinois, there are 264 school districts with only a single school, and the district board of education currently acts much like a site-based council. However, designing a school-based funding system for the state's other 700 districts entails solving a great number of problems now solved at the district level. These include decisions on facility utilization, the grade structure of individual schools, enrollment patterns, how to levy taxes for additional services, and new construction, among others. Until school-based solutions to these issues can be developed, it is advisable to pursue a more immediately available option.

Therefore I propose adopting the British pass-through model to distribute the vast majority of school resources directly to individual schools. Since many school districts in Illinois do not now allocate spending by school units, it is advisable to phase in this distribution scheme over 5 years. Therefore, in the first year, at least 75% of all school district revenues would be allocated directly to schools, 77.5% in the second year, 80% in the third year, 82.5% in the fourth year, and at least 85% in the fifth year.

Correspondingly, school districts would need to establish site-based budgeting and site-based management councils and to devolve authority over spending decisions to the individual schools. While school districts might continue to bargain with employee unions regarding compensation levels and general staffing patterns, individual schools should be able to diverge from districtwide patterns with the concurrence of a majority of the school staff. State mandates for required programs and staffing within schools should be significantly reduced, with waivers available for those mandates that are retained. However, the civil rights of individual students must continue to be respected. By phasing in the pass-through provision, individual school communities would be given a transition period during which to build their self-managing capacity.

Incentives for Innovation

While establishing a system of high-stakes accountability should encourage all existing schools to embark on a process of self-improvement, it should not be expected that many schools would embark on radical innovation under such a system. To encourage more dramatic change in schools, the state should provide opportunities for existing schools and newly created schools to organize themselves in completely different ways.

Therefore, as part of a comprehensive package to reorganize the operations and finances of its public schools, the state should adopt legislation allowing the creation of publicly supported charter schools accountable to meeting specified levels of student achievement. A system of such schools would both allow nontraditional forms of organization to emerge and present the state with an opportunity to solve the problems of moving to a statewide system of school-based, rather than district-based, finance.

A system of up to 200 charter schools should be initiated, with funding coming directly from the state; the charters should be granted by the state board of education under criteria designed to assure stability of operations, general admissibility of students, responsiveness to the local community, and continuance dependent on meeting, after a reasonable period, the state's learner-outcomes goals. Charter schools could be designed by existing school districts, groups of teachers, nonprofit organizations, or local governance bodies of existing public schools. They would have to meet the current nonsectarian criterion of public schools and be willing to accept a wide variety of students. They would be public schools established within the geographic boundaries of existing school districts, but they would not be subject to the governance or existing union contracts of those districts. Thereby the current geographic monopoly on public education would be ended. In this way, school districts would be forced to demonstrate that the support they provide to district schools is ultimately more valuable than the independence experienced by neighboring charter schools. The system of charter schools would then represent a pilot transition program either toward a new state system focused on individual schools or a new mixed system of governance in which the function of school districts is shifted dramatically from control to support.

Another arena of innovation that should be encouraged is the integration of community services and schools. For many families in Illinois, schooling is just one of the services being directly provided by the state. Of course, most of us take for granted the services the state provides in general: highways and roads, hospitals and mental health centers, facilities for recreation, support for economic development, and care for the environment. But in addition to these generally available services, many families need help with specific problems: finding a job and securing support until one can be found, meeting extraordinary health problems, and finding housing and support for families whose adult members need help in providing an adequate home for their children. Sometimes members of these families are involved in the court system and/or the criminal justice system. Characteristically, the various representatives of the state working with an individual family are unaware of other representatives of the state or local governments working with the same family. The family's problems are divided up by "turf" responsibilities, and each specialty grabs its share of the family's life and adds it to some worker's caseload. Nobody works with the family as a whole. But all of the family's problems are carried with the child to school, and all of those problems affect the child's ability to benefit from the educational setting in which he or she is placed.

It is time to overcome this "divide and destroy" policy of state services to our most needy citizens. This policy too narrowly defines the assistance that can be made available to individual families, it underestimates the impact of the community resources that can be mobilized to help individual families, and it understates the strengths and abilities that these families might have to address their own needs. Each state service now assumes the client family has no other needs than the ones it is designed to serve. Under this system, either the client qualifies for service or does not. As one wag has put it, "When the only tool one has is a hammer, every problem is forced to look like a nail."

We must overcome this specialization of services by the state in order to see families as wholes, as units whose needs must be comprehensively addressed. As the one state institution intended to provide continuous services to families for durations of more than a decade, it is logical for schools to play a central role in this coordination and integration of services. We must reorganize the family-oriented services of the state so that information is shared and services are integrated. This will not be an easy task. There are issues of confidentiality that must be overcome. There are worse problems of bureaucratic "turfism," with each state bureau and local department wanting to expand its own budget and staffing. The current system is designed more to satisfy the needs of the service providers than of the service recipients. States must take an aggressive posture in redefining their ways of providing services so that the focus is on meeting the needs of their citizens, not the needs of their bureaucrats.

An Altered Finance Package

For states in the Midwest at least, a new finance package must be based on an adequately established foundation funded primarily from state sources, include significant property tax relief, generate sufficient tax revenue, provide for some local liberty in setting service levels, assure that some of the yield from local taxes is equalized through state resources, and constrain spending growth in the highest-spending districts so that increases in lower-spending districts will narrow the current resource gap.

In Illinois, the State Board of Education conducted a survey of districts reputed to provide an adequate education and estimated the cost of their basic programs at $3,898 per pupil in 1991. The Illinois foundation level in 1994–95 was just over $2,800. Thus an adequate foundation level should be $3,898 plus cost adjustments for inflation since 1991. A reasonable plan might start by increasing the foundation to $3,898 and then escalating the foundation at roughly double the rate of inflation for 5 years so that at the end of that period the foundation would be equivalent to the 1991 estimate adjusted for inflation. Thereafter the foundation level should be indexed to inflation.

The foundation level should be fully funded from state revenues but should be adjusted to reflect regional differences in the cost of living. The McMahon Index (created by Professor Walter McMahon of the University of Illinois, Urbana-Champaign) establishes cost-of-living differences in each county in Illinois and, in a restricted range, could be used to index the foundation level for each county. By fully funding the foundation level from state sources, local property taxes for basic education could be eliminated. Property taxes might be retained for capital expenses, debt service, and funding the local liberty option for higher levels of educational services.

To fully fund the higher foundation level, a uniform state property tax of $2 per $100 of equalized assessed value (EAV) of property (assessed at 33% of market value) would be levied and collected by the state. The personal income tax, set at relatively low rates in Illinois, should be raised from 3% of adjusted gross income to 5%, with a corresponding increase in corporate income taxes. The current level of state resources directed to elementary and secondary education would also need to be maintained. Together these revenues would provide enough extra funds in the first year that currently overdue state bills could be paid and a graduated exemption system could be added to the income tax system to make it more progressive.

Together with the elimination of local property taxes to fund the basic level of school services, the state property tax would both equalize the tax burden for taxpayers across the state and reduce basic school property taxes by 50% ($2.6 billion statewide).

School districts would be allowed to add on a property tax levy adequate to sustain their current level of spending per pupil if it is above the new foundation level or to provide higher levels of service. The property tax revenue needed to increase the foundation level by up to 15% would be guaranteed, on a per-pupil basis, to the yield of a comparable tax on property in the school district at the 80th percentile.[1] Local liberty tax rates above that required to produce the 15% increase would require approval of the voters in the district, but revenues would not be allowed to exceed 45% of the foundation level. During the transition phase-in period, school districts that would need more than the permitted 45% variance to maintain existing funding levels could levy a higher temporary rate, again with the approval of the district voters, but their total revenues per pupil would be allowed to grow only at 1.5% per

---

1. The 80th percentile wealth per-pupil ratio would be calculated by ascribing both high school and elementary school students to the property wealth of high school districts and then rank ordering unit and high school districts together. This method would achieve an equalized target wealth per pupil (CWADA) for unit districts. For high school districts, the target would be divided by 0.39; for elementary districts, the target would be divided by 0.61.

year until the excess above the 45% cap was eliminated by increases in the foundation level. For most districts, this 1.5% limitation on growth would expire within 5 years. Thereafter, growth could occur at the rate of inflation, the basic growth rate of the state-supported foundation level.

With the constraint on revenue growth for the highest-spending districts and the annual increases in the foundation level during the phase-in period, the gap between rich and poor districts would be significantly narrowed during the transition. If all districts exercised their full local liberty only to maintain current spending levels, the statewide property tax relief would be decreased by $875 million, but these districts would gain back $500 million in property tax relief by the fifth year of the transition, due to growth in the foundation level. Thus, after 5 years, the net annual property tax relief would be $2.2 billion.

The special needs of students who are disadvantaged, handicapped, and limited in English proficiency would continue to be met through the current categorical funding programs, though the number of these programs might be significantly reduced. Recognizing the increased awareness of the importance of the first 4 years of schooling, cost adjustments for high school students would be reduced from 25% to 10% and a higher weighting for the critical early primary years could be added. However, the current funding scheme acts perversely to discriminate against school districts that have high concentrations of students from poverty-impacted homes. The best research indicates that schools with higher concentrations of low-income students have a more difficult task than do schools with lower concentrations of or few such students (Clune, 1994). Therefore the current cap on weighting low-income students in the existing Illinois formula would be raised from 0.625 to 1.0 while reducing the multiplier from 0.53 to 0.47. This would have the effect of producing about $2,000 extra for each low-income student in districts with higher-than-average concentrations of poor students, while gradually reducing the extra support for schools with lower-than-average concentrations of such students.

Prior to 1982, the Illinois Capital Development Board helped needy school districts adequately maintain appropriate facilities. Since the state stopped funding the development board, school facilities across the state have significantly declined and capital investment in computers and other technology has become unfairly imbalanced toward wealthy school districts. The state needs to restore funding to the development board to provide support to school districts needing to rehabilitate old buildings, build new facilities for replacement or to keep up with growing student populations, and invest in appropriate technology. The board should disperse funds on the same guaranteed yield basis described above.

A Coordinated Approach

Public education in the United States faces a major contradiction. The achievement levels of our students are not appropriate for life in the twenty-first century. Some critics see this problem primarily as a matter of international competition relating to the reduced productivity of the American work force. My own focus is on the failure of our nation's schools to adequately educate economically and culturally disadvantaged young people, whether in the inner city, depressed suburbs, or neglected rural areas of our country. Continuance of this failure brings with it the potential for increased violence in poverty-impacted communities that could ultimately be revolutionary in nature.

But to change schools across a whole state or across the nation requires a concerted, coordinated approach such as is outlined here. School staffs must be held accountable, with real consequences for their actions, for accomplishing the desired improvement in the achievement of our least successful students. The responsibility for improving student outcomes must be moved to the school level, but to do that requires providing those schools with the flexibility, support for change, and resources to do things differently. Resources must be provided to level the playing field instead of tilting the field to favor children of our most affluent citizens. Finally, some space must be created for more radical innovation that might produce schools that make more than incremental improvements.

Conclusion

At the close of the 1993–94 school year, the Chicago school reform effort reached the end of its initial 5-year implementation period. On the basis of evidence summarized in this volume and reported elsewhere (e.g., Hess, 1994a), it can be safely said that this reform effort has produced unprecedented change in Chicago schools. Not all schools have changed. Some schools that have changed may have changed for the worse. But in many more schools, creative change has been happening. The full effects of those changes on student achievement cannot yet be determined. Advocates have claimed that test scores show achievement is going up (Designs for Change, 1993). Detractors in the popular press have claimed that achievement is deteriorating (Polsby, 1993). A more realistic view is that the long-term achievement effects still are unknown. Given the pace of change in the city's schools, it is not surprising that the trends in achievement are not yet clear.

But change is happening in individual schools across the city. As indicated in Chapter 6, change was already well under way at Winkle Elementary School when the reform act was adopted. A threefold strategy was undertaken to upgrade teacher competence, enhance student responsibility for learning, and increase parent involvement. An intensive staff retraining process resulted in a curriculum shift that involved writing across all aspects of the school program and hands-on learning in math and science. The second leg of the construct, enhancing student responsibility, involved a restructuring of the seventh- and eighth-grade program to focus on project-oriented integrated learning, but with much higher outcome expectations for the students, including higher criteria for promotion to eighth grade and for graduation into high school. Students found themselves working much harder and achieving far more under this change. The third leg of the educational improvement strategy, increasing parent involvement, had not yet been implemented in 1993–94.

Progress was not as quick at Montgomery School, where the reform effort was not welcomed by the incumbent principal. He created a school improvement plan that contained many "sound-good" ideas, such as using computers across the curriculum, but made no actual effort to provide the computers such a plan required. In the plan he also revealed his negative feelings about the reform effort. During the next year, this principal was replaced by the Montgomery LSC. The new principal had little opportunity to change the second-year improvement plan already submitted to the LSC by her predecessor, but she did add three items strongly desired by teachers in the school: a full-day kindergarten program, an after-school program focusing on male responsibility, and a security officer. These changes encouraged the faculty, and during the third year of reform, they participated in a more extensive school-improvement-planning process that included both long-needed environmental projects and such instructional changes as a cross-grade whole-language program, a heterogeneously grouped primary program with classes ranging from 5- to 8-year olds, and the establishment of an African American resource center in the school. In the following year, a social service agency was invited to provide training for parents on the academic and social needs of students.

The Montgomery School experience is more typical of schools trying to change under school reform in Chicago than is Winkle's. It took several years for the process to really get underway, starting with the replacement of the incumbent principal in the second year. It took until the third year for the new principal to win the confidence of her staff and to engage them in significant improvement planning in the school. Only in the fourth year did real change begin to emerge. Understandably, student achievement testing at the end of the fourth year of reform reflected little change from the achievement levels of students prior to reform. In all likelihood, it will be several more years before measures of student learning are affected by the changes now being undertaken at this school.

The Chicago experiment is not a perfect testing of the school-based management strategy of school reform. The devolution of authority to the school level has been tentative and characterized by resistance for much of the initial implementation effort. Under Superintendent Kimbrough, whose administration spanned much of the first 4 years of reform implementation, schools seeking to make major changes were more likely to be sanctioned than praised. Local school councils continued to be severely regulated, both by rules implemented by the Chicago Board of Education and by rules promulgated by the Illinois Board of Education. Kimbrough's successor, Argie Johnson, has articulated a more supportive strategy for using central office resources, but at the end of her first year in office she had not yet implemented her plan.

It would not be stretching the truth to suggest that the bureaucrats in the state education agency were as reluctant to see real authority devolved to local schools as were the city's educational administrators. For example, when some schools voted to go to a year-round schedule to reduce overcrowding (an innovation strongly touted by Kimbrough, based on his previous experiences in California), the state board initially reduced the average daily attendance at those schools by one-quarter, reducing the city's claim for state financial support. It took extensive negotiation for the state to develop a new way of calculating attendance for purposes of state aid for schools in which not all students attended during the same 180 school days. If this was true for an innovation the city's general superintendent was touting, one can appreciate the difficulties for innovations the superintendent did not favor.

In addition, for most of the years of reform implementation, the school system was floundering through a persistent fiscal crisis occasioned by the signing of employee contracts calling for raises for which the board did not possess adequate revenues. This meant that the "base program" at each school was reduced each year. At the schools with heaviest concentrations of low-income students, discretionary funds could be diverted to keep the same level of program, but thereby the compensatory effect intended in reallocating the system's resources was weakened. At schools with fewer low-income students, the program levels simply deteriorated while they were attempting to restructure. Given these constraints of resources and continuing regulation, it is extremely significant that so many schools claimed the power of self-determination the reform act made available.

Still, under reform implementation, the pattern of inequitable funding of schools across the city was changed such that base-level funding is more equitably distributed and schools with higher proportions of low-income students are receiving extra funding. Resource allocations among schools, under reform, are more directed toward meeting differing student needs rather than benefiting primarily white and middle-class students. But the funding of schools across the state of Illinois clearly does not reflect this needs-based allocation approach. The most affluent students have double the state average spent on their educations, while poor rural students and minority students in poorer suburban areas and cities such as East St. Louis have about half the state average spent on their schools. A "savage inequality" marks the funding of public education in Illinois. Not surprisingly, these poorly funded schools also tend to be lower in student achievement, and the state is doing little to help these schools improve. Meanwhile, the Clinton administration was focused on other issues (tax increases and health care) and would not commit the political muscle to force Congress to concentrate its resources on the school districts where poverty is most intense. Efforts to swing federal support behind more equitable funding of public schools across the nation have met with but token success.

It is remarkable that, 5 years after the enactment of the Chicago school reform legislation, opposition is still very emotional among leaders in the nation's educational research and practitioner establishment. I think this is an indication of how trapped in unexamined assumptions these leaders are. It has been amazing for me to experience the virulence with which many academics and school practitioners react to the Chicago experiment. Such violent reactions are more understandable among Chicago's central office bureaucrats, whose jobs may disappear as previously centralized functions are devolved to the school level. But such immediate self-interest does not account for the passionate resistance of those living beyond the city's boundaries. Perhaps their reactions indicate how radical the Chicago experiment appears to lifelong educationists.

The educational psychologists and psychometricians, who gave us norm-referenced tests and bell curve student achievement distributions that arbitrarily designate half the student population as "below average," have so dominated educational thinking for the last half century that few educationists can think practically about making every student successful. Thus it is beyond their ken to think that schools, rather than the students themselves, might be to blame for students' lack of success. The changes necessary for schools to adequately serve a nonwhite, nonmiddle-class student body are too radical for them to conceive of; thus the students must be to blame for their own lack of success. To formulate a reform that suggests *schools*, rather than the students, are "at-risk" is to attack their fundamental intellectual comfort levels. Similarly, to reemphasize communities rather than large, hierarchical bureaucracies that can be controlled by benevolent philosopher kings (or queens) is to transgress the political correctness of midcentury liberalism. The rigid intolerance of some of those so-called liberals makes one wonder when that philosophical approach degenerated into a set of rigid dogmas that are above questioning. Questioning these assumptions is a critical first step toward redesigning public education for the twenty-first century, which will more likely be an information age than a manufacturing century.

But it must be remembered that the Chicago school reform effort was largely designed on the basis of the effective schools literature. From that perspective, one would not expect to find radically futuric school structures emerging in our city. The evidence to date does not suggest that there are a series of schools in Chicago that might prefigure the new shape of public education in the twenty-first century. The devolution of authority, if it becomes sustained and institutionalized, may still provide the opportunity for such harbingers of a different future to emerge, but the likelihood of such radical change is small. Those seeking such signs of the future may need to look to schools more completely divorced from current regulations and constraints, such as charter schools.

The Chicago experiment, while a radical assault on many current assumptions about public education, seems to be plowing the ground of more plebeian, incremental change and restructuring. Under that mode, the changes happening in Chicago schools are quite exciting. It is still too early to claim success or to proclaim failure. But schools are clearly changing across the whole city. They are changing at different paces, and not all changes are positive. However, the momentum for change is clearly increasing, and as former Chicago Board of Education member and 1994 Illinois Teacher of the Year Adela Coronado-Greely has said, "Nobody wants to go back to the way things were before reform! (personal communication)"

These conclusions provide support for efforts to maintain an open space for the decentralized school-based management strategy of school reform. But, in fact, it is still too soon to state definitively whether the Chicago effort points toward the future or represents another in the long line of educational experiments that have failed. The very nature of the effort, however, does raise some fundamental questions about our assumptions about public education, particularly in large urban centers, as we move into the twenty-first century. I have tried to raise several of those issues in this volume. I hope my efforts will spark further discussion, for it is not the ideas presented here that are of primary importance.

What is important is finding a way to successfully educate the 411,000 students attending the Chicago Public Schools and the millions of other students in similar large urban school systems. The record is clear that we have largely failed their predecessors, nearly half of whom have dropped out short of graduation. We cannot allow that level of failure to continue in our big-city schools! We must find better ways to be successful with inner-city young people. I hope this book contributes to that search.

Appendix A

Monitoring the Effectiveness of Chicago School Reform

In 1989 the Chicago Panel on Public School Policy and Finance (now known as the Chicago Panel on School Policy) launched a major effort to monitor the implementation of school reform in Chicago and to assess its effectiveness in meeting the goals of the reform legislation.* The monitoring effort was designed to run for 5 years, the period described in the legislation itself as the focus of reform. We intended to continue monitoring the effects of the reform effort far beyond the time period included within the act.

The Chicago Panel had previously released nearly 20 studies examining different aspects of the programs, practices, and policies of the Chicago Board of Education. Its early studies focused on the board's finances (Hallett & Hess, 1982; Hess & Greer, 1984) and management practices (Hess & Meara, 1984). As the board's fiscal crisis eased in the mid-1980s, the Panel's attention turned to the educational achievement of students in the system, particularly to the dropout problem. The Panel produced five dropout-related studies during the second half of the 1980s (Hess & Greer, 1987; Hess & Lauber, 1985; Hess et al., 1986; Hess et al., 1988; Hess et al., 1989). These studies included both large-scale quantitative studies (e.g., a cohort analysis of dropout rates system-wide and at each high school in the system that involved tracking 100,000 students through 6 years) and in-school qualitative research in four matched pairs of high schools with similar student bodies but differing dropout rates. Thus the Panel was familiar with the school system, had established working relationships with its staff, and had the expertise to design and implement a comprehensive monitoring project.

The original monitoring plan was composed of 11 subprojects organized under three basic rubrics. Four of the projects focused on school

---

*This description of our research methodology, while developed in 1989 and then later elaborated, was first published in Hess & Easton, 1994. Reprinted by permission of the State University of New York Press.

governance issues; 3 focused on school improvement issues; and 3 focused on the outcomes of reform:

I. School governance
    A. Local school council composition
    B. Local school council operation
    C. Principal contracts
    D. Personnel changes
II. School improvement
    E. School improvement plans
    F. Resource allocation
    G. Implementation of school improvement plans
III. Outcomes of school reform
    H. Student achievement
    I. Attendance and graduation
    J. Grade retention
    K. Teacher and parent attitudes

Thus the monitoring effort would focus on assessing what the actual change in governance was, how it operated, and the effects it has had on staffing, particularly at the school level. It would examine what improvements were planned at schools, what changes in resource allocation occurred, and whether real change followed from the effort to implement those plans. Finally, the project would monitor changes in student achievement and behavior, as measured by test scores, grades, retention rates, attendance rates, and graduation rates. It would also assess changes in the attitudes of teachers and parents as the restructuring effort proceeded.

An interrelated research plan was designed to examine the relationships among the various changes noted during the monitoring effort. A statistical school effects study would use regression techniques to assess changes in student achievement during reform implementation. Moving beyond simply tracking changes in median reading scores at each grade in each of the system's 542 schools, this approach allowed us to aggregate individual student improvement to the school level, accounting for individual characteristics of students. Further analyses would relate changes in achievement to other changes occurring in schools the students attended. The research project included surveying attitude changes in teachers and principals, which would be examined both as outcomes of the reform effort and as inputs into the change process. Ron Edmonds (1979) had identified the attitudes of staff as a critical characteristic of effective schools. Funding from the research project allowed greater in-depth examination of the change process in local schools, which would focus both on the planning and implementation of improvement efforts and on changes in classroom instruction. The ultimate focus of the monitoring and research plans was to be on the effects of school restructuring on classroom instruction. The monitoring and research design we created could be imaged as a huge funnel with massive data inputs at the systemwide level and more limited, but ethnographically richer, data from the school governance level, all focused on perceived changes in classrooms where children experience and engage in the instruction process. It is the Panel's hypothesis that reform must affect changes in classroom instruction if it is to be effective in changing student achievement on the multiple measures included in our plan.

The design of our monitoring and research efforts included both massive quantitative measures and more intense qualitative approaches. At one level we designed studies that emulate classical productivity studies, correlating changes in educational inputs with changes in outcomes. At the same time, we have been working intensely with a representative sample of 14 schools in which we have been attending every LSC meeting; observing faculty meetings; interviewing key staff, parents, and area residents; and observing classrooms. Through this combination of methodological approaches we intended to produce an assessment of the implementation and effects of school reform in Chicago that is rich in texture and comprehensive in results. Parts of this original research design were later undertaken by the Consortium on Chicago School Research, in which the Panel has participated.

ESTABLISHING THE QUANTITATIVE BASELINE

During the first year of reform implementation, the monitoring and research staff developed the database that would be used for the 5-year study on school reform. The initial database focused on the 1988–89 school year and contained the following information:

- *Basic information about each school*, such as the board of education unit number, the subdistrict number, the community area in which the school is located, school type (magnet, special education, vocational, etc.), whether the school has an LSC (some specialized school units were excluded from the school-based management mandate)
- *Characteristics of the student body*, such as racial composition, number and percentage of low-income students, percentage who had limited English proficiency

- *Data about the educational setting*, including enrollment; number of students from outside the school's attendance boundaries; attendance rate for the previous 4 years; mobility rate; average class size; percentage of elementary students not promoted in each grade and overall; high school students completing a general, vocational, or college-bound curriculum; high school students enrolled in various subject areas; high school graduation rate; and 1986 dropout rate
- *Data about achievement on standardized tests*, including third-, sixth-, and eighth-grade reading and math achievement on the Iowa Test of Basic Skills and the Illinois Goal Assessment Program test, eleventh-grade achievement on the Test of Achievement and Proficiency, and twelfth-grade achievement on the American College Test

The Panel recognized the limitations of standardized tests and saw the use of such test scores as providing only part of the evidence on school improvement. However, improvement on these test scores was an explicit goal of the reform act. This assessment was complicated by the Chicago Board of Education's decision to use a series of versions of the Iowa Test of Basic Skills during the 5-year reform period. These tests had not been equated to each other. To overcome this problem, with the cooperation of the board's Department of Research, Evaluation, and Planning, and the Center for School Improvement at the University of Chicago, the Panel has conducted a series of equating studies to relate the annually reported outcomes on these various tests. Annually, the monitoring and research staff would update this entire extensive database and calculate year-to-year changes for all data points.

The database was created using a variety of sources. One of the largest sources of information was the Illinois State Board of Education, which provided the data compiled for the Illinois School Report Card. The Chicago Board of Education has provided other information from its computer system, and the monitoring and research staff entered some of the data manually from printed board sources.

A number of reports have been generated in establishing the baseline data for the entire monitoring and research project. At the beginning of the first year of reform implementation, the Panel surveyed a sample of teachers from predominantly minority schools (Easton, 1989). Some 146 teachers (a 31.5% response rate) provided insights into the understandings and attitudes teachers brought to the initiation of reform efforts in these schools where reform was most needed but which skeptics suggested would be the most unlikely to be affected by the Chicago reform experiment (see Chapters 4 and 5).

The baseline data for student achievement was compiled in a resource book distributed to every principal and every LSC chairperson, *Chicago Public Schools DataBook* (Chicago Panel, 1990). The *Data-Book* provided basic data about student and staff characteristics in each school and listed relevant student performance data on test scores, attendance, and graduation rates. Since the reform law sets as a goal that at least half the students in each grade in each school will be performing at or above the national norms in reading and math by 1994, the *Data-Book* was organized to show what percentage of students were now achieving at that level and what percentage would have to improve their performance to reach that goal. The *DataBook* became a valuable resource for LSCs as they entered the school-improvement-planning process, and annual updates of the *DataBook* have been made available to all schools. Thus the process of monitoring has had some direct effect on the process being monitored.

The Panel has released several interim reports on the reallocation of resources during the first year of reform implementation (Hess, 1990a, 1990b) and during each ensuing year (see Appendix B). Despite the doubts of both reformers and critics, the board of education did dramatically reduce its expenditures and staffing at the central and district administrative offices and did make about $40 million available in new program resources at the local school level. Over 1,000 positions were cut from the administrative budget, and another 500 staff were now budgeted to the local schools they had previously served on an itinerant basis (e.g., speech therapists who might have served five different schools, each on a different day of the week). While this change in budgeting did not increase the number of personnel working in schools, the budget change indicated a change in supervisory authority and a more direct responsibility of staff to the principal of each school they were to serve. Resource utilization at the school level was tracked throughout the reform implementation period (see Appendix B; Rosen-kranz, 1994).

Two other baseline reports were issued toward the end of the first year of implementation, one assessing the level of grade retention in elementary schools in June 1989 (Easton & Storey, 1990b), the other examining attendance rates for the previous 4 years in all schools in the system (Easton & Storey, 1990a). Both of these reports played a dual function. The first function was to provide the Panel and each LSC with an objective report of the starting point for reform in these two areas in which the law mandated that improvement should be made (retention rates were to decline by 10% during the reform period and attendance rates were to improve annually by 1% over the previous year [P.A. 85-1418, Sec. 34-1.02.3 and 34-1.02.2]). The second function was to provide LSCs with a review of the literature on improvement efforts in each of those arenas.

The retention study showed a systemwide elementary school retention rate of 4.3%, considerably lower than in Boston (9.4%) or New York (6.1%). Retention rates were highest in the first grade (8.9%) and lowest in the sixth grade (3.0%). More troubling was the variation in retention rates from school to school. While 81 of 434 elementary schools retained fewer than 2% of their first graders, more than a third of the schools retained at least 10%. Twenty-three schools retained more than 20% of their first-graders, with one school retaining more than half. These statistics were particularly troubling given the Panel's previous findings that grade retention, even in the earliest grades, is directly associated with later dropping out of high school prior to graduation (Hess & Lauber, 1985; Hess et al., 1989).

The attendance study also showed a pattern of variation from school to school, but the major variation among elementary schools was restricted to specialty schools, known in Chicago as EVGCs (Education and Vocational Guidance Centers) in comparison with regular elementary schools. The median elementary school attendance rate for 1988–89 was 93.0%. However, EVGCs regularly had attendance rates in the 65% to 80% ranges, while most elementary schools had attendance rates above 90%. The picture changed dramatically at the high school level, where the median attendance was only 81.3%. In other research (Hess, 1986) we have shown that Chicago has operated an educational triage system in which the best-prepared elementary students are guided into magnet and selective-entrance specialty schools or neighborhood high schools in more affluent communities, while the least well prepared are trapped in "holding pen" high schools with high dropout rates. High school attendance rates across the system underscore this tracking of students into a two-tiered system. Attendance rates in 1988–89 varied from a low of 65.3% to a high of 91.3%.

These quantitative studies provided the baseline from which improvement would be achieved and measured. The Chicago Panel continued to monitor and track changes in these various measures during the 5 years of the educational reform effort. It has computed changes in these various measures on a school-by-school basis. These data have been reported both for their systemwide effects and for each school. In this way, the Panel hoped both to keep the wider public abreast of changes experienced by the Chicago schools under the reform effort and to keep individual local schools aware of the progress or lack of progress they had experienced in moving toward the goals articulated in the reform act.

QUALITATIVE ASSESSMENTS OF
SCHOOL-LEVEL IMPROVEMENT EFFORTS

As part of our overall monitoring effort, the Chicago Panel has worked closely with a sample of schools willing to be closely observed as they go through the reform process. The initial focus of the monitoring project was on the composition and operation of the LSCs, the development of school-based management and increased local governance, the expansion of leadership roles in the schools, and the development of the school improvement plans. During subsequent years of this study, the emphasis shifted from governance to implementation issues, including the implementation of any new instructional practices. During the final years of the project, the emphasis was on documenting improvements in the schools.

Our original plan for monitoring school reform in Chicago called for intensive study of 16 schools. Using a random sample stratified by race and geographic region, we identified 48 schools as possible participants—three sets of 16 schools meeting the sampling requirements.

Securing Entrance into Observed Schools

We first approached schools by phone and set up appointments to meet with the principal. Two Panel staff members met with the principal (and in many instances, the LSC chairperson) to discuss our study. One staff member subsequently remained in contact with each school, attempting to secure its participation.

Specifically, we explained that in order to conduct this monitoring and research project, we wanted to conduct interviews with the principal, selected teachers, staff, parents, and students and to observe all LSC meetings, some faculty meetings, gatherings of the Professional Personnel Advisory Committee (PPAC; the vehicle for faculty input into the school governance process), and other school events.

By March 1990, after discussing this study with 18 schools, a total of 12 schools had formally agreed to participate. At that time we decided to concentrate our efforts on studying these 12 instead of continuing to spend time on securing the participation of additional schools. (We also attended the LSC meetings at one other elementary school that had not yet been asked to participate.) The 12 schools that agreed to participate included 8 of the intended 12 elementary and all 4 projected high schools. Three schools officially voted not to participate. Two additional elementary schools agreed to participate beginning with the 1990–91 school year. In aggregate, the students enrolled in these 14 schools approximated the characteristics of students enrolled system-wide. Thus these 14 schools are a small but representative sample of the whole school system.

Findings from the Entrance Process

Although the process of securing the participation of schools proved more difficult than anticipated, much was learned from it, especially when the process is considered in light of the literature on school-based management.

The literature on school-based management emphasizes that this form of governance is a process that takes time to implement success-fully (David, 1989) and cautions that districts adopting this form of governance cannot expect to make major improvements in a short pe-riod of time. Consistent with this, we found that the process of request-ing schools to cooperate took more time, effort, and a higher degree of involvement than we had anticipated. This is in sharp contrast to the ease of entry during our earlier ethnographic study (Hess et al., 1986), when a deputy superintendent's decision and one interview with each principal was all it took to study eight schools. Most schools required 2 to 3 months to decide whether or not they wanted to be included in the study; for many of the LSCs, this was their first major, and sometimes controversial, decision.

We found that parent and community LSC members were more apt to want to participate in our study than were principals and teachers. Even with the support of parents and community members, securing a school's participation was often a long process. Generally, we visited each school four to six times between December 1989 and March 1990. A typical sequence of the process involved in securing a school's partici-pation follows:

- *December 5, 1989.* JE and JQ (two Panel staff members) met with the principal from School X to explain our study and request permission to make a presentation to the LSC. The principal was receptive, partly because of a positive reaction to a previous Panel study, and endorsed the idea of a presentation to the council.
- *January 10, 1990.* JQ presented our request to the LSC. He explained the study verbally and distributed written material about it and the Panel's other monitoring projects. Although the LSC seemed prepared to vote in favor of participating in the study at this meeting, they decided to table the request until the PPAC had been informed of and voted on the study. They took this action after one of the teacher members of the LSC raised several questions.

- *January 17, 1990.* JE and JQ attended a PPAC meeting that included the entire faculty. JE presented the study to a wary group concerned about possible intrusions from outsiders. After the meeting, a teacher leader discussed the negative reactions and suggested that we attend a second PPAC meeting.
- *February 2, 1990.* JQ returned to the PPAC. After the PPAC vented a great deal of frustration with school reform (primarily related to the low representation of teachers on the LSC), it voted to support the Panel's proposal.
- *February 7, 1990.* The LSC voted unanimously to participate in our study.

Although this represents a typical sequence, we also encountered the extremes. In one school, we met with the principal in the morning and secured LSC agreement to participate that evening. In another school, we made seven visits and presentations before finally gaining approval.

The above sequence identifies issues that seemed to be of key importance in securing the participation of schools. For example, the principal greeted us favorably and endorsed the idea of our making a formal presentation to the LSC. Generally, where the principal was supportive of participating in the study, we secured formal consent from the council. In 7 out of the 12 schools that agreed to participate, the principals expressed interest in our work and were willing to be included. In one school, the principal stated that she felt comfortable with our presentation, that she preferred to present our information to the council herself, and that she was confident that she could persuade the LSC to participate. Similarly, the principal in another school readily agreed to have the school participate in our study, stating: "The LSC is meeting tonight. I'll explain the study and they [LSC members] will approve it." The council vote to participate was unanimous.

By contrast, the schools where principals did not express an interest were less likely to participate. In one school where the LSC and its chair seemed receptive to participating in the study but the principal was hesitant, the council voted against participation. The LSC chair explained, "I think the school should participate in the study, but the principal does not want to because she has a policy that does not allow classroom observations." Continuing, the chair stated, "I don't agree with the principal's closed classroom policy, but she has a lot of other good programs at the school." In only one school did we find a council that voted to participate even though the principal was reluctant about the study.

The significance of the leadership of principals reflects the experience of those who have studied other systems using school-based management (Lindquest & Mauriel, 1989; Malen & Ogawa, 1988). The importance of the professionals, principals and teachers, in school decision making was underlined in both studies.

Several other interesting findings related to school reform emerged during our attempts to secure participation. Teachers played little role in shaping the reform legislation or in the initial planning for implementation. The initial attitude survey (Easton, 1989) showed teachers were skeptical of reform in general and concerned about intrusions by parents. However, the depth of their feelings was more fully revealed in the process of securing permission to observe these schools. For example, in one school that voted against joining the project, teachers were vehemently against participating. This became apparent during one of our formal presentations at that school when a teacher began to complain that teachers had been "shut out" of the school reform process. This teacher asked the presenter what the Panel would do if the teachers were opposed to the study but the council voted to participate. When the staff member stated that the Panel would accept the majority decision and go ahead with the study, the teacher became angry and stated that this was proof that no one respected teachers.

Similarly, teachers in another school expressed their dissatisfaction with school reform. At this school, we made a formal presentation to an unenthusiastic faculty during a PPAC meeting. At the invitation of a teacher representative on the LSC, we made a second presentation to the school's PPAC. During this presentation, the members of the PPAC vented their frustrations over school reform. They explained that their sense of powerlessness grew from their opinion that teachers are underrepresented on the LSC. Furthermore, they did not like the council's being composed of parents and community representatives who, in their view, were least equipped to make crucial decisions. Ironically, after venting these frustrations, PPAC members voted overwhelmingly to support our study. Interestingly, the LSC in this school was initially supportive of our study but would not vote to participate until after the PPAC had been informed of and voted on the study. After the PPAC voted to support the study, the LSC voted unanimously to participate. This indicates that in this school, the opinion of the "professionals"— the PPAC—carried weight and that the parent and community representatives on the council respected the opinion of the faculty, though the faculty members did not seem to appreciate this fact.

Another issue emerged in a school that voted to participate in the study even though the faculty did not seem eager. In an initial LSC vote, four members favored participating, four abstained from voting, and one member voted against participating. The one vote against was cast by a teacher member of the LSC who stated that he had to vote according to the wishes of his constituents, the majority of whom were against participating for all the familiar reasons. This illustrates an issue that recurs in all governing bodies—whether elected representatives are obliged to vote as their constituents would want or to vote their own conscience.

We found that some principals felt reform had actually reduced parental participation. One principal noted that a number of active parents in her school also held part-time jobs at the school. These parents were ineligible to serve on the LSC, due to their employee status. She also felt that the extensive time demanded for service would hinder parental involvement. Due to resource constraints, the Panel has not been able to assess actual changes in parent involvement at the school level.

We also learned that LSCs had been required to make many decisions in a short period of time; at times members on the council lost track of the decisions they had made. For example, in one school a researcher attended a meeting expecting the council to make a decision about participating in our project, but our study was not an agenda item and was not discussed during the meeting. After the meeting, the staff member asked the LSC secretary whether the council had decided to participate; she responded that a special meeting would have to be called to make that decision. The observer then asked the principal about the decision. The principal responded that the school had already voted to be a part of our study and that a letter stating this had just been mailed to the Panel. The secretary then apologized and said she just did not remember that the decision had been made. Similarly, the LSC chairperson added: "There are so many things going on, I forgot, too."

The process of securing the participation of schools in our observational study was useful in identifying issues that needed to be taken into account during our research. We intended to examine the role and influence of key council members: principals, chairpersons, and teachers. We would examine the development of the roles of the other parent and community members on the council. We would give further attention to the feelings of powerlessness and underrepresentation on the part of teachers. We wanted to assess whether some councils were able to make decisions in a more efficient manner than others and tried to identify why this was the case. Finally, we wanted to account for the possible nonrepresentativeness of the schools we were working with in that principal willingness was a key condition of our entry into these schools.

APPENDIX B

Financial Aspects: The Engine for School Reform

Frequently overlooked in the national debates about school reform strategies are the resources needed to implement the strategies. While additional money does not automatically lead to improvement or reform, the absence of additional funding frequently means reform strategies must be considered as replacements for existing programs rather than as new initiatives. This means that existing programs, each with their own supporters, must be targeted for elimination in order to embark on a new effort, thus making the decision to adopt a new direction doubly difficult.

In Chicago, as part of a larger effort to shift governance from the district to the school level, most schools received significantly increased funding in yearly increments during a 5-year implementation period for school reform that started in 1989–90. In this appendix, I trace the financial aspects of the reform effort, detailing the prereform growth of the bureaucracy that prompted the legislated reallocation of the system's funds. I then examine the changes in funding that occurred, the changes in the location of the system's funds, the greater equity that has resulted among individual schools in the system, and the effect of the resolution of the financial crisis affecting the budget for the 1993–94 school year.

THE GROWTH OF THE BUREAUCRACY

As the school reform movement in Chicago was moving toward a climax, the Chicago Panel presented testimony (Hess, 1987) that showed the misplaced priorities of the school administration. We reviewed the

Information in Appendix B first appeared in Hess, "Reallocating Resources for School-Based Management," *School Business Affairs*, May 1995. Reprinted by permission of ASBO International.

TABLE B.1. Bureaucratic Growth in the Chicago Public Schools (Operating Funds Only)

			Staff			Admin/
	Students		Admin		Percent	1,000
Year	Enrolled	Schools	Units	Total	Admin	Pupils
1981	458,497	29,339	2,884	32,223	9.0%	6.3
1982	442,889	27,822	3,036	30,858	9.8%	6.9
1983	435,843	28,855	3,043	31,898	9.5%	7.0
1984	434,042	29,185	3,156	32,341	9.8%	7.3
1985	431,226	29,418	3,295	32,713	10.1%	7.6
1986	430,908	29,462	3,470	32,932	10.5%	8.1
1987	431,298	29,919	3,598	33,517	10.7%	8.3
1988	430,000	29,964	3,708	33,672	11.0%	8.6

board's actions during the system's near bankruptcy in 1979–80, when more than 8,000 positions were eliminated; we reminded the current board members that at that time more than 17% of teachers and other student-contact staff were cut, while fewer than 13% of employees in the administrative units were eliminated (Hallett & Hess, 1982). The priorities of the administration at that time had been to protect administrative jobs while firing more school-level people who worked directly with students. We then traced the steady growth in the bureaucracy since the crisis.

Table B.1 shows that operating budget staff positions in the administrative units increased in every year from Fiscal Year 1981 (the 1980–81 school year) to FY 1988, the budget then being considered. In the proposed FY 1988 amended budget, the superintendent was recommending the elimination of more than 800 magnet school teaching staff, while continuing to increase staff in the administrative units by more than 150 positions. This budget proposal convinced the reform advocates that legislation would be required to alter the budget priorities of the school system's administration.

SHIFTING THE LOCATION OF CHICAGO PUBLIC SCHOOL FUNDS

Under the Reform Act, as explained in Chapter 3, the Chicago Board of Education is prohibited from spending a higher percentage of its budget on noninstructional costs than did the average of all other school districts in the state in the preceding year. That provision required a reduction in the central administrative budget of approximately $40 million and the elimination of nearly 550 bureaucratic positions in FY 1990. In successive years, fiscal crises led to further central office reductions, leaving the school district well below the mandated administrative cap. Together with a progressive reallocation of poverty-generated state aid (State Chapter I) resulting from a poverty weighting factor in the state aid formula and the requirement that these funds become progressively discretionary at the local school level, a significant reorientation of the school district's funding priorities was accomplished. Fortunately, the funding reallocation began during a period of dramatically increasing local tax revenues, cushioning somewhat the establishment of these new priorities.

Between the enactment of the reform act in December 1988 and the 1992–93 school year (FY 1989 and 1993), the Chicago board's operating revenues increased by $586 million (see Table B.2). The federal government provided $128 million more in support of free lunches and additional programs for low-income students. The state, over 4 years, increased its support of the Chicago Public Schools by a mere $3 million. Local property taxes increased by $456 million, double the projected 5-year costs of reallocating the State Chapter I funds. In sum, the Chicago Public Schools experienced an abundant revenue growth, far exceeding the mandates of the reform act. However, several financial crises occurred during the reform years. As these figures show, the crises did not result from the revenue shortfalls that had characterized the 1980 fiscal crisis, but from fiscally irresponsible expenditure decisions, mostly about compensation levels.

TABLE B.2. **Chicago Public Schools Operating Revenues FY 1989–1993 (in millions)**

Year	Local	State	Federal	Total
1989	$781.5	$920.9	$245.9	$1,948.3
1990	887.6	1,009.6	274.0	2,171.2
1991	951.3	929.3	293.1	2,173.7
1992	1,053.6	946.3	351.7	2,351.6
1993	1,237.0	923.7	374.0	2,534.7
Change 1989–93	$455.5	$2.8	$128.1	$586.4

FIGURE B.1. Administrators per 1,000 Students in the Chicago Public Schools, FY 1983–1993

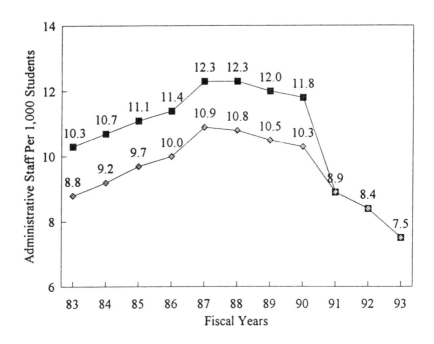

■ Total Administrators ◇ Itinerant Adjusted

One of the major concerns of reform advocates was where employees worked. The Panel's budget testimony during the fall of 1987, following the settlement of the system's longest teacher strike (19 days), had demonstrated the rising proportion of staff assigned to work in the system's administrative units and the corresponding declining proportion working in schools. Pressure from the growing reform movement forced the board of education to reject the superintendent's proposed FY 1988 budget with its projected teacher cuts in favor of smaller cuts in the administration. The pressure, later reinforced by passage of the reform act, held down the size of the central administration in the FY 1989 and FY 1990 budgets. Actions of the board during FY 1990, not ready for inclusion in the line-item budget, but implemented during the early part of that school year, are shown in Figure B.1 and Table B.3 as a significant reduction in the administration for FY 1991.

TABLE B.3. Staff Changes over 5 Years in the Chicago Public Schools

Year	Enrolled	Student Contact Staff			Administrative		Operatives		Total Staff	In Schools	Admin Units	Percent Admin
		Regular Teachers	Support Teachers	Aides	Admin	Profl	Clerks/ Lunchrm	Maint/ Trades				
1989	406,372	22,313	2,610	3,862	1,527	380	7,116	4,525	42,332	37,451	4,881	11.5%
1990	404,409	21,984	2,634	4,246	1,554	380	6,860	4,507	42,164	37,363	4,801	11.4%
1991	407,850	22,727	3,015	5,151	1,465	378	6,587	4,688	44,010	40,379	3,632	8.3%
1992	408,462	22,982	3,062	5,778	1,465	305	6,786	4,483	44,860	41,433	3,427	7.6%
1993	411,169	23,574	3,154	5,477	1,492	280	6,865	4,328	45,171	42,045	3,126	6.9%
CHANGE:												
FY89-93	4,797	1,261	544	1,615	-35	-100	-251	-197	2,839	4,594	-1,755	-4.6%
%	1.2%	5.7%	20.8%	41.8%	-2.3%	-26.3%	-3.5%	-4.4%	6.7%	12.3%	-36.0%	-40.0%

TABLE B.4. Changes in Government Funded Staff in the Chicago Public Schools, FY 1989–1993

Year/ Type	Student Contact Staff			Administrative		Operatives		Total Staff	In Schools	Admin Units	Percent Admin
	Regular Teachers	Support Teachers	Aides	Admin	Profl	Clerks/ Lunchrm	Maint/ Trades				
'89 Total	22,313	2,610	3,862	1,527	380	7116	4,525	42,332	37,451	4,881	11.5%
'89 Govt Fd	2,608	297	1,193	322	58	549	30	5,056	3,973	1,083	21.4%
% Govt Fd	11.7%	11.4%	30.9%	21.1%	15.3%	7.7%	0.7%	11.9%	10.6%	22.2%	
'93 Total	23,574	3,154	5,477	1,492	280	6865	4,328	45,171	42,045	3,126	6.9%
'93 Govt Fd	4,421	617	3,335	484	58	1,597	37	10,549	9,678	870	8.2%
%Govt Fd	18.8%	19.6%	60.9%	32.4%	20.7%	23.3%	0.9%	23.4%	23.0%	27.8%	
Total Chng	1,261	544	1,615	-35	-100	-251	-197	2,839	4,594	-1,755	-36.0%
Govt Chng	1,813	320	2,142	162	0	1,048	7	5,493	5,705	-213	-19.7%
Reglr Chng	-552	224	-527	-197	-100	-1,299	-204	-2,654	-1,111	-1542	-40.6%

Under the mandate of the reform act to reallocate resources toward schools with heavy enrollments of low-income students and to reduce noninstructional costs below the state average, and under fiscal pressure in the ensuing years, the Chicago Board of Education was forced, by 1992–93, to reduce staff in its administrative units by 1,138 positions beyond the 617 support staff itinerants transferred (see below). At the same time, the staff employed in local schools had increased by 3,977 (exclusive of 617 transferred itinerants). Whereas in December of 1988, 88.5% of the system's staff was budgeted to schools, by the fourth year of reform implementation (1992–93), the proportion had grown to 93.1%. This represents a significant reallocation of the system's resources.

In addition to the above-noted reductions, 617 teachers who were assigned as itinerants, providing specialized services on a part-time basis to a number of different schools, were rebudgeted to the school level. For example, a school nurse might serve five different schools, spending 1 day a week at each one. A speech therapist might serve 10 schools, spending only half a day in each. In the past, these itinerant staff were budgeted to district offices and were under the direct supervision of the district superintendents. Under reform implementation, these staff were budgeted to the schools they served and thereafter would be responsible, during that part of the week, to the school principal. While this arrangement did bring the itinerant staff more directly under the supervision of each school's educational leader, in most cases there was no significant change in services available to students. The lower line on the graph in Figure B.1 shows the estimated effect of deducting these itinerant staff from the administrative units to which they had previously been assigned. Even allowing for this anomaly, the administrative staff levels have been returned to well below those of FY 1983, a significant reversal of the trend during the mid-1980s.

An examination of the full staffing pattern (refer to Table B.3) shows some interesting developments during the initial years of reform implementation. It should be noted that enrollment had dropped sharply from the prestrike level of 431,298 to 404,409 2 years later (FY 1990), as reform was beginning. However, since that time, enrollment figures have increased slightly.

As Table B.3 shows, total staff increased by 2,839 positions between the beginning of reform and its fourth year. Staff with direct contact with students increased by 3,420 positions (1,261 more classroom teachers; 544 more educational support staff such as social workers, guidance counselors, librarians, etc.; and 1,615 additional classroom aides). Meanwhile, administrators (−35), professional and technical staff (− 100), clerks and lunchroom staff (− 251), and maintenance and trades persons (− 197) all decreased, for a total reduction of 585 nonstudent-contact positions. Again, this is a significant reallocation of the system's resources toward staff who have direct contact with students. In FY 1989, 68.0% of the staff had direct contact with students; by FY 1993, 71.3% did.

In addition to the offsetting loss of the budgeted itinerant teachers, the administrative units have lost a quarter (27.8%) of their administrators (ranging in rank from coordinator to deputy superintendent), nearly a third of nonteacher professional and technical staff (31.3%), and more than half (53.5%) of their clerks.

As already noted, most of the increase in staff occurred in schools, particularly for the student-contact staff. Most of that increase was in categorically funded positions not supported by the board's general operating funds. These positions were largely funded by the reallocation of State Chapter I moneys or by federal grants. In fact, general operating positions declined by 2,654, while categorical positions increased by 5,493 (see Table B.4). At the school level, operating positions declined by 1,111, while categorical positions increased by 5,705. Thus, these new positions were largely at the discretion of LSCs. The decrease in general operating positions reflects the persistent fiscal crises in the school system that derived from the unaffordable employee contracts offered in FY 1991 by the interim board's vice-president, William Singer (see Chapter 4). The schools were being forced to use their discretionary funds to offset cuts in their "basic" program, cuts necessitated by the ongoing fiscal crisis. This picture is clearer when school-level staffing is examined separately.

As shown in Table B.5, at the school level, significant increases in classroom teachers (1,226), educational support staff (1,078), and classroom aides (1,568) appear, despite decreases in regularly funded teachers (− 543) and aides (− 535). The decrease in regularly funded aide positions shows most clearly the administration's effort to diminish the effect of reallocating State Chapter I funds. In the FY 1991 budget, some 600 aides in the high schools, whose positions had been guaranteed for years in the board's contracts with the Chicago Teachers Union, were arbitrarily shifted onto each high school's State Chapter I funds budget. Because of the contract agreement, high schools could not dispense with these positions and thus rightfully considered these staff as part of their basic educational program. A similar shift happened with school administrative positions, as virtually every high school lost a funded vice-principal's position; these schools were then forced to use their State Chapter I funds to retain that administrative position if they

TABLE B.5. Changes in Government Funded Staff at the School Level, FY 1989–1993

| Year/Type | Student Contact Staff | | | Administrative | | Operatives | | Total In Schools |
	Regular Teachers	Support Teachers	Aides	Admin	Prof'l	Clerks/ Lunchrm	Maint/ Trades	
'89 Total	22,296	1,538	3,797	765	33	5,188	3,835	37,451
'89 Govt Fd	2,603	100	1,145	48	5	51	22	3,973
% Govt Fd	11.7%	6.5%	30.2%	6.3%	15.2%	1.0%	0.6%	10.6%
'93 Total	23,522	2,616	5,365	941	41	5,969	3,591	42,045
'93 Govt Fd	4,372	382	3,248	268	8	1,369	31	9,678
%Govt Fd	18.6%	14.6%	60.5%	28.5%	19.5%	22.9%	0.9%	23.0%
Total Chng	1,226	1,078	1,568	176	8	781	-244	4,594
Govt Chng	1,769	282	2,103	220	3	1,318	9	5,705
Reglr Chng	-543	796	-535	-44	5	-537	-253	-1,111

wanted to continue the same level of schoolwide leadership. Lunchroom and custodial positions were also cut between FY 1989 and FY 1993; schools did increase the number of office clerks to handle the increased responsibilities of local school governance. The increase in regular educational support staff reflects the rebudgeting of 617 itinerant staff from the district (administrative unit) budgets to the schools in which they had already been working. Thus, the real increase in support staff was 461 (1,078 − 617).

FY 1993 did see significant changes in the use of discretionary funds by schools. Schools doubled their increases in classroom teachers (up from only 620 new teachers through FY 1992) while dropping almost 300 aide positions from the previous year. Thus, for the fourth year of reform, schools shifted emphasis toward using their discretionary funds to buy more classroom teachers.

The average school had increased its staff by the fourth year under reform by about 8.5 staff, 3 of whom were likely to be aides. Two of the new staff were likely to be classroom teachers and 2 were providing educational support. One was likely to be a clerk in the school office.

LEVELING THE LOCAL PLAYING FIELD

The Chicago Reform Act also required that the resources of the school system be distributed more equitably among schools than it had been in 1988. The Chicago School Finance Authority was charged "to ensure the equitable distribution among the schools and programs of funds budgeted by the Board" (P.L. 85-1418, Sec. 34A-412 [a] [8]). This provision was included in the reform act to correct the inequitable distribution of funds to schools we had revealed early in 1988 (Chicago Panel, 1988).

During the 1987–88 school year, we discovered that per-pupil spending was $355 less in schools with between 90% and 99% low-income enrollments than in schools with fewer than 30% low-income students. In fact, per-pupil spending decreased progressively as the proportion of low-income students increased, except that schools with 100% low-income students (which received the bulk of desegregation, federal Chapter I, and other remedial programs) had spending levels, on average, comparable to those with few economically disadvantaged students (see Figure B.2).

In an equitable distribution of school support, basic program support would be the same for all groups of schools (appearing on a graph as a straight line across the graph at the average basic support level).

FIGURE B.2. Elementary Per-Pupil Expenditure in the Chicago Public Schools, 1987–88

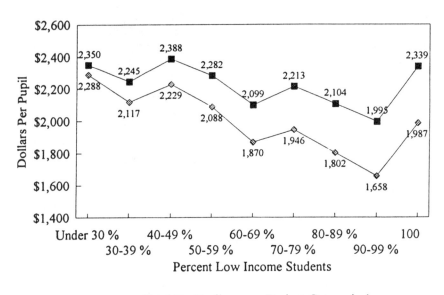

Percent Low Income Students

■ Total Per Pupil   ◇ Basic + Categorical

Special categorical programs that are designed to meet the special needs of qualifying students would be distributed on the basis of the enrollment of those students. Since economic disadvantage is a primary component in qualifying for many of those programs, they would tend to increase progressively as the proportion of low-income students increased (appearing on the graph as a line slanting upwards toward the right). Finally, State Chapter I funds, as they were phased out of providing basic programs and into being supplemental discretionary funds, would provide a larger increment for schools with higher proportions of low-income students (appearing as a line with an even steeper slant to the right). By FY 1993, this pattern was becoming apparent (see Figure B.3).

The distribution of funds to elementary schools during the 1992–93 year, when 80% of the State Chapter I funds were made supplementary, still showed more support for more affluent schools. The schools in groupings with less than 60% low-income students received higher than expected basic funding; for schools with more than 60% low-income students, the funding pattern was as expected. Schools with totally low-income enrollments received $917 more per pupil over their basic and categorical funding (note that the middle line on Figure B.3 [basic plus categorical] roughly corresponds to the lower line on the FY 1988 graph in Figure B.2). By comparison, schools with fewer than 30% low-income students received, on average, less than $200 above their basic and categorical level funding from State Chapter I sources. Even with the remaining skew in the basic funding, schools with entirely low-income enrollments had $1,000 more in total per-pupil support in 1992–93 than did those with less than 30% low-income students.

It should be pointed out, as Table B.6 shows, that more than two-thirds of all Chicago elementary school pupils attend schools that have low-income enrollments of higher than 80%. In FY 1993, only 12.3% of the city's elementary students attended the schools with less than 60% low-income students. Thus the skew in the lower end of the per-

FIGURE B.3. FY 1993 Elementary School Per-Pupil Expenditures by Percent of Low-Income Students

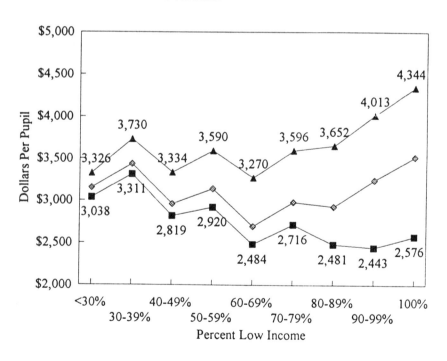

■ Basic Resources ◇ Basic + Categorical ▲ Total with Chapter I

TABLE B.6. Elementary School Enrollment and Support, 1992–93

Percentage Low Income	Number Schools	Average Size	Total Enrolled	Total Low Inc	Dollars Per Pupil	Less Chap I
100 %	85	630	53574	53574	4344	3427
90–99 %	154	742	114225	108650	4013	3141
80–89 %	68	683	46462	40044	3652	2862
70–79 %	51	647	33002	24937	3596	2903
60–69 %	28	700	19607	12741	3270	2674
Under 60%	72	521	37505	15313	3469	3095
Total	458	3923	304375	255259		

pupil graph benefits relatively few students (less than 38,000) and costs relatively few extra dollars. If the basic per-pupil cost (less Chapter I funds) in those schools had been held to $2,500 ($174 per pupil under the cost for the 60% to 69% low-income schools), the savings would have been about $22 million (37,505 students × $595 = $22,315,475) out of a budget of $2.6 billion. As the reallocation of funds continues and basic program levels are equalized, even this skew should disappear.

It appears that the differences in basic-level funding derive from two factors. The schools with fewer low-income students are, on average, smaller schools. The average size of the 72 schools with fewer than 60% low-income students in 1992–93 was 521; for the 20 schools with fewer than 30% low-income students, the average size was only 441 students, quite small by Chicago standards. However, the average size of all Illinois elementary schools outside of Chicago is about 350 students. (One of the disadvantages Chicago's students face is that they must attend larger, and more anonymous, schools than do their counterparts across the rest of the state; see Chapter 10 for a discussion of the effects of school size.) Smaller schools tend to be slightly more expensive, on a per-pupil basis, because staffing formulas and building costs are not quite so easily met. A second feature producing higher basic costs in those schools on the lower end of the low-income spectrum is the "hold harmless" feature of the school reform act. In order to force the board to fund the reallocation of State Chapter I funds from reductions in administrative expenses and from new revenues, the law required that individual schools suffer no loss in per-pupil support as a result of the reallocation (P.L. 85-1418, Sec. 18-8.5 [i] [1] [b]).

In high schools, the picture is clouded by the relative inaccuracy of the low-income measure through which State Chapter I funds are distributed: the free-lunch count. Because high school students are more reluctant to sign up for a free lunch, only 54.8% of high school students were counted as low-income, compared with 83.9% of elementary school students. Since it is highly unlikely that students' families become more affluent as the students graduate from eighth to ninth grade, the measure itself must be considered more dubious at the secondary level.

Still, as Figure B.4 shows, when high schools were grouped into four sets by percentage of low-income students, a significant change had occurred in per-pupil support, with schools with the most low-income students reported receiving about $760 more per pupil in 1992–93 than schools in the lowest quartile. As can be seen, the per-pupil funding line has moved significantly toward the intended lower-left to upper-right slant, indicating schools with more disadvantaged students were receiving extra support. Schools with fewer low-income students lost their financial advantage over schools with more disadvantaged students.

FIGURE B.4. **High School Per-Pupil Expenditures by Quartiles for FY 1989 vs. FY 1993**

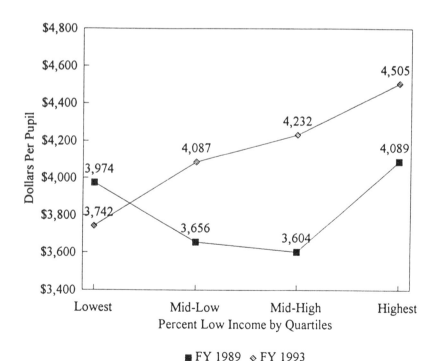

The significance of this State Chapter I reallocation is that it has provided schools with significant new resources for their discretionary use. In Chapter 5, I provided an indication of how this money had been used in some schools and indicated the Panel's concern that too frequently it had simply been used to fund add-on programs without creating schoolwide changes that would be experienced by every student (also see Rosenkranz, 1994, for a description of the use of discretionary funds in our sample of 14 schools). Still, the very amount of these discretionary funds is important to note.

As Figure B.5 shows, the average elementary school in FY 1993 received $459,000 in supplementary funds. Schools with fewer low-income students received less of these funds (about $76,000 for schools with less than 30% low-income students), while schools with more low-income students received more ($573,000 for those with 90% to 99% low-income students). The 100% low-income schools received less

FIGURE B.5. Average Supplementary Budgets for Chicago Elementary and High Schools, FY 1993

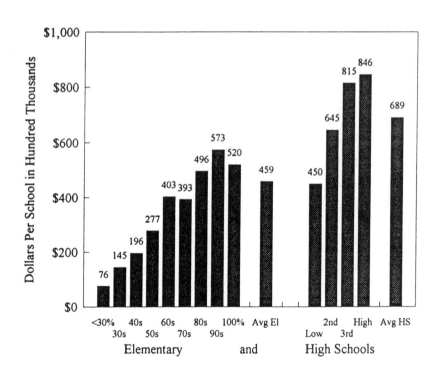

because they averaged 112 fewer students in total enrollments. At the high school level, the average supplemental funds were larger because the schools were much larger. The average for all high schools was $689,000, with the highest quartile averaging $846,000. Juarez High School, a large high school predominantly serving low-income Hispanic students, received the highest supplemental budget, $1,729,182. Nine other high schools received more than $1 million in discretionary funds.

EFFECT OF FY 1994 BUDGET RESOLUTION

A fiscal crisis in the fall of 1993 had severe repercussions for the budgets of individual schools, particularly high schools. Legislative remedies in the spring had reduced the board's projected deficit for FY 1994 from more than $400 million to under $300 million. As the opening of school approached, the board declared itself deadlocked in its negotiations with its employee groups after its "last, best offer" was rejected by the Chicago Teachers Union (CTU) membership. The deadlock allowed the board to institute staff cuts that would have violated the previous contract, reducing teaching positions by about 1,000, representing nearly the entire increase accomplished since FY 1989. These staff reductions reduced the deficit to about $200 million. An eventual contract agreement with the CTU rearranged the way in which these position cuts were accomplished and restored about 200 positions for the second semester of the year. A legislative bailout reduced the final-stage reallocation of State Chapter I funds by $16 million, further cutting into school-level resources for 1993–94; the final reallocation installment was postponed until the fall of 1995. Bond revenues to cover the remaining deficit were approved by the General Assembly in mid-November.

One factor that further reduced resources at the school level was the introduction of the 1990 U.S. Census count of poverty-impacted children. Although the system counted 326,183 students who qualified for a free or reduced-price lunch in 1993–94, a number that has steadily increased during the past 5 years, census takers could only find 162,752 children living in poverty in Chicago. This represented a drop of 23,726 children from the 1980 census. Since the census poverty count is used both by the federal government to calculate its compensatory aid and by the state in its poverty-impact formula, public schools in Chicago lost both federally supported programs and potential discretionary funds under State Chapter I. State funding dropped by $24.2 million, while federal compensatory aid funds dropped by $15.8 million. These were resources that would have provided services to the city's poorest children.

As Table B.7 shows, the Chicago Public Schools increased local revenues by $435 million during the 5 years after reform was launched. At the same time, federal support increased by $133 million. Meanwhile, state support declined by $52 million; however, the unrestricted state aid not attributable to the city's poverty count dropped by $146 million. Since virtually all of the rest of the state money had become restricted by FY 1994, the funds available to balance the board's general operating budget had declined sharply. The increase in local revenues was enough to completely cover the shifting of State Chapter I funds from general to discretionary use, which ranged from about $56 million in FY 1990 to about $264 million in FY 1994. However, the local revenue increase was not large enough to also cover the huge increases in salary costs connected with employee raises in contracts signed by the board of education in 1989 and 1990 (e.g., the 1990 contract called for teacher raises of 7% for each of 3 years). The resulting shortfall caused a major fiscal crisis in the fall of 1993.

The legislative bailout plan adopted in November 1993 put off a real solution to the continuing fiscal imbalance of expenditures and revenues for the Chicago Public Schools until after the 1994 gubernato-

TABLE B.7. **Total Resources for the Chicago Public Schools During Reform Years (in millions)**

	FY 89	FY 90	FY 91	FY 92	FY 93	FY 94	Change 1989–94
Local	$781.5	$887.6	$951.3	$1,053.6	$1,237.0	$1,216.9	$435.4
Tot State	920.9	1,009.6	929.3	946.3	923.7	868.7	(52.2)
State Aid	322.4	317.0	253.2	267.8	237.5	176.5	(145.9)
Chp I	249.0	277.9	291.6	294.1	303.1	278.8	29.8
Categ'l	349.5	414.7	384.5	384.4	383.1	413.4	63.9
Tot Federal	245.9	274.0	293.1	351.7	374.0	379.3	133.4
Chp I	106.1	113.2	130.2	170.4	191.6	175.8	69.7
Other	139.8	160.8	162.9	181.3	182.4	203.5	63.7
Other Fds	62.3	87.1	145.3	52.5	86.0	278.0	215.7
Tot Funds	$2,010.6	$2,258.3	$2,319.0	$2,404.1	$2,620.7	$2,742.9	$732.3

rial election and the spring 1995 mayoral election. Rather than act to solve a current problem, the major political actors delayed a final solution that would undoubtedly require a tax increase. Their inaction will cost untold additional dollars in interest payments and educational opportunities lost for FY 1994 and FY 1995.

SUMMARY

The data in this appendix show that, after 4 years, one of the goals of the reform act was clearly being met. The funds of the Chicago Public Schools had been reallocated to reduce the administrative bureaucracy and to equalize funding among schools; schools with high proportions of low-income students did have more resources, and schools had a significant amount of discretion in the programs they chose to provide. However, events during the early months of the fifth year of reform implementation cast a shadow on this finding. The continuing financial instability of the Chicago Public School system threatens to eclipse the progress made toward this goal of reform.

References

Adler, M. (1982, July). The Paideia proposal: Rediscovering the essence of education. *American School Board Journal, 169*(7), 17–20.

Andreoli, T. (1990). Councils stick with insiders in picking new principals. *Catalyst, 1*(4), 12–14, 16.

Appalachia Educational Laboratory. (1994). *1993–94 annual report: Appalachia Educational Laboratory study of KERA implementation in four rural Kentucky school districts (for review panel)*. Charleston, WV: Author.

Avishai, B. (1994). What is business's social compact? *Harvard Business Review, 72*(1), 38–48.

Ayers, W. (1993). *To teach: The journey of a teacher*. New York: Teachers College Press.

Bennett, A. L., Bryk, A. S., Easton, J. Q., Kirbow, D., Luppescu, S., & Sebring, P. A. (1992). *Charting reform: The principals' perspective*. Chicago: Consortium on Chicago School Research.

Berne, R., & Stiefel, L. (1984). *The measurement of equity in school finance*. Baltimore: Johns Hopkins University Press.

Board cuts it close—Schools will open. (1991, September 1). *Chicago Sun Times*, p. 1.

Board passes a wishful budget. (1991, Summer). *Panel Update: Newsletter of the Chicago Panel on Public School Policy and Finance*, pp. 1, 4.

Board's budget balanced by smoke and mirrors. (1990, October). *Panel Update: Newsletter of the Chicago Panel on Public School Policy and Finance*, pp. 3–6.

Board's fiscal mismanagement undermines long-term success. (1991, Fall). *Panel Update: Newsletter of the Chicago Panel on Public School Policy and Finance*, pp. 1, 4–6, 10.

Bradley, A. (1994, June 22). A quest for change. *Education Week*, pp. 34–35.

Brazil, R. D. (1988). *The engineering of the Paideia proposal: The first year*. Champaign, IL: School Design Group.

Brookover, W. B. (1991). So far, reform not so good. *Catalyst, 3*(3), 15–17.

Brookover, W. B., & Lezotte, L. W. (1979). *Changes in school characteristics coincident with changes in student achievement*. East Lansing: Michigan State University.

Bryk, A. S., Deabster, P. E., Easton, J. Q., Lupescu, S., & Thum, Y. M. (1994, May). Measuring achievement gains in the Chicago Public Schools. *Education and Urban Society*, pp. 306–319.

Bryk, A. S., Easton, J. Q., Kerbow, D., Rollow, S. G., & Sebring, P. A. (1993). *A view from the elementary schools: The state of reform in Chicago*. Chicago: Consortium on Chicago School Research.

Byrd defends school anti-dropout role. (1987, January 18). *Chicago Tribune*, Sec. 2, p. 2.

Camayd-Freixas, Y. (1986). *A working document on the dropout problem in Boston Public Schools*. Boston: Boston Public Schools.

Carnegie Forum on Education and the Economy. (1986). *A nation prepared: Teachers for the 21st century*. New York: Author.

Carroll, T. G. (1992). The role of anthropologists in restructuring schools. In G. A. Hess, Jr. (Ed.), *Empowering teachers and parents: School restructuring through the eyes of anthropologists* (pp. 189–206). Westport, CT: Bergin & Garvey.

Chicago Board of Education. (1985). *Racial/ethnic survey – students*. Chicago: Author.

Chicago Panel on Public School Policy and Finance. (1987). *Testimony be fore the Chicago Board of Education*. Unpublished paper distributed by author.

Chicago Panel on Public School Policy and Finance. (1988). *Illegal use of State Chapter I funds*. Unpublished paper distributed by author.

Chicago Panel on Public School Policy and Finance. (1990). *Chicago Public Schools databook: School year 1988–1989*. Chicago: Author.

Chicago Public Schools. (1990). *The school improvement plans of 1990: What the schools will do* (Report of the Department of Research, Evaluation, and Planning). Chicago: Author.

Chicago Public Schools. (1991). *High school dropout profile: A trend report on the graduating classes of 1982–1990*. Chicago: Author.

Chicago Teachers Union. (1986). *Perspectives from the Classroom – II*. Chicago: Author.

Chubb, J. E., & Moe, T. M. (1990). *Politics, markets, and America's schools*. Washington, DC: Brookings Institution.

Cibulka, J. G. (1975). School decentralization in Chicago. *Education and Urban Society, 7*(4), 412–438.

Cienkus, B. (Ed.). (1989). Size: The ultimate education issue [Special issue]. *Education and Urban Society, 21*(2).

Cippolone, A. (1986, April). *Boston compact in the schools: Does it make a difference?* Paper presented at the annual meeting of the American Educational Research Association, San Francisco.

City school reform plan is ruled illegal. (1990, December 1). *Chicago Tribune*, Sec. 1, pp. 1, 6.

Clune, W. (1994). The shift from equity to adequacy in school finance. *Educational Policy, 8*(4), 376–394.

Coleman, J. S. (1966). *Report of Commission on Equal Educational Opportunity*. Washington, DC: U.S. Goverment Printing Office.

Commission on Chapter I. (1992). *Making schools work for children in poverty*. Washington, DC: American Association for Higher Education.

Committee for Educational Equality et al. v. *State of Missouri et al.* (1993). *Memorandum Opinion and Judgment.* No. CV190-1371CC. Circuit Court of Cole County.

Cooper, B. S. (1990, April). *A tale of two cities: Radical school reform in Chicago and London.* Paper presented at the annual meeting of the American Educational Research Association, Boston.

Cooper, B., Sarrel, R., & Tetenbaum, T. (1990, April). *Choice, funding, and pupil achievement: How urban school finance affects students – particularly those at risk.* Paper presented at the annual meeting of the American Educational Research Association, Boston.

Council of Great City Schools. (1987). *Challenges to urban education: Results in the making.* Washington, DC: Author.

Crain, R. L., & Strauss, J. (1985). *Student desegregation and black occupational attainment: Results from a long term experiment.* Baltimore: Johns Hopkins University Press.

Cubberley, E. P. (1906). *School funds and their apportionment.* New York: Teachers College Press.

Daley's teacher settlement has a familiar ring. (1991, November 18). *Chicago Tribune,* Sec. 1, pp. 1, 17.

Darling-Hammond, L. (1994). Policy for equality: Towards equalization of educational opportunity. In *Resources for Restructuring.* New York: National Center for Restructuring Education, Schools, and Teaching.

David, J. L. (1989). Highlights of research on school based management. *Educational Leadership, 46*(8), 50.

Deming, W. E. (1982). *Quality, productivity, and competitive position.* Cambridge, MA: MIT Press.

Designs for Change. (1985a). *All our kids can learn to read.* Chicago: Author.

Designs for Change. (1985b). *The bottom line: Chicago's failing schools and how to save them.* Chicago: Author.

Designs for Change. (1991, February). The first year. *Closer Look: Newsletter of Designs for Change,* pp. 1–5.

Designs for Change. (1993). *Chicago achievement scores and graduation rates rise since reform.* Chicago: Author.

Deyhle, D., Hess, G. A., Jr., & LeCompte, M. (1992). Approaching ethical issues for qualitative researchers in education. In M. LeCompte, W. L. Millroy, & J. Preissle (Eds.), *The handbook of qualitative research in education* (pp. 597–641). New York: Academic Press.

Dropout program is sought at elementary school level (1988, August 24). *New York Times,* Sec. B, p. 3.

Easton, J. Q. (1989). *Teacher attitudes toward school reform.* Chicago: Chicago Panel on Public School Policy and Finance.

Easton, J. Q., Bryk, A. S., Driscoll, M. E., Kotsakis, J. G., Sebring, P. A., & van der Ploeg, A. J. (1991a). *Charting reform: The teachers' turn.* Chicago: Consortium on Chicago School Reform.

Easton, J. Q., Flinspach, S. L., Ford, D. J., Qualls, J., Ryan, S. R., & Storey, S. L. (1991b). *Decision making and school improvement: LSCs in the first two years of reform*. Chicago: Chicago Panel on Public School Policy and Finance.

Easton, J. Q., & Hess, G. A., Jr. (1990). *The changing racial enrollment patterns in Chicago's schools*. Chicago: Chicago Panel on Public School Policy and Finance.

Easton, J. Q., & Storey, S. (1990a). *Attendance in Chicago Public Schools*. Chicago: Chicago Panel on Public School Policy and Finance.

Easton, J. Q., & Storey, S. (1990b). *June 1989 grade retention in Chicago public elementary schools*. Chicago: Chicago Panel on Public School Policy and Finance.

Easton, J. Q., & Storey, S. L. (1990c). *Local school council meetings during the first year of Chicago school reform*. Chicago: Chicago Panel on Public School Policy and Finance.

Edgar signs 2 school council bills. (1991, September 12). *Chicago Sun Times*, p. 32.

Edmonds, R. (1979, October). Effective schools for the urban poor. *Educational Leadership*, pp. 15–18.

Elmore, R. F. (1978). Organizational models of social program implementation. In D. Mann (Ed.), *Making change happen* (pp. 185–224). New York: Teachers College Press.

Elmore, R. F. (1979). Backward mapping: Implementation research and policy decisions. *Political Science Quarterly, 94*, 601–616.

Elmore, R. F. (1990). Conclusion: Toward a transformation of public schooling. In R. F. Elmore (Ed.), *Restructuring schools: The next generation of educational reform* (pp. 289–297). San Francisco: Jossey-Bass.

Elmore, R. F. (1991). Foreword. In G. A. Hess, Jr., *School restructuring, Chicago style* (pp. vii–ix). Newbury Park, CA: Corwin.

Etheridge, C. P., & Collins, T. W. (1992). Conflict in restructuring the principal-teacher relationship in Memphis. In G. A. Hess, Jr. (Ed.), *Empowering teachers and parents: School restructuring through the eyes of anthropologists* (pp. 89–102). Westport, CT: Bergin & Garvey.

Fecho, B. (1994). Language inquiry and critical pedagogy: Co-investigating power in the classroom. In M. Fine (Ed.), *Chartering urban school reform: Reflections on public high schools in the midst of change* (pp. 180–191). New York: Teachers College Press.

Fine, M. (1990). Making controversy. *Journal of Urban and Cultural Studies, 1*(1), 55–68.

Fine, M. (1991a). *Framing dropouts: Notes on the politics of an urban high school*. Albany: State University of New York Press.

Fine, M. (1991b, November). *Interrupting the structured silence: Trying to talk about race and class in education*. Paper presented at the annual meeting of the American Anthropological Association, Chicago.

Fine, M. (Ed.). (1994). *Chartering urban school reform: Reflections on public high schools in the midst of change*. New York: Teachers College Press.

Finn, C. E., Jr. (1989, Summer). The high school dropout puzzle. *The Public Interest*, pp. 3–22.

Finn, C., & Clements, S. K. (1990). Complacency could blow "grand opportunity." *Catalyst, 1*(4), 2–6.

Finn, C. E., Jr., & Rebarber, T. (Eds.). (1992). *Education reform in the '90s.* New York: MacMillan.

Fliegel, S. (1989). Parental choice in East Harlem schools. In J. Nathan (Ed.), *Public schools by choice* (pp. 95–112). Minneapolis: The Institute for Learning and Teaching.

Flinspach, S. L., & Ryan, S. P. (1992). *Vision and accountability in school improvement planning.* Chicago: Chicago Panel on Public School Policy and Finance.

Flinspach, S. L., & Ryan, S. P. (1994). Diversity of outcomes: Local schools under school reform. *Education and Urban Society, 26*(3), 292–305.

Ford, D. J. (1991). *The school principal and Chicago school reform: Principals' early perceptions.* Chicago: Chicago Panel on Public School Policy and Finance.

Fullan, M. G. (with S. Stiegelbauer). (1991). *The new meaning of educational change.* New York: Teachers College Press.

"Fuzzy" school plan rejected. (1990, August 15). *Chicago Tribune,* Sec. 2, pp. 1, 8.

Glass, T. E., & Sanders, W. D. (1978). *Community control in education: A study in power transition.* Midland, MI: Pendell.

Gomez, M. L. (1988). *The National Writing Project: Creating community, validating experience, and expanding professional opportunities* (Research Report IP 88-2). East Lansing, MI: Michigan State University, The National Center for Research on Teacher Learning.

Greenwald, R., & Hedges, L. V. (1994, November 16). In schools, money matters if it's spent wisely. *New York Times.* Sec. A, p. 18.

Guskey, T. R. (Ed.). (1994). *High stakes performance assessment: Perspectives on Kentucky's education reform.* Thousands Oaks, CA: Corwin.

Guthrie, J. W., Garms, W. I., & Pierce, L. C. (1988). *School finance and education policy: Enhancing educational efficiency, equality, and choice.* Englewood Cliffs, NJ: Prentice-Hall.

Habermas, J. (1971). *Knowledge and human interest* (J. J. Shapiro, Trans.). Boston: Beacon.

Habermas, J. (1978). *Theory and practice* (J. Viertel, Trans.). Boston: Beacon.

Hallett, A. C., & Hess, G. A., Jr. (1982). *Budget cuts at the board of education.* Chicago: Chicago Panel on Public School Finances.

Hammond, R., & Howard, J. P. (1986). Doing what's expected of you: The roots and the rise of the dropout culture. *Metropolitan EDUCATION, 1*(2), 53–71.

Hanson, M. K., Morris, D. R., & Collins, R. A. (1992). Empowerment of teachers in Dade County's school-based management pilot. In G. A. Hess, Jr. (Ed.), *Empowering teachers and parents: School restructuring through the eyes of anthropologists* (pp. 71–87). Westport, CT: Bergin & Garvey.

Hanushek, E. (1986). The economics of schooling: Production and efficiency in public schools. *Journal of Economics Literature, 24*(3), 1141–1177.

Hanushek, E. A. (1989). The impact of differential expenditures on school performance. *Educational Researcher, 18*(4), 45–51.

Hargreaves, A. (1989). *Curriculum and assessment reform*. London, UK: Open University Press.

Hargreaves, A. (1994). *Changing teachers, changing times: Teachers' work and culture in the postmodern age*. New York: Teachers College Press.

Harrington, D., & Cookson, P. W., Jr. (1992). School reform in East Harlem: Alternative schools vs. "schools of choice." In G. A. Hess, Jr. (Ed.), *Empowering teachers and parents: School restructuring through the eyes of anthropologists* (pp. 177–186). Westport, CT: Bergin & Garvey.

Harris, M. (1981). *America now: The anthropology of a changing culture*. New York: Simon & Schuster.

Hedges, L., Laine, R. E., & Greenwald, R. (1994, April). Does money matter? A meta-analysis of studies of the effects of differential school inputs on student outcomes. *Educational Researcher*, pp. 5–14.

Henderson, A. T., Marburger, C. L., & Ooms, T. (1986). *Beyond the bake sale: An educator's guide to working with parents*. Columbia, MD: National Committee for Citizens in Education.

Herrick, M. J. (1984). *The Chicago schools: A social and political history*. Beverly Hills, CA: Sage.

Hess, G. A., Jr. (1984). Renegotiating a multicultural society: Participation in desegregation planning in Chicago. *The Journal of Negro Education, 53*(2), 132–146.

Hess, G. A., Jr. (1986, Fall). Educational triage in an urban school setting. *Metropolitan EDUCATION*, pp. 39–52.

Hess, G. A., Jr. (1987, October 14). Testimony before the Chicago Board of Education. Unpublished testimony distributed by the Chicago Panel on Public School Policy and Finance.

Hess, G. A., Jr. (1990a, April). *Changing illegal use of state compensatory aid*. Paper presented at the annual meeting of the American Educational Research Association, Boston.

Hess, G. A., Jr. (1990b). Testimony before the Chicago Board of Education. Unpublished testimony of July 16 distributed by the Chicago Panel on Public School Policy and Finance.

Hess, G. A., Jr. (1991). *School restructuring, Chicago style*. Newbury Park, CA: Corwin.

Hess, G. A., Jr. (1992a, Summer). Chicago and Britain: Experiments in empowering parents. *Journal of Education Policy*, pp. 155–171.

Hess, G. A., Jr. (Ed.). (1992b). *Empowering teachers and parents: School restructuring through the eyes of anthropologists*. Westport, CT: Bergin & Garvey.

Hess, G. A., Jr. (1992c). Midway through school reform in Chicago. *International Journal of Education, 1*(3), 270–284.

Hess, G. A., Jr. (1992d). Reorienting a school district's funding priorities by state mandate. *Network News & Views, 11*(5), 70–80.

Hess, G. A., Jr. (1992e). *School restructuring, Chicago style: A midway report*. Chicago: Chicago Panel on Public School Policy and Finance.

Hess, G. A., Jr. (1994a). The changing role of teachers: Moving from interested spectators to engaged planners. *Education and Urban Society, 26*(3), pp. 248–263.

Hess, G. A., Jr. (1994b). School based management as a vehicle for school reform. *Education and Urban Society, 26*(3), 203–219.

Hess, G. A., Jr., & Easton, J. Q. (1992). Who's making what decisions: Monitoring authority shifts in Chicago school reform. In G. A. Hess, Jr. (Ed.), *Empowering teachers and parents: School restructuring through the eyes of anthropologists* (pp. 157–176). Westport, CT: Bergin & Garvey.

Hess, G. A., Jr., & Easton, J. Q. (1994). Monitoring the implementation of radical reform: Restructuring the Chicago Public Schools. In K. M. Borman & N. P. Greenman (Eds.), *Changing American education: Recapturing the past or inventing the future?* (pp. 221–248). Albany: State Unversity of New York Press.

Hess, G. A., Jr., Flinspach, S. L., & Ryan, S. P. (1993, Fall). "Case studies of Chicago schools under reform." In R. P. Niemiec & H. J. Walberg (Eds.), *Evaluating Chicago School Reform* (pp. 43–55). New Directions in Program Evaluation, No. 59. San Francisco: Jossey-Bass.

Hess, G. A., Jr., Green, D. O., Stapleton, A. E., & Reyes, O. (1988). *Invisibly pregnant: Teenage mothers and the Chicago Public Schools.* Chicago: Chicago Panel on Public School Policy and Finance.

Hess, G. A., Jr., & Greer, J. L. (1984). *Revenue short falls at the Chicago Board of Education.* Chicago: Chicago Panel on Public School Finances.

Hess, G. A., Jr., & Greer, J. L. (1987). *Bending the twig: The elementary years and dropout rates in the Chicago Public Schools.* Chicago: Chicago Panel on Public School Policy and Finance.

Hess, G. A., Jr., & Lauber, D. (1985). *Dropouts from the Chicago Public Schools.* Chicago: Chicago Panel on Public School Policy and Finance.

Hess, G. A., Jr., Lyons, A., & Corsino, L. (1989). *Against the odds: The early identification of dropouts.* Chicago: Chicago Panel on Public School Policy and Finance.

Hess, G. A., Jr., & Meara, H. (1984). *Teacher transfers and classroom disruption.* Chicago: Chicago Panel on Public School Finances.

Hess, G. A., Jr., & Warden, C. A. (1987). *Who benefits from desegregation?* Chicago: Chicago Panel on Public School Policy and Finance.

Hess, G. A., Jr., & Warden, C. (1988). Who benefits from desegregation now? *The Journal of Negro Education, 57*(4), 536–551.

Hess, G. A., Jr., Wells, E., Prindle, C., Kaplan, B., & Liffman, P. (1986). *"Where's room 185?" How schools can reduce their dropout problem.* Chicago: Chicago Panel on Public School Policy and Finance.

Holland, D. C., & Eisenhart, M. A. (1990). *Educated in romance.* Chicago: University of Chicago Press.

Hopfenberg, W. S., Levin, H. M., Meister, G., & Rogers, J. (1991). Accelerated schools. *Reform Report, 2*(2), 1–6.

Howe, H. (1988, November 30). *Update: Newsletter of Designs for Change.*

Howe, K., & Eisenhart, M. (1990). Standards for qualitative (and quantitative) research: A prolegomenon. *Educational Researcher, 19*, 4–9.

Interim board accomplishes four of five miracles. (1989, October). *Panel Update: Newsletter of the Chicago Panel on Public School Policy and Finance, 4*(3), 1, 4–6.

Jacobsen, S. L., & Berne, R. (Eds.). (1993). *Reforming education: The emerging systemic approach* (AEFA Yearbook for 1993). Thousand Oaks, CA: Corwin.

Jencks, C., Smith, M., Acland, H., Bane, M., Cohen, D., Gintis, H., Heyns, B., & Michelson, S. (1972). *Inequality: A reassessment of the effect of family and schooling in America*. New York: Basic Books.

Johnston, J. A., Bickel, W., & Wallace, R. E., Jr. (1990, May). Building and sustaining change in the culture of secondary schools. *Educational Leadership*, pp. 46–48.

Katz, M. B. (1992). Chicago school reform as history. *Teachers College Record, 94*(1), 56–72.

Kimbrough reads the riot act, but Daley, legislators doubt need for big school cuts. (1991, May 2). *Chicago Tribune*, Sec. 1, p. 4.

Kozol, J. (1968). *Death at an early age*. Boston: Houghton Mifflin.

Kozol, J. (1991). *Savage inequalities*. New York: Crown.

Lareau, A. (1991, November). *Social class and race differences in parents' structuring of children's leisure activities*. Paper presented at the annual meeting of the American Anthropological Association, Chicago.

LeCompte, M., Wiertelak, M. E., & Eilletto, A. (1991, November). *"It's a bird; It's a plane; It's a . . . " How one school defined restructuring*. Paper presented at the annual meeting of the American Anthropological Association, Chicago.

Legislators patch school reform. (1991, January 9). *Chicago Tribune*, Sec. 1, p. 1.

Lieberman, A. (Ed.). (1988). *Building a professional culture in schools*. New York: Teachers College Press.

Lieberman, A. (in press). Practices that support teacher development: Transforming conceptions of professional learning. *Phi Delta Kappan*.

Lieberman, A., & McLaughlin, M.W. (1992). Networks for educational change: Powerful and problematic. *Phi Delta Kappan, 73*(9), 673–677.

Lieberman, M. (1989). A brief analysis of the Illinois education reform act. *Government Union Review, 10*(2), 23–30.

Lindquest, K., & Mauriel, J. (1989). School-based management—Doomed to failure? *Education and Urban Society, 21*(4), 403–416.

Little, J. W. (1993). *Teacher's professional development in a climate of educational reform*. New York: National Center for Restructuring Education, Schools, and Teaching.

Louis, K. S., & Miles, M. B. (1990). *Improving the urban high school: What works and why*. New York: Teachers College Press.

Lytle, S. L., Christman, J., Cohen, J., Countryman, J., Fecho, B., Portnoy, D., & Sion, F. (1994). Learning in the afternoon: When teacher inquiry meets school reform. In M. Fine (Ed.), *Chartering urban school reform: Reflections on public high schools in the midst of change* (pp. 157–179). New York: Teachers College Press.

Malen, B., & Ogawa, R. T. (1988). Professional-patron influence on site based governance councils: A confounding case study. *Educational Evaluation and Policy Analysis, 10*(4), 251–270.

Mann, D. (Ed.). (1978). *Making change happen*. New York: Teachers College Press.

Marburger, K. (1985). *One school at a time*. Columbia, MD: National Committee for Citizens in Education.

Marcus, G. E., & Fischer, M. (1986). *Anthropology as cultural critique*. Chicago: University of Chicago Press.

Marshall, C. (Ed). (1993). *The new politics of race and gender*. Washington, DC: Falmer.

Massachusetts Advocacy Center. (1988). *The way out: Student exclusion practices in middle schools*. Boston: Author.

Maxwell, J., & Pitman, M. A. (1992). Qualitative approaches to evaluation: Models and methods. In M. D. LeCompte, W. L. Millroy, & J. Preissle (Eds.), *The handbook of qualitative research in education* (pp. 729–770). New York: Academic Press.

McCarthey, S. J. (1992). *Teachers' changing conceptions of writing instruction* (Research Report 92-3). East Lansing: Michigan State University, National Center for Research on Teacher Learning.

McLaughlin, M. W. (1978). Implementation as mutual adaptation: Change in classroom organization. In D. Mann (Ed.), *Making change happen* (pp. 19–32). New York: Teachers College Press.

McLaughlin, M. W. (1987). Learning from experience: Lessons from policy implementation. *Educational Evaluation and Policy Analysis, 9*(2), 171–178.

McLaughlin, M. W., & Talbert, J. E. (1993). *Contexts that matter for teaching and learning*. Stanford, CA: Center for Research on the Context of Secondary School Teaching.

Mirel, J. (1990). What history can teach us about school decentralization. *Network News & Views, 9*(8), 40–47.

Monti, D. J. (1986, Spring). Brown's velvet cushion: Metropolitan desegregation and the politics of illusion. *Metropolitan EDUCATION*, pp. 52–67.

Moore, D. R. (1992). The case for parent and community involvement. In G. A. Hess, Jr. (Ed.), *Empowering teachers and parents: School restructuring through the eyes of anthropologists* (pp. 71–87). Westport, CT: Bergin & Garvey.

Moore, D. R., & Radford-Hill, S. (1982). *Caught in the web: Misplaced children in Chicago's classes for the mentally retarded*. Chicago: Designs for Change.

Morris, V. C., Crowson, R., Porter-Gehrie, C., & Hurwitz, E. (1984). *Principals in action: The reality of managing schools*. Columbus: Merrill.

Moynihan, D. P. (1969). *Maximum feasible misunderstanding: Community action in the war on poverty*. New York: Free Press.

Muncey, D. E., & McQuillan, P. J. (1992). The dangers of assuming a consensus for change: Some examples from the Coalition of Essential Schools. In G.

A. Hess, Jr. (Ed.), *Empowering teachers and parents: School restructuring through the eyes of anthropologists* (pp. 47–70). Westport, CT: Bergin & Garvey.

National Commission on Excellence in Education. (1983). *A nation at risk: The imperative for educational reform*. Washington, DC: U.S. Government Printing Office.

Needed: A new spirit. (1990, January). *Panel Update: Newsletter of the Chicago Panel on Public School Policy and Finance*, pp. 1, 4.

Nelson, F. H., Yong, R., & Hess, G. A., Jr. (1985). *Implementing educational reform in Illinois*. Chicago: Chicago Panel on Public School Finances.

Oakes, J. (1985). *Keeping track: How schools structure inequality*. New Haven, CT: Yale University Press.

Odden, A. (1994). Decentralized management and school finance. *Theory into Practice, 33*(2), 104–111.

O'Dowd, S. (1991). Newcomers dominate new local school councils. *Catalyst, 3*(4), 18–19.

Ogbu, J. (1978). *Minority education and caste: The American system in cross-cultural perspective*. New York: Academic Press.

Olson, L. (1992, September 9). Fed up with tinkering, reformers now touting "systemic" approach. *Education Week*, pp. 1, 30.

Orfield, G. (1986, Spring). Knowledge, ideology, and school desegregation: Views through different prisms. *Metropolitan EDUCATION*, pp. 92–99.

Orfield, G. (1991). Foreword. In P. Scheirer, *Poverty, not bureaucracy: Poverty, segregation, and inequality in metropolitan Chicago schools* (pp. 1–11). Chicago: University of Chicago.

O'Rourke, P. (1987, Spring). Shared decision making at the school site: Moving toward a professional model. *American Educator*, pp. 10–17.

Payzant, T. W., & Pendleton, B. O. (1993). Partnerships through interagency collaboration. In J. Learmonth (Ed.), *Teaching and learning in cities* (pp. 200–211). UK: Lamort Gilbert.

Perpich, R. (1989). Foreword. In J. Nathan (Ed.), *Public schools by choice* (pp. 1–3). Minneapolis: The Institute for Learning and Teaching.

Peters, T. J., & Waterman, R. H., Jr. (1982). *In search of excellence: Lessons from America's best-run companies*. New York: Harper & Row.

Poinsett, A. (1990). School reform, black leaders: Their impact on each other. *Catalyst, 1*(4), 7–11, 43.

Polsby, D. (1993, December 2). School reform? Figures don't lie. *Chicago Tribune*, Sec. 1, p. 17.

Purkey, S., & Smith, M. S. (1983, March). Effective schools: A review. *The Elementary School Journal*, pp. 426–452.

Raudenbush, S. W., & Bryk, A. S. (1986). Hierarchical model for studying school effects. *Sociology of Education, 59*, 1–17.

Reformers say schools deficit is overestimate. (1991, June 25). *Chicago Tribune*, Sec. 2, p. 1.

Rogers, D. (1968). *110 Livingston Street: Politics and bureaucracy in the New York City schools*. New York: Random House.

Rogers, D., & Chung, N. (1983). *110 Livingston Street revisited: Decentralization in action*. New York: New York University Press.

Rosenbaum, J. E. (1980). Social implications of educational grouping. In D. C. Berliner (Ed.), *Review of research in education* (Vol. 8; pp. 361–401). Washington, DC: American Educational Research Association.

Rosenbaum, J. E., Kulieke, M. J., & Rubinowitz, L. S. (1987). Low-income black children in white suburban schools: A study of school and student responses. *Journal of Negro Education, 56*(1), 35–43.

Rosenkranz, T. (1994). Reallocating resources: Discretionary funds provide engine for change. *Education and Urban Society, 26*(3), 264–284.

Rossi, R. (Ed.). (1994). *Schools and students at risk: Context and framework for positive change*. New York: Teachers College Press.

Ruenzel, D. (1993, August). Woman on a mission. *Teacher Magazine*, pp. 26–31.

Sartre, J. P. (1955). *Literary and philosophical essays* (A. Michelson, Trans.). New York: Criterion Books.

Schlechty, P. C. (1990). *Schools for the twenty-first century: Leadership imperatives for educational reform*. San Francisco: Jossey-Bass.

Schwartz, R., & Hargroves, J. (1986). The Boston compact. *Metropolitan EDUCATION, 3*, 14–24.

Senate kills bid to sap Chapter I funds. (1991, June 30). *Chicago Sun Times*, p. 58.

Singer, W. S. (1993). Chicago's fiscal crisis. In D. Simpson (Ed.), *Chicago's future in a time of change* (pp. 414–417). Champaign, IL: Stipes.

Sizer, T. (1984). *Horace's compromise: The dilemma of the American high school*. Boston: Houghton Mifflin.

Sizer, T. (1988). Letter to all coalition schools [Quoted in Muncey & McQuillan, 1992].

Sizer, T. R. (1989). Diverse practices, shared ideas: The essential school. In *Organizing for Learning: Toward the 21st Century* (pp. 1–8). Reston, VA: National Association of Secondary School Principals.

Slavin, R. E. (1988). Synthesis of research on grouping in elementary schools. *Educational Leadership, 46*(1), 67–74.

Smith, M. S., & O'Day, J. (1991). Systemic school reform. In S. H. Fuhrman & B. Malen (Eds.), *The politics of curriculum and testing* (pp. 233–267). New York: Falmer.

Stephenson, R. S. (1985). *A study of the longitudinal dropout rate: 1980 eighth-grade cohort followed from June 1980 through February, 1985*. Miami: Dade County Public Schools.

Strayer, G. D., & Haig, R. M. (1923). *Financing of education in the state of New York*. New York: Macmillan.

Swadener, B. B., & Niles, K. (1991, Spring). Children and families "at promise": Making home-school-community connections. *Democracy and Education*, pp. 13–18.

Tatel, D. S., Lanigan, K. J., & Sneed, M. F. (1986, Spring). The fourth decade of *Brown*: Metropolitan desegregation and quality education. *Metropolitan EDUCATION*, pp. 15–35.

Teachers union OKs contract. (1989, July 27). *Chicago Tribune*, Sec. 1, pp. 1, 20.

300 school custodian and clerical jobs restored to avoid court fight. (1991, September 23). *Chicago Tribune*, Sec. 2, p. 3.

Tyack, D. B. (1974). *The one best system: A history of American urban education*. Cambridge, MA: Harvard University Press.

van den Berghe, P. L. (1973). Pluralism. In J. Honigman (Ed.), *Handbook of social and cultural anthropology* (pp. 959–977). Chicago: Rand McNally.

Verstegan, D. (1994, November). The new wave of school finance litigation. *Phi Delta Kappan*, 243–250.

A view from the schools: Reform gains real—but fragile. (1993). *Panel Update: Newsletter of the Chicago Panel on School Policy, 8*(5), 1, 6–10.

Walberg, H. J., & Fowler, W., Jr. (1988). *Expenditures and size efficiencies of public school districts*. Chicago: Heartland Institute.

Watkins, J. (1992). Critical friends in the fray: An experiment in applying critical ethnography to school restructuring. In G. A. Hess, Jr. (Ed.), *Empowering teachers and parents: School restructuring through the eyes of anthropologists* (pp. 207–228). Westport, CT: Bergin & Garvey.

Wehlege, G. G., & Rutter, R. A. (1986). Dropping out: How much do schools contribute to the problem? *Teachers College Record, 87*, 374–392.

Weis, L. (1991, November). *White male working class: An exploration of relative privilege and loss*. Paper presented at the annual meeting of the American Anthropological Association, Chicago.

With teachers laid off, some students are idle. (1991, September 11). *Chicago Sun Times*, Sec. Metro, p. 3.

Index

About the Author

G. Alfred Hess, Jr., is the executive director of the Chicago Panel on School Policy, a nonprofit, multi-ethnic research and advocacy organization. He has studied the Chicago Public Schools for more than a decade, using both qualitative and quantitative approaches. He is the president-elect of the Council on Anthropology and Education and has served on the board of directors of the American Education Finance Association. From 1991 to 1994, he was the president of the Coalition for Educational Rights, a statewide organization of groups seeking to reform the school finance scheme in Illinois. He is the author of a book describing the inception of the school reform effort in Chicago, *School Restructuring, Chicago Style* (Corwin, 1991). He has edited a volume of studies about school restructuring efforts across the United States, *Empowering Teachers and Parents: School Restructuring Through the Eyes of Anthropologists* (Bergin & Garvey, 1992), and a special edition of the journal *Education and Urban Society* (May 1994) on the "Outcomes of Chicago School Reform."